"Values work is at the core of many forms of modern psych
team of authors has produced a real gem that will illuminate how a focus on values
can inform every aspect of psychotherapy, from case conceptualization to the
therapeutic relationship. At once accessible and profound, it dances effortlessly
between basic behavioral science and the deepest clinical issues in a way that will
leave no serious reader unchanged. Highly recommended."

—Steven C. Hayes, Ph.D., University of Nevada Foundation Professor of
   Psychology at the University of Nevada, Reno

"This invaluable and inspirational guide to helping clients live meaningful and
passionate lives is replete with conceptually clear explanations and high-impact
exercises. This book belongs in the library of any practitioner who yearns to make
a difference personally and professionally."

—Mavis Tsai, Ph.D., independent practitioner and clinical faculty
   member at the University of Washington

"Helping clients identify their values and move toward acting on them is one of the
central components of ACT and, sometimes, a challenging task for therapists. This
book provides practitioners with all the knowledge and tools required to accomplish this in therapy. Readers will appreciate the wealth of new information, exercises, worksheets, and suggestions related to enhancing value-guided behavior in
their clients. This book is a great resource for any therapist who wants to help
clients live richer, more fulfilling lives."

—Georg Eifert, Ph.D., professor and chair of the department of
   psychology at Chapman University in Orange, CA

"This book is a guide to putting meaning, heart, and inspiration into therapy. The authors skillfully illustrate how basic research on language and cognition applies to clinical situations. This book is a must-read for anyone who is interested in values and meaning in therapy or for those interested in how relational frame theory applies to clinical practice."

—Jason B. Luoma, Ph.D., psychologist at Portland Psychotherapy Clinic, Research, and Training Center, and coauthor of *Learning ACT*

"*The Art and Science of Valuing in Psychotherapy* is an exciting book for therapists! This well-written and accessible book guides the therapist through the process of helping the client to contact and instantiate a values-based life in a thoughtful and straightforward fashion. The authors truly brought valued living to life. It was a pleasure to read and I look forward to using it in my own therapeutic practice."

—Robyn D. Walser, Ph.D.

The Art & Science of Valuing

in Psychotherapy

Helping Clients Discover, Explore,
and Commit to Valued Action Using
Acceptance and Commitment Therapy

JOANNE C. DAHL, PH.D.
JENNIFER C. PLUMB, MA
IAN STEWART, PH.D.
TOBIAS LUNDGREN, MS

New Harbinger Publications, Inc.

Publisher's Note

This publication is designed to provide accurate and authoritative information in regard to the subject matter covered. It is sold with the understanding that the publisher is not engaged in rendering psychological, financial, legal, or other professional services. If expert assistance or counseling is needed, the services of a competent professional should be sought.

Distributed in Canada by Raincoast Books

Copyright © 2009 by Joanne Dahl, Jennifer C. Plumb, Ian Stewart, & Tobias Lundgren
New Harbinger Publications, Inc.
5674 Shattuck Avenue
Oakland, CA 94609
www.newharbinger.com

FSC
Mixed Sources
Product group from well-managed
orests and other controlled sources

Cert no. SW-COC-002283
www.fsc.org
© 1996 Forest Stewardship Council

Acquired by Melissa Kirk; Cover design by Amy Shoup;
Edited by Jasmine Star; Text design by Tracy Marie Carlson

Library of Congress Cataloging-in-Publication Data

The art and science of valuing in psychotherapy : helping clients discover, explore, and commit to valued action using acceptance and commitment therapy / JoAnne C. Dahl ... [et al.].
    p. ; cm.
Includes bibliographical references and index.
ISBN-13: 978-1-57224-626-3 (hardcover : alk. paper)
ISBN-10: 1-57224-626-X (hardcover : alk. paper)
1. Acceptance and commitment therapy. 2. Values. I. Dahl, JoAnne, 1951-
[DNLM: 1. Cognitive Therapy--methods. 2. Adaptation, Psychological.
3. Social Values. WM 425.5.C6 A784 2009]
RC489.A32A78 2009
616.89'1425--dc22
                    2009014693

11   10   09

10   9   8   7   6   5   4   3   2   1   First printing

To my Dad, Walter, who has always been and still is an inspiration of vitality in my life. Your daughter number 2,

    – JoAnne

To my family, friends, and labbies for living and loving with vitality. You are my valued action team.

    – Jen

To my family and friends—sources of much-appreciated intrinsic reinforcement.

    – Ian

To Mom and Dad, for your never-ending love and support, YNWA.

    – Tobias

Contents

Dear reader,

Welcome to New Harbinger Publications. New Harbinger is dedicated to publishing books based on acceptance and commitment therapy (ACT) and its application to specific areas. New Harbinger has a long-standing reputation as a publisher of quality, well-researched books for general and professional audiences.

As part of New Harbinger's commitment to publishing books based on sound, scientific, clinical research, we oversee all prospective books for the Acceptance and Commitment Therapy Series. Serving as series editors, we comment on proposals and offer guidance as needed, and use a gentle hand in making suggestions regarding the content, depth, and scope of each book.

Books in the Acceptance and Commitment Therapy Series:

- Have an adequate database, appropriate to the strength of the claims being made.

- Are theoretically coherent. They will fit with the ACT model and underlying behavioral principles as they have evolved at the time of writing.

- Orient the reader toward unresolved empirical issues.

- Do not overlap needlessly with existing volumes.

- Avoid jargon and unnecessary entanglement with proprietary methods, leaving ACT work open and available.

- Keep the focus always on what is good for the reader.

- Support the further development of the field.

- Provide information in a way that is of practical use to readers.

These guidelines reflect the values of the broader ACT community. You'll see all of them packed into this book. This series is meant to offer professionals information that can truly be helpful, and to further our ability to alleviate human suffering by inviting creative practitioners into the process of developing, applying, and refining a better approach. This book provides another such invitation.

Sincerely,

John Forsyth, Ph.D., Steven C. Hayes, Ph.D., Georg H. Eifert, Ph.D., and Robyn Walser, Ph.D.

Foreword

Acceptance and commitment therapy (ACT) is part of a larger effort to create a psychology more adequate to the challenge of the human condition. Making progress toward such a distant goal is inherently slow, but many hands make light work. Over the last few years, it has become increasingly evident that a worldwide community is forming that takes this challenge seriously. The hands are arriving, and the work is being done. No longer content to write protocols for specific problems, ACT leaders are increasingly writing about issues that cut across applied domains. This book is an example.

This book is also a striking example of something else. Let me explain.

ACT is a modern form of behavioral and cognitive intervention that combines acceptance and mindfulness processes with commitment and behavior change processes, in order to produce psychological flexibility. It is based on a functional contextualistic philosophy of science and modern learning theory, as is expanded by relational frame theory (RFT). It is based on a model of scientific development we call contextual behavioral science (CBS). As such, ACT is more a unified model of behavior change—linked to a specific philosophy, theory, and development strategy—than it is a specific set of methods.

The book you are holding reveals some of the most remarkable features of the community that is fostering this work. The authors are from Sweden (JoAnne Dahl and Tobias Lundgren), Ireland (Ian Stewart), and the United States (Jen Plumb); they include clinical researchers and educators (JoAnne Dahl, Jen Plumb, and Tobias Lundgren) and basic behavioral scientists (Ian Stewart); the pages of this book dance back and forth between extremely practical yet profound issues encountered in the consulting room and current findings in modern learning theory. Empirical but also accessible, applied but also grounded in basic science, this book is a microcosm of the transformative values and strategies underlying the ACT/RFT/CBS community itself.

There are possibilities that are opened up by that level of diversity and that depth of focus. This book contains a different kind of conversation than most applied volumes. The reader is invited to benefit from what has been learned in a very practical and accessible way, but the reader is also invited to understand where these innovations came from and how they work at such a level that new connections can be made and new methods can be created. Instead of being a passive recipient of information, the reader of this important new book is led on a path to expertise.

Expertise makes new things possible. This book is at one level about ACT, but at another level it is about all of psychotherapy and indeed all of behavior change. The entire world culture is becoming more sensitive to the issue of values and purpose. Once relegated primarily to spiritual and religious institutions, values conversations are now part of work, health, home life, and, yes, therapy. You can see that in the popular media and in the speeches of political leaders.

The importance of becoming expert in a way that goes beyond mere technology is twofold. For one thing, it is becoming much clearer how profoundly values work can modify traditional clinical work. Values work is powerful. It reorganizes everything, from assessment to case conceptualization to intervention. When you see its possibilities and begin to understand its centrality, a new vista of clinical intervention opens up. Seeing that is more than a matter of technology. It is a matter of appreciation and understanding.

The second major reason that expertise is critical is that clinicians and behavioral health specialists are being looked to by the community at large to help the culture learn how to address the issue of values. We cannot do it in the same way as religious leaders or politicians. We cannot do it in the same way as advocates or organizers. We have to learn how to speak in a practical way about values on the basis of what behavioral science and practice reveals. It is still early. We have a lot of work ahead of us to discover how to do this, but one thing is clear: for the behavioral science professions to participate in the process, expertise is required.

The ACT community has been working for nearly a decade to get on top of the issue of values. Leaders such as Kelly Wilson and the authors of this book have been at the forefront of developing new assessment methods and styles of intervention. Finally, the expressions of that work are becoming available.

Be forewarned: you will not be left unchanged. This book will make a difference in your life, but more importantly, in the lives of those you serve.

Steven C. Hayes, Ph.D.
University of Nevada
Reno, Nevada
March 2009

Acknowledgments

This book is a waypoint on a journey of teamwork that has not ended with this publication. We thank our families and colleagues for their patience, their subtle (and not-so-subtle) suggestions, and their steadfast support throughout the writing of this book.

We thank Steve Hayes for his never-ending support and broad vision of the work, John Forsyth for his early and insightful feedback, and the many folks in the ACT community who have continually inspired and shaped our interest in values, including Kelly Wilson, Robyn Walser, Carmen Luciano, J. T. Blackledge, Dermot Barnes-Holmes, Yvonne Barnes-Holmes, Louise McHugh, Joe Ciarrochi, Lance McCracken, Kevin Vowles, Rikard Wicksell, Todd Kashdan, Ann Branstetter, and all of their students. Countless exercises in this book were shaped by our exposure to workshops, our students' and colleagues' creativity, and our clients themselves. Without all of them, this book would not be possible.

We thank New Harbinger for the opportunity to share what matters to us as researchers and therapists in the writing of this book. We were blessed with Melissa Kirk, Jasmine Star, and Jess Beebe, whom we thank for their gentle, caring, and informed editing.

JoAnne Dahl is grateful to those who have taught her the value of valuing: Mavis Tsai, Bill Miller, Steve Hayes, Kelly Wilson, Sten Rönnberg, and Lennart Melin.

Jen Plumb thanks Sue Orsillo, Jennifer Block Lerner, Steve Hayes, Kelly Wilson, Robyn Walser, and the labbies for sharing their values. She is eternally grateful to Roger Vilardaga, Jennifer Boulanger, and Mike Levin for being such wonderful sounding boards for this work.

Ian Stewart thanks Dermot Barnes-Holmes, Bryan Roche, Steve Hayes, the members of the ACT/RFT and BA communities more generally, and hais fellow authors—for sharing their values with him over the years.

Tobias Lundgren would also like to acknowledge Lennart Melin and Sten Rönnberg for their creativity and wisdom, Steve Hayes for his support, and all our students for much creativity.

CHAPTER 1

An Introduction to Values in ACT

Fundamental questions of life are questions of values. Questions pertaining to meaning and purpose for humans ultimately revolve around values, which can guide and define our lives. Philosophers have been examining the concept of values for centuries, demarcating questions of fact from questions of value and asking how such differences affect human behavior. How is morality established? How do we make choices about our behavior? What shapes our life's purpose? In acceptance and commitment therapy (ACT), values are used to help clients select directions for their lives that are congruent with what is deeply important to them and establish goals supporting movement in those directions. Using values as the context of therapy, the ACT therapist asks the question "In a world where you could choose to have your life be about something, what would you choose?" (Wilson & Murrell, 2004, 135). Values continue to provide useful guidance for clients once therapy is over, facilitating the living of a vital life.

This book aims to make a contribution to the use of values generally in psychotherapy and specifically within acceptance and commitment therapy, a modern, functional analytic approach to the treatment of human suffering that is explicitly linked to an empirically validated conceptualization of human language and cognition known as relational frame theory (RFT; Hayes, Barnes-Holmes, & Roche, 2001). Other social science fields have examined values across sociological contexts, and within psychology itself, and thus we certainly don't present the only approach or even the only psychological approach to values. However, we do believe that we have something unique and valuable to offer. An ACT perspective on values differs from many other conceptualizations of values in important ways. ACT is built upon explicitly stated scientific theory and philosophical assumptions, including relational frame theory, a basic behavioral account of human language and cognition. RFT and ACT both rest on the foundation of the basic scientific philosophy of functional contextualism. As such, RFT and functional contextualism have helped shape the development and implementation of ACT. Hence, our analysis of values directly links to psychological intervention, is based on behavioral principles and a theory of human language and cognition, and sits atop the foundation of a well-developed philosophy of science. In addition, we have an increasing quantity of data suggesting that our perspective on values can be helpful and may enrich your clients' lives.

While we don't have data to support each and every intervention presented in this book, the ACT model as a whole and its purported processes of change have been empirically validated for many psychological problems, across cultures and populations (see Hayes, Luoma, Bond, Masuda, & Lillis, 2006, for a review). Additionally, since ACT is an applied extension of a basic behavioral model of language, almost any method, technique, or intervention strategy based upon ACT or sufficiently congruent with it will be linked with similar processes and principles and is thus likely to be helpful. Therefore, ACT can be a very creative endeavor once you understand the model and principles upon which it is based.

This book is intended to be a stand-alone, step-by-step guide to doing ACT from within a values context. However, you may find your ACT work all the more powerful if you read other books and articles or if you seek further training.

Before we begin to discuss in detail the practical processes and interventions characterizing values-based psychotherapy, we will first introduce you to functional contextualism, the philosophy underlying our science, and then introduce you to relevant principles of behavior analysis. In the first half of chapter 2, we will examine the fundamentals of relational frame theory, particularly those RFT concepts related to values and applicable to clinical intervention, while in the latter half of the chapter we will present ACT. We ask you to bear with us as we provide the sometimes challenging or technical background for ACT, as becoming acquainted with this background will put what we do in ACT into perspective. While we don't assert that having an in-depth knowledge of the roots of ACT is absolutely necessary to practice ACT itself, we believe it can help you become more flexible and increase the impact of your psychotherapeutic interventions.

Philosophical Assumptions

Why is a scientific philosophy important to applied psychologists and practicing clinicians? It is the stance of some philosophers that there are sets of assumptions about the world that affect all human endeavors, including scientific or therapeutic ones. Imagine this: You want to know why the sky is blue. The very question you ask is affected by your history, including the way you learned about the world and its physical properties, which leads you to consider that this is a good question to ask. Also consider how you could go about answering that question. If your worldview focuses on the role of deities in creating the Earth, you would seek to answer the question by prayer, consulting with priests, or reading holy texts. If your worldview focuses on the role of the human in perceiving the sky, you might study the eye or the brain. In his discussion of the role of the scientist, B. F. Skinner suggested that there is no such thing as "objective" observation of the world (Skinner, 1974). As soon as humans get involved, we bring with us all sorts of beliefs and previous experiences that shape the way we interact with whatever we are observing.

This is true for your therapeutic work as well. You may not realize that there are many assumptions that affect your work, but indeed there are. The fact that you are a practitioner of some sort, the type of therapy you do, and the clients you choose to see are all affected by a long line of historical events in your life. In ACT, we choose to be up front with the assumptions that affect our work from the outset, starting with the most basic philosophical assumptions. That's why we spend some time on this issue now.

Worldviews

Steven Pepper (1942) described a *worldview* as a set of assumptions about the world and about science as a methodology for discovering truth in the world. All worldviews are characterized by a root metaphor or commonsense way of understanding the world, and a *truth criterion*, which is a means for distinguishing truth in the world. These characteristics of any particular worldview fundamentally shape any scientific approach based on that worldview and make for fundamental differences between scientific approaches that are based on differing worldviews. Two prominent worldviews are *mechanism*, which is the worldview of much of mainstream psychology, and *contextualism*, which is the worldview of RFT and ACT.

MECHANISM

The root metaphor of the mechanistic approach is the machine. For mechanists, the world is like a machine made up of parts and forces, and the job of the scientist is to analyze that machine down to its component parts and explain how those parts work together. The truth criterion for this approach is correspondence between theory and reality; the better the fit, the truer the theory. An example of this approach within psychology is traditional cognitive theory, which provides the basic scientific background for mainstream cognitive behavioral therapy (CBT). In the context of traditional CBT, the job of the scientist is to break down units of thought and behavior into their component parts and understand how these parts influence one another. Through such research, the scientist can build accurate models of the normal working mind, including normal working thoughts. Meanwhile, as an applied cognitive scientist the psychotherapist works to analyze minds that operate with dysfunctional thoughts and beliefs and aims to fix them essentially by modifying or replacing those thoughts and beliefs. For example, in Beck's traditional CBT-based model of depression, there are core belief templates inside the mind that when maladaptive create dysfunctional or irrational automatic thoughts, which negatively affect mood and behavior (e.g., Beck & Emery, 2005). Intervention requires modification of the maladaptive core beliefs as well as of the irrational thinking that arises from them, thus facilitating positive mood and adaptive behavior.

CONTEXTUALISM

The root metaphor of the contextualistic approach is the event in context, or act in context. From this perspective, we can understand any event or phenomenon by understanding the context in which it happens. The truth criterion for this approach is successful working. In other words, if an explanation of an event allows us to achieve some preset goal, then it is true, otherwise not. Behavior analysis is an example of functional contextualism within psychology, and so also are RFT (which is behavior analysis applied to language and cognition) and ACT (which is psychotherapy based on the RFT analysis of language).

Behavior analysis, as a broad field subsuming both ACT and RFT, represents the application of functional contextualism in psychology. The fundamental behavior analytic unit is the operant, or three-term, contingency, involving antecedents (those stimuli that come before or set the scene for responding), behavior, and consequences (those stimuli that follow the behavior). This deceptively simple concept is used to examine behaviors ranging from the very basic to the very complex. Most important in the current discussion is the fact that the context of the behavior being analyzed is a fundamental and inseparable aspect of the analysis, and hence this unit coheres with the act-in-context conception of contextualism. With regard to truth criteria, the contextualist emphasis on scientific goals is captured both within the behavior analytic unit itself vis-à-vis the importance of consequences, and by the pragmatic character of behavior analysis, in which a prespecified level of prediction and influence over behavior is regarded as sufficient to establish the finality of any analysis. Thus, truth in behavior analysis is goal-based, and the nature of the goal in this case makes behavior analytic psychology a form of functional contextualism.

This relates to ACT and RFT because we are not interested in analyzing a behavioral event (overt action, thought, or feeling) by breaking it down into its component parts. Rather, we are interested in seeing how behaviors occur within the context of a person's unique personal history and the influences of the present environment. How we change behavior in ACT is related to understanding context, as opposed to changing the content of thought or the form of feelings. We work to change not a person's thoughts about her painful history, but rather her relationship to those very thoughts, so that she might live a meaningful life guided by her values, as opposed to her past or current private experiences.

In addition, as a consequence of the radically pragmatic nature of the functional contextual behavioral approach upon which both ACT and RFT are based, analysis focuses always on the function of behavior (its environmental consequences) as opposed to its form, or appearance. In ACT and RFT, this is the fundamental basis upon which we categorize and distinguish between all types of behaviors. Thus, based on this specialized perspective, two behaviors may look different but be functionally similar in that they have the same consequences for the person. For example, working late might be functionally similar to drinking alcohol if both patterns of responding involve avoiding depressive thoughts. On the other hand, behaviors that are similar in form might be functionally different. For example, one person might work late to avoid depressive thoughts, whereas another might do so to get a promotion. Therefore, in this book, whenever we are assessing whether a particular behavior is congruent with values or not, we always focus on whether the behavior functions to pursue or realize those values or whether it functions to diminish or negate them.

Summing Up Philosophical Assumptions

In summary then, whereas mechanism provides the assumptions and aims of mainstream cognitive psychology, functional contextualism provides the assumptions and aims of behavior analysis and RFT, and their application in the practice of ACT. We hope that this brief introduction to the functional contextual assumptions underlying behavior analysis, RFT, and ACT will help you understand and appreciate the contextualistic and pragmatic nature of these approaches, which provide the theoretical background for the perspective on values presented in this book. We concluded our examination of functional contextualism by describing a few of the general features of behavior analysis, RFT, and ACT that derive from a functional contextual philosophy. In the next section we will examine a number of the important principles of behavior analysis that are relevant to values.

Behavior Analysis and Values

Because ACT and RFT have their theoretical and empirical roots in behavior analysis, it will be useful to first introduce behavior analysis and its approach to values before examining ACT and RFT and how we conceptualize values within their framework. As we shall see, the traditional behavior analytic approach to values was somewhat simplistic in that it omitted an analysis of complex human behavior, including language. Identified values are verbal by definition, and even in the case of values that are implicit or of which we are unaware, verbal processes play a large role. Hence, in order to discuss these aspects of values in technical detail, it will be necessary to introduce the language of RFT, which we do in chapter 2. Despite the role of verbal processes, however, all values arguably have a basis in the nonverbal environment and, more specifically, in nonverbal reinforcement.

Reinforcement: Positive and Negative

Reinforcement is a behavioral concept defined as an increase in responding that produces particular consequences (e.g., Skinner, 1974). Reinforcement is conceptualized as being either positive or negative. In *positive reinforcement*, the consequence in question is the presentation of an *appetitive* stimulus, or, in less technical terms, a stimulus that is motivating or desirable in some way. For example, parental praise is a powerful appetitive consequence for a young child, so forms of responding that produce this consequence, such as the child's repetition of a parent's spoken sounds, will tend to increase under certain circumstances. In *negative reinforcement*, the consequence in question is the removal of a stimulus that's aversive or undesirable in some way. An example of a negatively reinforced response might be a person putting her hands to her ears to block out a loud or grating noise. Negative reinforcement can further be broken down into two forms—escape and avoidance. *Escape* is a response that occurs to stop an aversive stimulus that is already present, whereas *avoidance* is a response that occurs to prevent something aversive from happening. The example we just used illustrates escape, since the person is escaping an aversive sound that's already there by blocking her ears. An example of avoidance might be putting up an umbrella when you see dark clouds in the sky. In this example, you aren't escaping the aversive stimulus of getting wet, since it isn't raining yet. Instead, by putting the umbrella up, you're avoiding getting wet.

This distinction between positive and negative forms of reinforcement is an important one in regard to the issue of values. From the current behavioral, ACT, and RFT perspective, values are defined in terms of what motivates us, what we find reinforcing, or what we will work toward gaining, rather than what we are escaping from or avoiding. Hence, values are defined in terms of positive rather than negative reinforcement. Indeed, from an ACT perspective maladaptive avoidance is seen as the primary cause of psychopathology, while acting in pursuit of those things we value in life is seen as the sign of a healthy and vital personality. Things are arguably more complex than that, since pathological avoidance and values-based action are more complex in some respects than the simple forms of avoidance and reinforcement that have often been studied in behavioral laboratories, but this is a good conceptual starting point.

So if values are related to positive reinforcement in some way, perhaps it is appropriate to consider positive reinforcement in a bit more detail at this point.

Positive Reinforcement and Values

Behavior analysts, including B. F. Skinner, have discussed the reinforcing quality of stimuli. Skinner (1938) referred to primary and secondary reinforcement. *Primary reinforcers* include food, drink, sex, sleep, and so on. For our ancestors, it was evolutionarily advantageous to be biologically attuned to finding such stimuli reinforcing with minimal learning, so we have inherited these biological proclivities. *Secondary reinforcers* acquire their reinforcing qualities through processes of conditioning; in other words, by being associated with primary reinforcers. In this case, the proclivity to be conditioned is inherited, but what is conditioned depends on the context and the person's specific life experiences. This allows flexibility with regard to what becomes reinforcing and means that different people may find different things reinforcing.

Money, good grades, attention, approval, and affection are all examples of conditioned reinforcers. These are all are associated more or less directly with primary reinforcers such as food or sexual contact. Money is associated directly with the provision of primary reinforcers such as food, and good grades are also associated, though less directly, with the attainment of primary reinforcers; for example, good grades enable academic success, which facilitates employment, which enables financial self-support, which allows the purchase of necessities and makes one more attractive as a marriage partner.

Attention, affection, and social approval become conditioned reinforcers through their association with socially mediated primary reinforcers. Children learn to associate approval and attention from their parents with primary reinforcers such as food, warmth, and cuddling. Later on in life, people learn that attention, approval, and affection from potential sexual partners are likely to be associated with sexual contact. A few conditioned reinforcers, such as money or approval, are referred to as *generalized reinforcers* because they're associated with more than one primary reinforcer.

Another very important reinforcer for humans is success in manipulating the environment. According to Skinner, simply "being effective" or "being right" may be innately reinforcing. Again, being effective or being right is often associated with gaining primary reinforcers. This association might be mediated by a generalized reinforcer such as social approval, which is itself associated with gaining primary reinforcers, or it might be established more directly, on the basis of successful manipulation of the environment resulting in access to primary reinforcers.

Hence, from a Skinnerian perspective, a wide variety of stimuli can attain reinforcing properties through their association with primary reinforcers, and these conditioned reinforcers can then function independently to control behavior.

Values: Beyond Simple Reinforcement

Having previously suggested that values are associated with reinforcement, based on what we have just discussed we can perhaps be more specific and say that values might be thought of in terms of aspects of life (such as meaningful relationships) that involve particular types of conditioned reinforcers (for example, affection), which are themselves linked both directly and indirectly with primary reinforcers. This behavioral approach does indeed provide a useful starting point for our current approach to values. It combines the idea that values have a connection with our biology, in terms of primary reinforcers, while also suggesting that there may be flexibility in the values we learn, since different histories will produce variations with regard to the conditioned reinforcers toward which we strive. Having said that, however, there are still some important elements missing.

First, we've implied that conditioned reinforcers provide an explanation of values, but we haven't provided enough detail about how the conditioning processes involved work. We've suggested that initially neutral stimuli become conditioned somehow, and that through this conditioning process, stimuli that aren't biological reinforcers can acquire status as reinforcers. However, we argue that simple behavioral processes involving explicit pairing of stimuli cannot be expected to account for the production of the highly complex and differentiated systems of values seen in human beings. Second, apart from the issue of complexity of values, the consequences of abstract high-level values (such as world peace) are often temporally distant or outside the lifetime of a particular individual and hence are unlikely to function as actual reinforcers. Third, we've mentioned that conditioning can create secondary reinforcers such as money, approval, and so on. However, reinforcers such as these can often actually be antithetical to what we understand by values. As many psychotherapeutic and philosophical traditions have suggested, seeking wealth or social approval can detract from the pursuit of psychologically healthy values. Indeed, this can often be true in the case of biological reinforcers, as well, such as when overeating or sex addiction, for example, block the development of genuine values. As we shall argue in later chapters, long-term sustainability is key to psychologically healthy values, and certain patterns of pursuit of secondary and even primary reinforcers can be antithetical to this end.

In conclusion, there must be something more than processes of simple reinforcement at work to allow the development of complex, long-term, sustainable values from simple processes of reinforcement. We believe there is, and we believe that verbal behavior, or language, provides the answer. In chapter 2, we introduce RFT and discuss how RFT conceptualizes values by retaining the idea of conditioning but also introducing the concept of conditioning through language. Furthermore, this theory of verbal behavior makes it possible to provide technical accounts of the functional patterns that distinguish long-term valued behavior from other behavior that is only apparently based in values.

Having provided some of the key foundations of ACT, both philosophical (functional contextualism) and scientific (behavior analysis), we will conclude chapter 1 with a brief overview of some of the core features of the ACT approach to values.

ACT, Values, and Modern Psychotherapy

As ACT clinicians, we can help a client identify her values, as well as cultivate and enhance value-consistent living. One key feature of ACT that sets it apart from some other forms of CBT is its explicit focus on values and building patterns of action that are consistent with one's values. As a functional contextual intervention, ACT has a greater focus on functioning than on symptom reduction. Helping a client function more effectively in her current environment, even with the experiences, predispositions, and problems in her past history, is the overall goal of the ACT therapist. Symptoms are important in ACT; an ACT therapist doesn't ignore the fact that her client is having daily panic attacks, for example, or has been so depressed at times that she couldn't get out of bed. However, in the ACT approach symptoms are examined in context. Depression, for instance, is viewed not as a discrete problem, but as having a contextual, historical basis and as being maintained at least in part by lack of valued action. ACT involves several processes that work together not to change a client's experiences directly, but rather to help her relate to her experiences in a different way so that she may engage more fully within valued life domains. This focus on function and processes as opposed to reducing symptoms means that ACT clinical researchers often work in areas outside the scope of traditional mainstream psychotherapy, such as behavioral medicine, severe mental illness, workplace stress and burnout, and preventing psychological problems.

An Introduction to an ACT Definition of Values

Recently, the ACT definition of values has been refined from what was originally presented in the first book on acceptance and commitment therapy, *Acceptance and Commitment Therapy: An Experiential Approach to Behavior Change* (Hayes, Strosahl, & Wilson, 1999). We will spend a great deal of time examining the implications of each part of this new definition in chapter 2, but for now we present the definition without detailed explanation. *Values* are now defined as "freely chosen, verbally constructed consequences of ongoing, dynamic, evolving patterns of activity, which establish predominant reinforcers for that activity that are intrinsic in engagement in the valued behavioral pattern itself" (Wilson, 2009, 66). In essence (and ignoring technical terms) this means that values are chosen concepts linked with patterns of action that provide a sense of meaning and that can coordinate our behavior over long time frames. Examples of such patterns might be acting lovingly toward one's partner or being present with one's children. Values in this sense can never be fulfilled, satisfied, or completed; rather, they serve to give us purpose or direction in each instance of behavior. In chapter 2 we thoroughly examine both the ACT definition of values and the other processes at the core of the ACT model.

Values Work as the Cornerstone of Psychotherapy

As you will see in the next chapter, there are many components of an ACT intervention, but values work is the one component that can provide a useful framework within which much of therapy can be conducted. Metaphorically, values are like the compass for therapy, providing a constant sense of direction for clients as they engage in therapeutic work. Specifically, values work supports the following processes:

- Helping clients clearly define what matters to them

- Creating a sense of meaning and purpose

- Providing a framework for setting specific goals in both the short term and the long term

- Providing a context in which a client may be more willing to experience difficult thoughts and feelings as she moves in valued directions

- Helping clients practice being more aware of the reinforcing qualities of behaviors in the moment that are related to a larger value

There are three important steps in values work. First, values clarification is the process of developing values statements that guide client behavior. This is a process that is ongoing throughout therapy. When a client enters therapy, she may not have a clear sense of her values or may have difficulty engaging in behaviors consistent with her values. As therapy progresses, a client's chosen values and value-directed behaviors may shift as her behavior becomes more flexible. Just as someone might periodically check her compass bearing to make sure she hasn't strayed too far from her intended direction, a client in therapy should engage in values clarification throughout the course of therapy to help ensure that her behavior is values-congruent. Second, clients and clinicians work together to develop goals: discrete behaviors that can be evaluated and completed to move the client in the direction of her stated values. Choosing particular goals that are in line with one's values can take practice. To determine whether a particular goal is in line with her values, the client must practice becoming aware of the reinforcing properties of her values-consistent behaviors. Third, clients build larger and larger patterns of behavior in line with their values, building meaning and developing a purpose to work toward in each moment.

The characteristics of these patterns are important. We would suggest that when a person's behavior is guided by avoidance or excessively rigid rules, that person's ability to behave flexibly decreases. For example, if a woman is terrified of heights, she may avoid situations where she would have to cross a bridge and may even believe that she couldn't stand the anxiety of doing so even if something important to her (say her daughter's graduation) was on the other side. In this case, if the person doesn't cross the bridge, we would say that she has very little flexibility in responding to her fear; she simply avoids it at all costs.

In contrast, when a person is more accepting of her uncomfortable thoughts and feelings as fleeting experiences that need not determine behavior, she is more likely to be able to choose a variety of different behaviors. Instead of avoiding the bridge, the woman might choose to cross it, and she might even find that she's willing to be in other situations that evoke her fear of heights. In short, behavior under control of aversive stimuli (for example, fear and avoidance) is likely to lead to a narrow repertoire of behavior, whereas behavior under control of appetitive stimuli (for example, acceptance and values-based choices) is likely to lead to a broad, flexible repertoire. As therapists, our overarching goal is to help clients build and maintain flexible, meaningful repertoires of behavior over long periods of time.

Summary

In this first chapter we have introduced and discussed some theoretical background to the concept of values. Specifically, we have presented functional contextualism as the philosophical foundation upon which ACT and RFT are grounded. Because ACT is a behavioral therapy, we have also provided you with some key behavior analytic principles relevant to ACT in general and values in particular. Finally, we have provided a brief introduction to values as conceptualized from an ACT perspective. In the next chapter, we'll introduce you to RFT, thoroughly examine the ACT definition of values, and take a closer look at the other core processes involved in the ACT model.

CHAPTER 2

ACT and RFT

The aim of this chapter is to help you understand, in more detail, the theory and principles of ACT and RFT that support and enhance our understanding of values. In the previous chapter, we introduced functional contextualism as the philosophy of science underlying ACT and RFT, with behavior analysis providing their basic theoretical background. In this chapter we will present ACT and RFT themselves in detail, which will require a fair amount of technical language. We think this is important for the purposes of gaining a thorough understanding of values as conceptualized from an ACT perspective. We believe you should gain some minimum familiarity with both ACT, the psychotherapy underlying the values approach we adopt, and RFT, the behavioral theory of language upon which ACT is based. After this chapter, however, our discussion of values will continue with a minimum of technical language.

We turn first to relational frame theory. We will introduce RFT and describe RFT concepts that bear on the issue of psychopathology. That will set the stage for the introduction of ACT.

Relational Frame Theory

In chapter 1, we described the traditional behavior analytic conception of values in terms of operant reinforcement. We suggested that the concept of reinforcement might provide a useful starting point for the analysis of values, since both biologically based primary reinforcers and conditioned secondary reinforcers play important roles in valued areas of our lives. However, traditional concepts of conditioning don't seem adequate to explain the nature of the learning that would appear to underlie the very complex and highly abstract nature of human values. An important reason why the traditional analysis might not be sufficient is that it fails to adequately characterize human language, which we believe is central to the understanding of values. Hence we turn to RFT, a relatively recent theoretical approach within behavior analysis that focuses specifically on language and cognition.

Relational Framing

Relational frame theory (RFT; Hayes et al., 2001) is a behavior analytic approach to the phenomena of language and higher cognitive functioning that explains these phenomena as *arbitrarily applicable relational responding*, also referred to as *relational framing*. This concept is explained as follows: Many nonhuman animals can be trained to respond to physical relationships between objects; for example, they can be trained to consistently pick the biggest object from an array. Humans also can do this, of course, and are able to do so from a very early age. However, RFT argues that verbally able humans show an additional type of relational responding that other animals don't in which they relate objects based not upon the physical relation between them but upon contextual cues that determine which relation is appropriate.

For example, imagine a verbally able child is given an exercise involving the hypothetical characters Mr. A. and Mr. B in which she is told that "Mr. A is taller than Mr. B." If subsequently asked to say which person is shorter, she will likely say, "Mr. B," without needing to be told anything further. This response is based upon the contextual cues "taller" and "shorter" rather than on physical relations. Since the taught relation need not depend in any way on physical relations and hence is arbitrarily applicable to any stimuli no matter what their physical properties, this type of responding is referred to as arbitrarily applicable relational responding.

According to RFT, learning language is based on learning many different patterns of arbitrarily applicable relational responding, referred to as relational frames. Examples include sameness ("0.5 is equal to one-half"), opposition ("Big is the opposite of small"), difference ("A boat is different from a ship"), comparison ("An elephant is bigger than a mouse"), and perspective taking ("I am here, and you are there"). There is an increasing quantity of empirical support for the existence of these and other frames (e.g., Dymond & Barnes, 1994, 1995, 1996; Roche & Barnes, 1996, 1997; Steele & Hayes, 1991) and for the human capacity to be trained in these frames (e.g., Barnes-Holmes, Barnes-Holmes, & Smeets, 2004; Berens & Hayes, 2007; Luciano, Gomez-Becerra, & Rodriguez-Valverde, 2007).

RFT posits that relational frames are forms of operant behavior that humans learn through multiple exposures to interactions with their native language community involving these patterns. (For detailed descriptions of the learning processes involved, see, for example, Barnes, 1994, 1996; Hayes, 1991, 1994; Hayes & Hayes, 1989, 1992.) All relational frames involve three defining features: mutual entailment, combinatorial entailment, and transformation of functions. *Mutual entailment* refers to the fact that a relation in one direction between two objects automatically gives rise to a second relation in the opposite direction. For example, if a person is given two foreign coins and told that coin 1 is worth more than coin 2, he will derive that coin 2 is worth less than coin 1. In other words, the first relation entails the appropriateness of the second relation, and this works no matter which of the two is trained first; that is, it is mutual. *Combinatorial entailment* is the phenomenon in which two relations are combined to form a third relation. For example, given three foreign coins, if coin 1 is worth more than coin 2, and coin 2 is worth more than coin 3, a "more than" relation is entailed between coins 1 and 3, and a "less than" relation is entailed between coins 3 and 1.

Transformation of functions (or, to be more precise, *transformation of stimulus functions*) is extremely important in terms of the psychological relevance of relational framing since, from an RFT perspective, it is the process by which language can control our behavior. In technical terms, if two stimuli, A and B, participate in a relation and stimulus A has a psychological function, then under certain conditions the stimulus functions of B may be transformed in accordance with that relation. For instance, imagine a child who is shown a coin and told that she can use it to buy candy in the store. Telling her that she can use the coin to buy candy gives it value and thus makes it desirable (in technical terms, this gives the coin an appetitive function). If she is then shown a second coin and told that this coin is worth more than the first one, the psychological functions of the second coin may be transformed such that it is now more desirable (or more appetitive) than the first, and if given a choice between the two coins, the child will choose the second. Transformation of function is a particularly important phenomenon in explaining clinical phenomena, as we shall see shortly.

As we derive relations through our interactions with the socioverbal community, we elaborate the relational network of stimuli that are in derived relations for us. The expansion of this relational network happens rapidly from the time we first encounter language and continues throughout our lives. The well-documented "language explosion" that happens for small children is an obvious and salient example of the elaboration of the relational network. This happens once children have acquired the ability to derive just a few simple relations, allowing them to name an expanding set of new objects and events and derive relations involving those new objects and events. As children grow into adulthood, continued verbal interactions produce an increasingly complex and multirelational network involving vast numbers of different objects and events and the relations between them. For human beings, everything we encounter and think about, including ourselves, our thoughts and emotions, our prospects, other people, and our environment, becomes part of this elaborate verbal relational network. Thus, for human beings the world is verbal, and we can never get away from language except under very unusual circumstances. Language has vast advantages for us including our ability to think about and mold our environment to suit our needs but also has potential disadvantages such as our susceptibility to uniquely human forms of psychopathology. There are already a large number of empirical studies that have used RFT to investigate and model language processes in the laboratory, including processes that bear directly on psychopathology and ACT. In the following sections, we'll look at some fundamental aspects of the RFT analysis of language that are relevant to psychology, psychopathology, and psychotherapy, and that set the scene for ACT.

Bidirectional Stimulus Relations

Language allows bidirectional or mutually entailed relations between stimuli, such as between words and objects such that if an object is related to a word, then the word is related to the object, and vice versa. This provides the basis for an important difference between humans and other animals. Consider, for example, an experimental setup in which a pigeon must peck a red disk for food if it previously received a shock. The pigeon will easily learn this. The shock may have been aversive, but reporting the shock via the red disk is not. For nonverbal animals, conditioning a neutral stimulus (e.g., a red disk) to acquire some of the functions of a psychologically potent stimulus (e.g., a shock) will occur only if the neutral stimulus comes before the potent stimulus, not if it comes after it. In other words, nonverbal conditioning is based on unidirectional stimulus relations.

Now consider a real-life situation involving an adult human who suffers a traumatic car accident. Afterward he fears and avoids car travel, and this avoidance begins to interfere with his life and values. For example, he might value his career, and not being able to drive to work may make it more difficult for him to make it in on time. He can "report" the car accident by talking to a therapist, just as the pigeon could report the shock by pecking the red disk. Furthermore, this man probably knows that talking about the accident may well be reinforced as it helps him get his life back together, just as pecking the red disk was reinforced with food for the pigeon. Will he actually talk to a therapist though? He might not. One key difference between his situation and that of the pigeon is that for him it isn't just the traumatic event that was aversive; talking about it is also aversive. This is due to the bidirectional relations and transformation of functions between talking about the event and the traumatic event itself. Some of the aversive functions of the crash transfer to talking about the crash, so he finds such talk itself aversive.

For example, if he attempts to talk about or even think about the crash, he may reexperience at least some of the same intense fear he experienced just before impact, or some of the unpleasant visual or auditory experiences of the aftermath. Since talking about or even thinking about the crash causes him to reexperience these aversive phenomena to some degree, he might avoid situations, including therapy, that require these actions. However, although verbal reexposure to these aversive psychological experiences may be uncomfortable, it is also likely to be helpful. By exposing himself to the aversive psychological functions of talking about the experience, some extinction of the functions conditioned by the experience of the crash will occur—both for the talk itself and for the object of that talk, including cars and car travel. This may help him to resume his previous level of contact with cars and car travel and thereby help him to live more fully in accordance with his values again.

Relational Coherence

could be innate as it has survival value

From an RFT perspective, a very important part of our learning at all ages involves reinforcement for maintaining coherence in our relational responding. This is largely socially mediated at first, in that parents and other authority figures, such as teachers, provide attention and praise for coherence between what we say and what we do (for example, telling the truth) and between our verbal descriptions and "reality" (descriptive accuracy). Later on, reinforcement for coherence is also mediated by the nonsocial environment through the ability to solve problems. For example, learning to master a new piece of computer software might produce conditioned reinforcement, such as faster completion of work-related tasks. Hence, relational coherence—figuring things out or getting the right answer—becomes very reinforcing for us.

Figuring things out can be a very important and useful element in our lives and in living congruently with our values. Solving problems is often necessary in order to achieve goals connected with the pursuit of our values. For example, a man might value helping other people by becoming a doctor. If he values this goal, then he will need to achieve the many subgoals associated with becoming a doctor, including getting into medical school, passing medical exams, and so on. Hence relational coherence can be extremely useful in our lives.

However, our learned need for relational coherence can also effectively cut us off from our values. For instance, consider the case of a car crash victim whose face is badly scarred. His values might include an intimate relationship, marriage, and a family. After the accident, however, he might give up dating, reasoning that he will probably always be scarred, that potential dates will now find him much less attractive, and that he will therefore continue to suffer anxiety about his face in future dating situations. He may diagnose this situation accurately and then cling to his correctly reasoned story as a basis for avoiding dating. He may reason philosophically that life is unfair, that there are winners and losers, and that he needs to resign himself to losing.

Apart from apparently justifying his avoidance of the high levels of anxiety and discomfort involved in dating, one other important reason why his story may be reinforcing for him is because, as RFT suggests, reinforcement is often contingent on simply gaining a good understanding and having that understanding confirmed by events. In this case, his story coheres with well-established relational networks concerning sex and attraction, success and failure, and possibly even ideals such as stoicism. However, no matter how good it might sometimes feel to be right, acting in accordance with his values by continuing to date will arguably be critically important for this man.

Rules and Rule-Governed Behavior

Skinner contrasted rule-governed behavior with contingency-shaped behavior (e.g., Skinner, 1989). Whereas nonhuman animals seem to learn about their environment primarily through *respondent conditioning* (pairing or association of stimuli) and *operant conditioning* (learning to respond to situations through the consequences of their behavior), verbal humans seem to show the ability to learn very rapidly through "rules" specifying how they should behave.

Rules are important because we can't always learn the most effective ways of responding to the world through our direct experience. For example, we have all heard and followed rules such as "Don't walk on thin ice," but most of us have not had the experience of falling into a freezing cold lake before we learned to avoid thin ice. It is much more efficient (and sometimes even lifesaving) to be able to learn from rules rather than just our direct experience. Imagine trying to learn to drive a car or operate a computer without any rules for operating them! In fact, rules apply to almost everything we do, because we are constantly learning from others and abstracting rules for behavior.

An example of a rule might be "If you stand outside the entrance to the town hall at three in the afternoon, then I'll be there to meet you." This rule specifies spatial and temporal antecedents, the form and context of the response, and the nature of the consequence. A verbally competent human could hear this rule once and act in accordance with it without any other training, despite the relative precision of the behavior required. It was for this reason that Skinner thought that rules as contingency-specifying stimuli were extremely important.

Much basic research supports this view, suggesting that rules and rule-governed behavior are indeed influential on our behavior (e.g., Weiner, 1970; Lowe, 1979). Furthermore, while rules can be influential in a positive way, they can also be influential in a negative way. In other words, they are relevant to the development of psychopathology. While rules can help people navigate their world more effectively, we also know that human behavior can come under the influence of rules to the exclusion of other sources of environmental control (e.g., Kaufman, Baron, & Kopp, 1966). Consider a child who, in response to a number of initial mistakes while learning to play the piano, generates the rule "I will never be able to play the piano." He might subsequently act according to this rule by giving up trying to learn during lessons, or by giving up on taking lessons altogether. If he had continued to try in spite of failures, he would probably eventually experience the reinforcement provided by hearing himself play well. However, obeying the rule prevents him from contacting this reinforcement. Much basic empirical work has documented this phenomenon of rule-based insensitivity to contingencies, wherein humans under the influence of a rule are much less likely to adapt to changes in their environment (e.g., Hayes, Brownstein, Haas, & Greenway, 1986; Matthews, Shimoff, Catania, & Sagvolden, 1977; Shimoff, Catania, & Matthews, 1981). Furthermore, recent RFT-based research (McAuliffe, Barnes-Holmes, & Barnes-Holmes, 2004) has suggested that depressed individuals may be more likely to come under the control of rules provided by others, referred to as *pliance*. For example, clinically depressed individuals were more likely than nondepressed controls to follow experimenter-provided rules specifying how to respond on a matching-to-sample task even though breaking the rule produced monetary reinforcement.

RFT ANALYSIS OF RULES

Despite the apparent importance of rules as suggested by Skinner and by empirical studies on their effects, basic behavior analysis could not provide a satisfactory definition of what a rule was. However, this has changed with the advent of the RFT approach to language. RFT provides an analysis of rule-governed behavior in terms of the relational frames involved and the cues that occasion the derivation of those relations, and also in terms of the psychological functions transformed through those relations and the cues that occasion those transformations of function (e.g., Barnes-Holmes et al., 2001). From this perspective, an analysis of the rule about meeting someone outside the town hall entrance would involve the following specific relational frames: coordination relations between words (town hall) and actual objects or events; before-after relations specified in terms that indicate a temporal antecedent; perspective (I-you) relations; and if-then relations that specify a contingency. As regards transformation of functions, the words "stand outside" alter the behavioral functions of the town hall building such that the listener is more likely to stand near it in the context specified in the rule (e.g., 'three in the afternoon').

RFT suggests that an individual provided with a rule can determine whether or not the rule is being followed by the extent to which the rule coordinates with actual behavior. More technically, for the rule follower, the coordination between the relational network constituted by the rule and the relations sustained among the objects or events specified by the rule acts as an ongoing source of behavioral regulation. In other words, if the listener sees that events in the nonarbitrary environment specified by the rule are indeed in the relations specified by the rule, then the rule is being followed. In our example, if the listener perceives that he is standing outside the town hall when his watch indicates it's three in the afternoon, then he is following the rule correctly.

CONTINGENCIES PRODUCING RULE-GOVERNED BEHAVIOR

Complementing the RFT analysis of the basic language processes involved in rule-governed behavior, Robert Zettle and Steven Hayes (1982) provide a therapeutically useful categorization of three different kinds of contingencies that produce rule-governed behavior: pliance, tracking, and augmenting. In each case, the process just explained—deriving a relation of coordination between a rule and one's behavior—occurs; however, an additional pattern determines the behavioral effect. *Pliance* is rule-governed behavior under the control of a history of socially mediated reinforcement for following rules. In other words, the person follows a rule because in the past he has received reinforcement for doing so. For example, if after being told, "Wear your coat; it's cold outside," a child wears his coat only because not doing so has previously resulted in punishment, this is pliance. *Tracking* (or *tracking a rule*) is rule-governed behavior under the control of a history of coordination between the rule and the arrangement of the environment independent of the delivery of the rule. For example, if a child wears his coat in response to the rule "Wear your coat; it's cold outside" because he wants to keep warm, this is tracking.

Augmenting is rule-governed behavior due to behavior that alters the degree to which events function as consequences. It takes two forms, motivative augmenting and formative augmenting. *Motivative augmenting* changes the effectiveness of a stimulus already functioning as a consequence. For example, if I say, "How would you like a delicious Snickers bar?" and this increases the reinforcing effect for you of receiving a Snickers bar—without Snickers bars actually becoming more accessible—this is a motivative augmental rule (we return to this concept and provide a theoretical explanation of how it works later in this chapter). *Formative augmenting* generates consequential functions for a stimulus where they did not previously occur. For example, the rule "These tickets are worth money" might transform the functions of previously neutral pieces of paper so as to make them reinforcing.

This categorization of rule-governed behavior into three functionally distinct patterns—pliance, tracking, and augmenting—is important in the therapeutic context. For example, given research evidence indicating the excessive influence of rules on behavior, and the role of such excessive influence in psychopathology in particular, ACT and RFT suggest the importance in psychotherapy of attenuating the influence of rules. In our approach to psychotherapy as ACT practitioners, we are aware of the particular need to de-emphasize therapist-provided rules that must be followed (pliance) and are concerned instead with enabling the client to contact the contingencies in his situation himself. For example, a typical example of a traditional therapist-presented rule might be "That's an irrational thought you've been having. You should focus on the positive instead." In this example, apart from providing the client with a thought-control type of rule, which basic research (e.g., Wegner, 1994) shows might actually backfire in the longer term (i.e., trying not to think the thought might actually increase the frequency of the thought), the therapist is encouraging further pliance on the part of the client (e.g., 'you should') and also underlining the importance of coherence in the verbal relational network (i.e., by suggesting the thought is 'irrational'). Hence, explicit provision of rules is often likely to be unhelpful from an ACT perspective. ACT therapists, on the other hand, attempt to avoid, for the most part, providing rules that must be followed. Rather, they conduct defusion or deliteralization exercises, which undermine the regulatory functions of language. Furthermore, communication with clients is often accomplished through indirect means, such as metaphors and experiential exercises, which tend to be less directly prescriptive than directly stated rules and can induce the client to examine his own behavior and find out for himself whether his behavior is likely to be effective in allowing him to contact his values.

Though excessive influence by pliance in particular may cause problems (as we will see when we discuss the ACT model), rules of all three functional types are also an important source of regulation in psychotherapy. This is particularly the case with regard to motivative augmental rules prescribing values, which we will discuss a bit later. However, it is also the case with rules prescribing behavior likely to bring the client into contact with valued consequences. Imagine in the case of our example of a rule about meeting someone outside the town hall that the rule is being followed by an agoraphobic and that the person who tells him she will meet him is a potential date. In this case, following the rule might be difficult and anxiety provoking for this person, but if he values a potential relationship enough, the reinforcing value of the consequence may make it more likely that he will follow the rule, particularly if he has learned about the importance of acting in accordance with his values, for example, in the context of therapy. Following such rules might be relatively pliance-based in the initial stages of therapy. However, as therapeutic progress is made, more tracking-type behavior should emerge.

SELF-RULES

In addition to analysis of rules provided by others, RFT also allows for the analysis of self-rules, which depends to some extent on an analysis of the concept of self. Relational frame theory suggests that a verbal self-concept emerges over time through multiple interactions with the linguistic community. On the basis of numerous questions and answers concerning his own behavior and that of others (for example, "What did you do yesterday?" or "What am I doing now?") the child learns to respond in accordance with deictic relations ("I-you," "here-there," and "now-then") that depend on the perspective of the speaker. I am always "here" and "now," whereas you or other people in general are more likely "there" and "then." Hence, the child develops a sense of a unique perspective that is different from that of other people and thereby also develops a concept of self.

In fact, relational frame theory indicates the emergence of a number of psychologically different categories of self, including self-as-content, self-as-process, and self-as-context. The *self-as-content* is a relational network that includes such self-descriptions as "I am twenty years old" or "I am male." *Self-as-process* involves the ongoing discrimination of psychological processes occurring in the context of "me," including patterns of emotion ("I feel angry") or thought ("I'm thinking about food a lot right now"). *Self-as-context* is the discrimination that there is continuity in the context in which the other selves (self-as-content and self-as-process) occur; in other words, whenever I describe my behavior, I describe it as "here" and "now," and this is always the case. Throughout this book, we also use other terms for this phenomenon, such as a "transcendent sense of self" and the "observer perspective."

We spend a great deal of time on the concept of self-as-context later in this chapter and throughout the book, so don't worry if it isn't completely clear just yet.

Relational framing makes verbal self-knowledge extremely useful. For example, humans can verbally construct their future and plan for it in minute detail. Such future planning involves self-rules, such as "I have to get up at seven tomorrow." This self-rule refers to strategic behavior that will occur relatively close in time to when the person makes the rule. This is an example of a *strategic self-rule*. However, self-rules can also refer explicitly to longer-term valued objectives that are more overarching, such as "I'd like a more intimate relationship with my partner." The latter is an example of a *valuative self-rule*. Both strategic and valuative self-rules refer to future behavior, though there tend to be immediately noticeable differences between them. For example, in strategic rules such as having to get up at seven, the behavioral terms specified by the rule tend to have relatively precise functions. In this instance, both the behavior involved ("getting up") and the antecedent conditions ("at seven") are clearly defined. In valuative rules, however, this often isn't the case. In the other example, the meaning of the term "a more intimate relationship" is more complex than that of "getting up at seven." Furthermore, the nature of the behavior required by the rule is also much less obvious than in the case of the strategic rule.

MOTIVATIVE AUGMENTAL RULES

As defined earlier, motivative augmental rules alter the degree to which previously established reinforcers function as consequences. Hence, in RFT, valuative statements or self-rules may be analyzed as motivative augmental rules. They function to augment the reinforcing functions of a valued direction. Value statements, such as "I'd like a more intimate relationship with my partner," are undoubtedly much more complex in terms of the relational network and the reinforcement involved; however, they work in a similar way to the simpler case involving the Snickers bar. Words such as "more intimate" present some of the emotional, sensory, and perceptual functions of greater intimacy, and therefore tend to increase the likelihood of behavior that works to produce this consequence.

Acceptance and Commitment Therapy

The preceding discussion of some of the important features of relational frame theory sets the scene for introducing the theory of acceptance and commitment therapy. In the rest of this chapter, we will present the ACT model of psychopathology, which ACT sees in terms of six primary problem areas, and the six core ACT processes, which are designed to target each of these areas. At the end of the discussion of each process, we briefly examine how RFT conceptualizes that process. For those enthusiastic to learn more about the RFT connection with ACT, these will be of interest, while others may skip over them.

Language (relational framing) is an extremely useful skill, allowing us to communicate, remember the past, solve problems, plan for the future, consider risks, discuss our options, decide on a course of action, and calculate a probability of success. However, language is a double-edged sword. Just as we are able to remember being on the beach last summer, we are also able to remember all of the times we've been hurt. Being able to remember the past is important for planning for the future, but it also allows us to ruminate about our mistakes, berate ourselves for our perceived failures, and defend our long-established conceptualizations of who we are. The ACT approach rests on the idea that normal processes of human language and cognition can play a major role in the development and maintenance of psychopathology.

Relational framing can become a problem when it overrides actual cues in the environment. For instance, based on frames of coordination and comparison an agoraphobic client may begin to avoid not only the place in which he suffered a panic attack, but other places where he might be likely to meet people. Over time, this can lead to a narrowing of behavior, usually at the expense of the person's values (e.g., Hayes, 1989). It isn't too much of a stretch to see that, over time, we all can start to respond to our own thoughts as if they were actually a threat to the self. You may have heard the phrase "Guns don't kill people; people kill people." This is exactly the case with our thoughts. They can't harm us, but our behavior in response to them may indeed do just that. Problematic verbal constructions can facilitate behavior patterns that are inconsistent with our values.

The traditional ACT conceptualization of psychological problems includes six fundamental processes—experiential avoidance, cognitive fusion, lack of contact with the present moment, attachment to a conceptualized self, unclear values, and lack of commitment to engaging in valued activity—all of which lead to psychological inflexibility. In turn, ACT offers six intervention strategies, each the flip side of one of these problem areas. Each of the other four pieces of the ACT model can impact valuing and commitment to values-consistent behaviors. A primary focus of this book is on how each of these problems impacts valuing, and to that end we provide strategies to help you help your clients build psychological flexibility as they live more values-consistent lives. In the sections that follow, we touch only briefly upon how each of these problems can impact values and values-consistent behaviors, as the rest of the book will cover this in depth. As we examine the ACT model in the following sections, we also introduce some of the core intervention techniques that may be employed to foster values-consistent behaviors; again, these techniques will be discussed in much greater detail in later chapters.

Experiential Avoidance and Acceptance

One verbal contingency that is particularly problematic for humans is the rule that private (internal) events cause other behaviors. This can create a verbal rule that negatively evaluated private events are dangerous and must be controlled, which can lead to responding characterized by experiential avoidance (e.g., Hayes et al., 2006). *Experiential avoidance* refers to a person's attempts to control, alter, or escape from private experiences even when attempts to do so may cause harm (Hayes, Wilson, Gifford, Follette, & Strosahl, 1996). From an ACT perspective, what is important is not the form of experiential avoidance, but rather the function of the behavior. In other words, many behaviors can serve to help people avoid their own experiences: getting angry, drinking alcohol or using drugs, avoiding particular people or places, engaging in compulsive behaviors, withdrawing from valued activities, or sleeping excessively. As varied as these behaviors are, each can serve a similar function: providing temporary relief from something unpleasant.

There are many physical and psychological experiences that may be evaluated as unwanted or uncomfortable. In certain circumstances, and in part based upon our individual histories, we may experience feelings, memories, or bodily sensations as threatening or harmful to us. As a result, we may learn to cope with these private experiences by trying to avoid them.

This ability to predict and avoid circumstances where fear, pain, or isolation is likely to occur is very adaptive for survival, and historically it has served humans well. For example, those who responded to fearful situations by avoidance or escape survived to pass on their genes to the next generation. From an ACT perspective, we would say that a behavior has the function of experiential avoidance if the avoidance and escape behaviors occur when the threat is only verbally derived, as opposed to actually being present in the nonverbal environment. Consider a trauma survivor whose hypervigilance served him well in a war zone, but upon returning home he finds every little noise or disturbance threatening. The context has changed, but the behavior remains the same. Some avoidance behaviors can be intrinsically harmful or even fatal, such as substance abuse, self-harm, or bingeing and purging.

Unfortunately, experiential avoidance tends to work extremely well to help us avoid and escape from undesirable experiences in the short run, making it more likely that we will continue to use it as a coping strategy. For example, in the short term the agoraphobic's avoidance of the shopping mall means lower levels of anxiety. In the long run, however, an increased sensitivity to the unwanted experiences is likely, so the person may engage in larger and larger patterns of avoidance and escape in order to remain out of contact with such experiences. Experiential avoidance as a rigid, pervasive pattern of behavior can lead to excessive narrowing of options and lead people down a path of not being willing to experience ever-smaller levels of uncomfortable experiences. In the long term, experiential avoidance doesn't lead clients down a valued path. For example, a drug addict may successfully avoid feeling sad in the moment by using, but the long-term consequences of this behavior might be very negative.

From a functional contextual perspective, it isn't what we experience that is the problem, but how we relate to those experiences. Our sensations and experiences themselves are not inherently good or bad; rather, it is the context in which private experience occurs that affects how willing we are to experience certain things at a particular point in time. For example, a person might be willing to feel the fear of skiing down a black diamond slope (in fact, he might speak of that type of arousal as excitement, not fear). However, that same person might not be willing to feel the fear related to speaking in front of a large audience. In the first case, the context is one in which he may be willing to feel fear, whereas in the second his fear is something to be avoided, even though the second event is much safer from a logical standpoint. What is notable is that the physical sensations of excitement and fear are almost identical; only the context and the person's relation to the sensations are different between the two scenarios.

How does experiential avoidance relate to values? Imagine a client who lives his life on the safe side, choosing to engage life only when it is comfortable and easy, and avoiding anything that offers real vitality. How many of us have seen clients who say they aren't living consistently with some of their values because they find the future too uncertain, the unknown too disquieting? It isn't that unusual to see clients who avoid things or experiences they have become conditioned to fear, such as dogs (following a serious dog bite) or heights (after falling from a ladder). What also tends to happen is that clients may start to avoid areas of life that are truly vital to living a meaningful life. It's hard to imagine a client who hasn't been in a relationship that has ended, whether through death, a breakup or divorce, or a fight with a friend, or because someone moved far away. Most people have experienced, and may well remember, the pain of losing someone close to them. Let's imagine then, that a client has lost a loved one and subsequently begins to avoid becoming close to others. He may do so to avoid feeling sad, lonely, a sense of loss, or any of the other feelings that could come from losing someone he cares for deeply. In order to avoid this anticipated private experience of loss, he may start to narrow his range of friends and close relationships. Or, for another example, imagine a client who fears failure so much that he doesn't take any risks, even if those risks are associated with valued domains. It's risky to live consistently with the value of making a difference at one's job or in the community, so he may find it simpler, easier, and more comfortable to settle for less than his heartfelt values.

These familiar examples illustrate that some people would rather live quietly than vitally. We don't mean to imply that anyone should value certain things (such as intimacy or making a difference at one's job or in the community, as in the previous examples), or even that people should behave in any particular prescribed way (such as taking risks in pursuit of one's values). What we are suggesting is that it can create a sense of meaninglessness or self-doubt when people don't live consistently with their values in an attempt to avoid negative experiences.

In ACT, acceptance is taught as an alternative to experiential avoidance. *Acceptance* refers to behavior rather than a belief or state of mind and involves the active and aware embrace of private events without unnecessary attempts to change their frequency or form. It is important to note that acceptance doesn't change the nature of private experiences (anxiety is still anxiety), but rather the person's experience of those events (willingness to experience anxiety). As clinicians, we hope to change the function of anxiety (as just one example) from something that must be avoided to something that can be embraced actively (not passively resigned to) in the service of an effective, values-driven life within the context of one's own history and within the context of each moment.

Acceptance is fostered in clients through the use of metaphors, experiential exercises, and emotionally relevant examples from the client's own life. As a client discusses the difficulties he experiences in life, the therapist examines ways in which the client is unwilling to experience his thoughts, feelings, memories, and bodily sensations. Metaphors and experiential exercises help the client see that trying to control, escape, or avoid his experiences comes at a cost to his life. For example, if a client struggles with feeling socially inadequate and becomes extremely nervous around others, he may stop seeking to interact with others even if it means giving up something important to him. Through acceptance work, as well as defusion work (which we will describe in a moment), clients learn to accept aversive private experiences as things that can be lived with as they engage in valued activities.

ACCEPTANCE AND RFT

From an RFT perspective (e.g., Barnes-Holmes, Barnes-Holmes, McHugh, & Hayes, 2004), acceptance at its core may be conceptualized as follows:

1. The provision of a rule or relational network that specifies taking an action that will bring the listener into contact with a possibly aversive event (for example, "Acceptance means that I'll attend the party, even though I may feel uncomfortable if I do").

2. The rule is followed and the person comes in contact with the event (attending the party) and with discomfort in the context of that event.

3. A relational network describing that contact is derived ("I am at the party and I feel uncomfortable").

4. A relation of coordination is derived between the derived network in point 3 and the original rule ("I thought that I might feel uncomfortable at the party and I do feel uncomfortable, so I was right").

From a relational frame perspective, the coordination between the two networks that occurs in point 4 probably plays an important role in the efficacy of the strategy of acceptance. The relational coherence of the networks is itself a reinforcing event since, as suggested earlier, coherence is a powerful generalized reinforcer for verbal humans. Hence, although the acceptance rule refers to an aversive situation, it does at least successfully predict the aversiveness of the situation, and this aspect alone may be enough to increase the likelihood that acceptance will be employed again. This is particularly the case when the alternative is a strategy of control of private events that may have been experienced as not working and hence as incoherent at some previous point in time.

You may understand this RFT explanation and yet feel that it is an unusual example of acceptance. However, this is an RFT explanation of pure acceptance, in isolation from other ACT processes. Naturally, acceptance is never actually isolated like this in ACT; it is always practiced in the context of the other ACT processes, such as values. If the example occurred within an ACT context, values such as friendship and social interaction would probably be guiding this action, and the person would also be deriving relations in regard to those values. (For example, "Feelings of discomfort don't have to stop me from doing this. I'm doing this because friendship with others is important to me.") However, for our current purpose of using RFT language to describe each ACT process as a separable entity, it is necessary to focus on this process in isolation.

Cognitive Fusion and Defusion

Based on our socioverbal learning history, we human beings tend to experience our thoughts as literal truths or as things that must be responded to. Experiencing thoughts as literal truths that must be responded to, which is referred to as *cognitive fusion* or sometimes simply *fusion*, is especially problematic for many clients. Commonly, those suffering from depression describe being consumed by ruminative thinking, and those struggling with anxiety often find that their thoughts about their fear feed the problem even more.

Consider a client with a history of depression and who finds himself ruminating for considerable amounts of time. One thought that might be particularly sticky for such a client is "I deserve to be miserable and alone." If he responds to this thought as "truth" each time he has it, one of two things could happen: He may engage in behaviors that conform with such thinking, such as staying home and not engaging with others in his life, even though this isn't consistent with his values. Alternatively, he may fight with the thought, telling himself, "Cheer up. You have friends; you should just go out." But then other negative thoughts may crop up as is common in depression, such as "Remember yesterday? Sandra didn't seem thrilled to see you. You're never going to fit in with that crowd." If he goes back and forth with this line of thinking, he's more likely to miss out on the things around him, and subsequently will be less likely to engage in valued activities.

Fusion can lead to a way of life governed by a constant need to respond to private experiences at the expense of responding to the outer world. From this fused stance, the person organizes his overt behavior to try to reduce the form or frequency of such thoughts. If he's organizing his world around managing his thinking, he'll be less behaviorally flexible and therefore less likely to be living a life consistent with his values.

Cognitive fusion and experiential avoidance are often related for many of us. The more we negatively evaluate our private experiences and the more fused we become with them, the less willing we are to experience them. Further, fusion with evaluations about private experiences (for example, as unwanted or bad) can build unwillingness. For example, people experiencing anxiety often have thoughts associated with that anxiety such as "This isn't good," "I must not feel this way," or "I can't stand this!" These thoughts are also experienced as literal truths, which necessitates attempts to manage the experience or escape from the situation. Taking the stance that private experiences are causal and threatening, as many clients do, only strengthens the pattern of experiential avoidance.

Cognitive fusion also plays a big role in lack of clarity about values. As we learn and grow, others teach us rules to keep us safe and to help us be more efficient. However, we can also become rigid in our application of certain rules and apply them when they aren't needed, and we may do things based only upon what others think or want for us. In upcoming chapters, we will discuss at length how rigid, inflexible behaviors based upon fusion with rules and morals taught to us by others can take us farther away from our valued directions.

Cognitive defusion is the process by which people come to experience thoughts as simply events that occur fleetingly and that need not be directly responded to, challenged, or controlled. Cognitive defusion techniques deliteralize language by attempting to alter the undesirable functions of thoughts, rather than by trying to alter their form, their frequency, or the contexts that occasion them. The goal of defusion techniques is to reduce the dominance of the literal functions of private experiences by creating or strengthening alternative responses to such experiences. Some examples include repeating feared words out loud until only the sound remains, watching thoughts go by as if they were written on leaves floating down a stream, or giving thoughts a shape, size, color, texture, or form. A client may be asked to engage in tasks such as walking across the room while repeating out loud "I cannot walk"; practicing labeling the process of thinking ("I am having the thought that I am worthless"); or "thanking his mind" for a thought. The result of defusion is usually a decrease in the believability of or attachment to thoughts or other private events, rather than an immediate change in their frequency. This ability to recognize thoughts as thoughts can be helpful when clients move toward their values. Rather than buying into the thought "I could never succeed at that, so I won't try," the client can learn to notice the thought and choose to behave consistently with his values.

DEFUSION AND RFT

From an RFT perspective, language involves speaking with meaning and listening with understanding based on contextually controlled derivation of relations and transformation of function through those relations. Contextual cues that control which relations are derived are referred to as C_{rel} cues, and those that control which functions are transformed are referred to as C_{func} cues. The standard socioverbal conditions under which these forms of contextual control operate produce fusion with language so that language (in the form of thinking, for example) occurs without awareness of the process of thinking, reasoning, evaluating, and so on. This fusion with language is harmless and even useful in many contexts and indeed is necessary in order to facilitate environmentally efficacious language-guided human behavior. However, fusion with language can become a problem when verbal stimuli begin to dominate behavior regulation to the detriment of other needed sources of behavior regulation. The result is a narrowing of the behavioral repertoire, which then makes values-based action less likely. Cognitive defusion is the inverse of cognitive fusion. From an RFT perspective, this involves manipulating the functional context (C_{func}) of verbal events so as to disrupt the process of transformation of functions and thus diminish their capacity to regulate behavior. For example, during ACT self-as-context interventions, the therapist attempts to establish I-here-now as the locus or perspective from which a client may observe his thoughts (the products of relational action) as events occurring there and then. This changed context for these thoughts results in lower levels of transformation of function, including such problematic functions as values-impeding avoidance.

Contacting the Present Moment

Mindful awareness of what's happening on a moment-to-moment basis is necessary for responding adaptively and flexibly to one's experiences. Oftentimes, however, people become so caught up in their emotions, memories, bodily sensations, worries, or ruminations that they lose awareness of what else might be happening in a given moment, especially opportunities for living consistently with their values.

Lack of contact with the present moment can lead to problems for people in recognizing that they are thinking or feeling, even though such experiences may guide their overt behavior. A person may be responding to his thoughts seemingly automatically, without awareness of a thought or experience, in essence, behaving "mindlessly." Much of our thinking is in reference to events that have happened in the past or is related to predictions or problem solving for the future. Often these private experiences can capture our attention and continually take us out of the moment and away from the world around us. Let's look at one relatively common example of mindless behavior.

Have you ever driven or traveled home only to realize you have no awareness of how you got there? If you drove, you were at least somewhat effectively responding to stop signs and the cars around you, otherwise you would have been in an accident. If you took public transportation, you made choices about which bus or train to take, where to sit, and when to get off. Yet all of these behaviors occurred without you realizing you were "languaging" (thinking and applying rules) about it. On some level, the verbal processes of making decisions and rule following were operating, but you weren't in contact with them at the time. Maybe you were thinking about dinner while you were in the car—to the extent that it was almost as if you were already at home and cooking. In this way, the future can be experienced in the here and now although it is really there and then. Similarly, while you traveled on the train, you may have been replaying a conversation you had with your boss earlier in the day. In this way, the past is alive in the here and now even though it has already occurred.

In some ways this is a relatively innocuous example, but in other ways it conveys the dangers of being unaware of what we are experiencing and what is going on around us. Many clients may mindlessly engage in behaviors that are as dangerous as driving home mindlessly, if not more dangerous, including suicide attempts, self-harm, and substance abuse. Even in its mildest and least overtly dangerous forms, lack of contact with the present moment has costs. Especially pertinent here is losing the opportunity to contact reinforcement gained from engaging in valued behaviors. It is very difficult to be aware of and gain reinforcement from values-consistent behaviors if a person is largely out of touch with his experiences and the world around him.

ACT therapists actively promote ongoing nonjudgmental contact with both the internal and the external world, rather than continuing to live mindlessly. The goal of *present moment awareness* is to have the client experience the world more directly so that his behavior is more flexible and thus his actions are more consistent with his chosen values. Clients are encouraged simply to note and describe events (both private events such as thinking and external events such as situations) rather than evaluate them. The process of awareness is actively encouraged in hopes of fostering a stance from which the client can engage in defused, nonjudgmental observation of his thoughts, feelings, and other private events. Such a stance enables the client to see how values-based behaviors function.

CONTACTING THE PRESENT MOMENT AND RFT

From a behavior analysis and RFT perspective, being centered in the present involves following a rule that prescribes deliberate attending to the immediately present environment so as to increase the regulatory effects of this environment on behavior and to decrease typical levels of transformation of function. If this rule is followed on an ongoing basis, it is likely to increase the person's ability to discriminate aspects of his environment that may have been less salient previously but that may be important with respect to his valued goals (for example, his own behavior and that of others in everyday social interactions). Ongoing practice in following this rule will also facilitate the weakening of the regulatory effects of language on behavior, which is an important element of the ACT approach. With sufficient ongoing practice, the positive effects of being centered in the present may be discriminated and act to strengthen the operant, thus producing a positive feedback loop.

Self-as-Content vs. Self-as-Context

As we experience events in our lives, we tend to construct stories of who we are that persist over time. As humans, we seek coherence. We tend to look for evidence that confirms these conceptualizations of self and discount evidence that doesn't fit with them. Predicting and controlling our behavior is only possible when we are able to access a stable sense of self that encompasses all of our experiences, but we can easily become attached to or invested in particular experiences over others. A rigid, literal attachment to the conceptualized self, or self-as-content, can limit the varieties of behavior in which we engage. For many clients, attachment to a conceptualized self can be problematic in that particular symptoms or problems may be experienced as threatening to the self, or clients may develop an attachment to the belief that their problems control their life at the expense of living consistently with their chosen values.

Imagine a client who has developed a conceptualization of himself as highly ambitious. He always tries to be the best, never slowing down to examine whether he enjoys the projects he takes on or the rewards he gets from being an achiever. There's nothing wrong with achievement, but for this client, none of his behaviors are linked to a valued domain. If pressured, he would tell you (as his therapist) that he's terrified of failure. He only feels good about himself for brief moments, and they always occur when he accomplishes an achievement, is first to finish a project, or is the best at work. When he isn't the first to buy the newest electronic gadget, he worries that his boss will think him cheap. When he makes a mistake, he tends to go to great lengths to lie and cover it up, as he's terrified of admitting to himself and others that he is less than perfect. His concept of self as ambitious and perfect makes for a highly structured existence that doesn't feel vital for very long. A client such as this is likely to show up for therapy when he becomes exhausted, a crisis has occurred (a pending divorce, being laid off from work, or financial problems), or he suddenly feels like he has every "thing" he wants but feels no connection to those around him.

In contrast with a focus on self-as-content, ACT therapists work to foster a transcendent sense of self, or self-as-context. Both observing one's experiences and describing them without evaluation can help foster a sense of perspective from which thoughts and other private experiences occur. As a result of relational frames such as I-you, now-then, and here-there, human language allows the development of a sense of self as a locus or perspective, and provides a transcendent sense of self. This perspective can help clients recognize that they aren't defined, threatened, or controlled by their private experiences; that they can be aware of their flow of experiences without attachment to them and without investing in which particular experiences occur. In ACT, self-as-context is fostered by acceptance, defusion, and mindfulness exercises, including metaphors and experiential processes. From the perspective of this open, defused, transcendent sense of self, values-consistent behavior is much more likely to be experienced as reinforcing and meaningful.

SELF-AS-CONTEXT AND RFT

The RFT perspective on the transcendent self or self-as-context has already been mentioned in the earlier section on the self and self-rules. ACT and RFT explain the emergence of the self in terms of the verbal discrimination of one's own behavior. By subsequently learning to respond appropriately in accordance with relations of perspective, or deictic relations (I-you, here-there, and now-then), the child develops a sense of perspective. Once an appropriate level of perspective taking has developed, a person can discriminate a consistent locus of relational behavior such that "I" am always seen to be responding in the "here" and "now," whereas "you" (other people in general) are always seen as "there," and often "then." This locus of behavior, which ACT and RFT refer to as the transcendent self, provides the context for all thoughts and emotions.

Valuing

In the previous chapter, we presented a revised ACT definition of values as "freely chosen, verbally constructed consequences of ongoing, dynamic, evolving patterns of activity, which establish predominant reinforcers for that activity that are intrinsic in engagement in the valued behavioral pattern itself" (Wilson, 2009, 66). Now let's examine exactly what this means, bit by bit.

FREELY CHOSEN

The idea that values are freely chosen might seem to contradict the behavioral underpinnings of ACT and RFT. Don't behavioral psychologists believe that patterns of behavior are ultimately determined by the person's history of interacting with his environment? Well, actually, from a functional contextual perspective, neither free will nor determinism is ultimately "true." Rather, from this perspective, it is workability that determines how we describe behavior. In psychotherapy, when our goal is to encourage flexible and possibly novel behavior, it is more useful to talk to a client as if his behavior can be freely chosen.

Even within a strictly scientific context, it makes sense to analyze situations in which people are more likely to describe their behavior as freely chosen. From a Skinnerian perspective, freedom is mainly indicated when people are free from aversive control. We feel more free when we are acting to produce positive reinforcement for ourselves than when we are trying to avoid or escape aversive situations. As we have suggested previously, language makes things more complex than simple processes of reinforcement and punishment, but this Skinnerian conceptualization provides a fundamentally important insight, so we adopt the same approach and regard freedom from aversive control as centrally important in defining what it is for behavior to be freely chosen. Furthermore, the more sources of long-term positive reinforcement that are available to us, the less likely we are to become satiated with any one source. Therefore, variety and long-term sustainability are also important when pursuing positive reinforcement in the context of values.

VERBALLY CONSTRUCTED CONSEQUENCES

Now, what about the phrase "verbally constructed consequences"? This simply means that values involve a linguistic concept of the consequences of valued action. For example, if intimacy in a relationship is one of a person's values and he is asked to describe what this involves, he might say something like "being able to talk honestly and openly to someone else about my feelings and my experiences." This is a verbal construction or linguistic description based to some extent on previous real-life experiences of intimacy, as well as on extrapolations from or generalizations about some of the qualities of such experiences. Verbally constructed consequences such as this are a core element of what we mean by values, since they essentially motivate us to act in particular ways (engage in valued actions) in order to achieve them.

ONGOING, DYNAMIC, EVOLVING PATTERNS OF ACTIVITY

The meaning of "ongoing, dynamic, evolving patterns of activity" is relatively straightforward. We engage in many different patterns of activity in our life-time, and some of these are particularly relevant to values in that they produce the kinds of verbally constructed consequences discussed in the previous section. For example, we can engage in certain patterns of behavior that are more likely to produce intimacy in a relationship. When seeking to initiate and establish the conditions for an intimate relationship, patterns of behavior that will be important include socializing, going on dates, identifying and reinforcing honesty within a burgeoning relationship, and opening up emotionally to someone at appropriate moments as the relationship develops. As a person goes through adulthood, he may experience many dating situations and relationships, and his experiences and verbal descriptions of those experiences will form ongoing, dynamic, evolving patterns of activity that may bring him closer to his verbally constructed values, which will also evolve over time and in accordance with this experience. In other words, as a person experiences and describes dating and romantic situations, not only will his idea of intimacy motivate him to continue to engage in such patterns of activity, those patterns of activity will also allow his verbal conception of intimacy to evolve to some extent, though the core idea of what intimacy involves (trust, honesty, closeness) will remain relatively constant.

ESTABLISHING PREDOMINANT REINFORCERS

Values are verbally constructed consequences that establish predominant reinforcers for particular patterns of behavior. To understand what "establish

33

predominant reinforcers" means, recall that values are essentially motivative augmental rules, which may be defined as verbal relational networks that serve to alter the degree to which previously established consequences function as reinforcers or punishers. More simply stated, values are ideas that serve to make particular consequences of our actions even more motivating. So, returning to our example of a man who values intimacy in a relationship, when he thinks about or is reminded of the valued idea of intimacy, that value can make the typical and predominant consequences of engaging in dating and relationships even more attractive and motivating. As a result, he might experience an increased desire to engage in emotionally intimate conversations. Stating or being reminded of one's values makes the typical consequences of acting in accordance with those values even more motivating and therefore makes it more likely that a person will act in accordance with them.

INTRINSIC IN ENGAGEMENT IN THE VALUED BEHAVIORAL PATTERN

"Intrinsic in engagement in the valued behavioral pattern" is an elaborated description of the predominant reinforcers mentioned in the previous paragraph. This phrase simply suggests that these predominant or typical reinforcers are ones that are intrinsic or inherent in certain types of behavior. The word "intrinsic" simply highlights the fact that the reinforcers resulting from certain patterns of values-committed action, which are likely to have increased motivational power, are typical, natural, or sustainable, as opposed to atypical, artificial, or short-term. Returning to the example of intimacy in relationships, examples of intrinsic reinforcers would be social acceptance, emotional support, physical touch, and sexual arousal. Each of these reinforcers is a typical and natural aspect of an intimate relationship, and as such, they might also be expected to be sustainable for as long as the relationship lasts.

Other Aspects of Values

In addition to the preceding explanation of the basic definition of values from an ACT perspective, there are a number of additional qualities of values that we should discuss briefly.

Values develop within a socioverbal context. Although values are not defined by what others tell us, they do develop within a socioverbal context. Others shape our statements about what is "good" or "bad," what is important, and what we might want. Our social communities teach us to describe what we want (hopefully accurately). A mother can't read the mind of her child, but she may make a guess that her son wants something if he moves a kitchen chair up to a cabinet and tries to get at something. She may ask, "What do you want there?" and he may answer her by saying, "I want cereal." Over time, we do the same with increasingly complex things and learn how to develop statements about what we want, our purpose, and a direction for our lives.

Values can never be completely attained. Values are defined within ACT as chosen, verbally constructed consequences that can never be fulfilled; rather, they function as motivation for certain behavioral directions. For example, a value of being a caring person in intimate relationships can never be fulfilled. Even if the person gets married (a concrete goal), it would be silly to say, "Now that I'm married, I've accomplished caring. Now I'll move on to the next thing." Caring as a value is based on behaviors such as sharing personal information, asking about one's partner's day, and anticipating a friend's wishes, which aren't about fulfilling concrete goals; they're behaviors in the direction of the value.

Values as rules. Values, if taken literally, can be viewed as statements of truth or rules that must be adhered to at all costs. While they are technically rules, they are freely chosen and do not prescribe any particular behavior. In other words, if a client has a value of nurturing in relationships, this rule of nurturing does not indicate precisely how, with whom (or what), or how often one engages in nurturing behaviors. Values as rules simply orient us to general patterns of purposeful behavior that will ideally be meaningful and reinforcing. We must learn how to choose particular behaviors that comport with those values by tracking the reinforcing consequences of our behavior. Hence, values give us a direction, but we must learn to monitor the course. Despite the connotation of a rule being rigid, flexibility is also important for living consistently with one's values. Even as the underlying value stays relatively the same, behaviors that embody that value may change in form over the years in response to different life circumstances.

RFT AND VALUES

The ACT definition of values provided earlier in this chapter states that they are "freely chosen, verbally constructed consequences of ongoing, dynamic, evolving patterns of activity, which establish predominant reinforcers for that activity that are intrinsic in engagement in the valued behavioral pattern itself" (Wilson, 2009, 66). From an RFT perspective, the two core features of values are that they are motivative augmental rules, and they involve hierarchical relational networks. Let's take a closer look at these two concepts as they pertain to values and show how they cohere with the ACT definition.

Motivative Augmental Rules

The RFT approach to values builds on and adds to earlier behavioral approaches. In chapter 1, we discussed an early behavior analytic approach to the concept of values that described values in terms of reinforcers. This approach suggested that many of the reinforcers associated with human values acquire their appetitive functions through verbal conditioning, but it could not describe the processes through which this verbal conditioning might occur.

Psychologist Sam Leigland (2005) suggests that apart from reinforcement, another behavioral concept that appears relevant to values is the *establishing operation* (e.g., Michael, 1982), in which the actual reinforcing effect of a particular reinforcer is manipulated. The classic example of an establishing operation in the behavioral laboratory is food deprivation, which increases the reinforcing power, or value, of food. More generally then, the establishing operation may be thought of as a historical variable that affects how valuable something is. Leigland suggests however, that in the context of the complexity of human values, we must refer to the "verbal establishing operation," and in that context he refers to the concept of the motivative augmental rule, which is central to the RFT approach to values.

According to our current definition, values are verbally constructed consequences that establish predominant reinforcers for particular patterns of behavior. According to RFT, values are essentially motivative augmental rules, that is, verbal relational networks that serve to alter the degree to which previously established consequences function as reinforcers or punishers. In the case of values, the verbal relational networks are verbally constructed consequences (for example, "community") that increase the degree to which particular events typically associated with that valued domain (for example, well-organized community activities or recognition by fellow members of the community) function as reinforcers for particular values-based actions (inviting members of the community to one's house, organizing community gatherings, and so on).

Hierarchical Relational Networks

In the ACT definition provided, values are described as "verbally constructed consequences" that serve to "establish predominant reinforcers." We've explained that establishing predominant reinforcers is based on motivative augmental rules. What do these "verbally constructed consequences" involve from an RFT perspective?

A verbal consequence is a stimulus whose consequential functions are based to at least some extent on its participation in a relational frame. Consider, for example, a teacher telling a young child that he will get a colored sticker for every correct answer he produces and that the colored stickers can be exchanged for candy at the end of the week. In this case, the colored stickers have now acquired consequential functions by their participation in a derived relation with candy, and the child might show an increase in the number of correct answers he produces. However, this is simply a verbal consequence. What about "verbally constructed consequences"? Verbally constructed consequences are similar in some respects to verbal consequences in that derived relational responding is involved and the concept of consequences for certain types of behavior is at issue. However, use of the term "verbally constructed" suggests that the derived relational responding involved is much more extensive and complex and that the consequences may be relatively abstract. From an RFT perspective, the derived relational network involved is hierarchical. An example of a verbally constructed concept in this sense is the idea of justice, which is a term in a hierarchical relation with a vastly extended and complex relational network including other concepts such as equity, criminality, and the legal system. If justice or a just world is a value for someone, then this verbally constructed concept might function as a consequence for that person to the extent that, under certain circumstances, actions believed to be congruent with this derived relational network might be made more likely. For example, if someone believes that writing a letter to a newspaper in support of a particular cause somehow supports justice, then he might be more likely to do so.

Important Note on Values as Rules

It should be noted that from an RFT perspective, acting in accordance with values involves following rules. This may be a little confusing to some readers, since we have discussed rule following in a somewhat negative light. However, behaving in an ACT-consistent way doesn't mean that one never again acts in accordance with rules. From an RFT perspective this would be impossible, since it would mean that we stop using language! In fact, it is often important to behave in accordance with rules, particularly when those rules prescribe core values or values-consistent behavior. Hence, ACT is not against rule-following behavior. It simply suggests that we respond to rules in a more flexible way, and that we track rules that tend to make future psychological flexibility more likely.

Lack of Commitment vs. Putting Values into Action

Many people have difficulty living consistently with their chosen values over long periods of time. Particular psychological experiences, such as feelings, may function as barriers to engaging in valued activities because the person's psychological symptoms impact one or more areas of functioning. Clients commonly report a lack of values-consistent living when entering therapy. Usually, clients come to therapy reporting that their behavior is controlled by the desire to remove or lessen their symptoms. They usually try to avoid or escape their unwanted experiences by following ineffective rules that aren't sensitive to their chosen values or changes in their environment.

Further, clients may believe that they must remove or manage their psychological experiences *before* they can attempt to live a more values-consistent life. They may spend time attempting to manage anxiety at the expense of engaging in behaviors consistent with valued directions. Some clients may report feeling like they spend their lives "walking on eggshells," trying not to come into contact with feared or previously avoided private experiences. Overall, lack of engaging in patterns of behavior that are consistent with values can lead clients to feel that their life is lacking a sense of purpose or meaning or that it is excessively painful.

In contrast to lack of action, *committed action* refers to behavior in accordance with large sets of concrete goals that are consistent with a person's values. ACT protocols almost always involve therapy work and homework linked to both short-term and long-term goals for behavior change. These efforts to change behavior in turn lead to contact with psychological barriers that are addressed through other ACT processes. Small and large steps can be mapped out to encourage increasing amounts of values-consistent behaviors. Taking steps in a valued direction can make additional steps in that direction easier over time. To this end, some acceptance of the discomfort that might come from trying and failing at something related to the person's values is important.

Valued living can take many different forms but still be functionally purposeful. Particular choices of values-consistent behaviors are based on what is most effective for the goals related to a client's values. In ACT, we use the term *workability* to describe what is effective for a client in relation to a particular value. No behavior is perfect or ideal, and the suitability of any behavior is based upon a functional analysis of that behavior. The clinician's job is to help clients be functional analysts of their own behavior. By developing that skill, clients become better prepared to commit to larger patterns of valued behaviors after therapy and throughout their lives.

For example, consider a client who feels consistently berated when in the company of his extended family. This client may state that his value is enjoying a peaceful day in the company of his relatives, and as such, workability for him might look like disengaging from the conversation when they become belligerent because he doesn't want to say mean things back to his family. However, if the client wants to develop a closer relationship with these same family members, he may choose to try to engage his family members even when it's difficult, in the service of cultivating more honest, and hopefully more intimate, relationships with them. Workability is what's effective, but effectiveness can only be evaluated in terms of one's goals and values.

COMMITTED ACTION AND RFT

Committed action is essentially responding in accordance with rules that prescribe action consistent with a hierarchical relational network with a core value at its highest point. For example, if family closeness is a core value for someone and time at home is a goal that will facilitate greater contact with his family, then that person might formulate a rule prescribing greater time at home ("I will spend every Saturday at home with my children"). If he subsequently acts consistently with this rule, he's demonstrating commitment to his values.

Psychological Flexibility

Problems in each of the six core areas described in this chapter create *psychological inflexibility*, which refers to a rigid, narrow repertoire of behavior that isn't directed by the person's values. We see many forms of inflexibility in behavior among our clients: rigid rule following not guided by values, experiential avoidance, excessive fusion, attachment to a conceptualized self, persistence in nonvalued directions, or lack of values-consistent behavior.

The goal of ACT work is to foster *psychological flexibility*, which is characterized by broad repertoires of behavior that move the person in valued directions. Taken as a whole, each of ACT's six basic intervention processes supports the others, and all target psychological flexibility: the process of contacting the present moment fully as a conscious human being and persisting or changing behavior in the service of chosen values.

Values: A Fundamental Part of ACT

Just as the functions of problematic behaviors are examined in ACT, so are the functions of valued behaviors. Each of the ACT processes is connected to values, and for useful and powerful ACT work to occur, each of the ACT processes should be involved in values work. It's best not to conceptualize the ACT processes as discrete and separate, but rather as processes that interact with and influence each other. The diagram on the following page illustrates how they fit together.

Values and committed action, taken together, are considered the behavior change processes in this diagram. Meaningful long-term behavior change is more likely when the psychological variables that clients struggle with have been addressed through each of the other ACT processes. This is not to say that values can't be a fundamental part of the ACT work; in fact, they are often addressed early on in therapy, and this is a strategy that we ourselves endorse and will describe later in this book. Much of the ACT work centers around what clients most want to work toward in their lives. Values can dignify the difficult thoughts, feelings, memories, and so on that they undoubtedly will experience as they move toward what matters to them.

Take a moment to consider what matters most to you. Now imagine the last time living consistently with this value created some pain in your life. Perhaps you missed out on doing something with someone you care about or you made a mistake at work. If there is something in your life that matters to you, chances are there have been situations where things didn't go the way you planned in regard to that value. Perhaps a relationship ended prematurely, a job was offered to someone else, a family member got angry with you, or an unforeseen financial situation cropped up. Many times even the things we plan and work hard for don't work out the way we hoped, and this can cause psychological pain. Further, even when we behave consistently with our values, we may sometimes find that this behavior is difficult in the moment. For example, if having honest relationships matters to you, then sometimes you may need to tell someone else that you're upset with them, which can be uncomfortable in the moment.

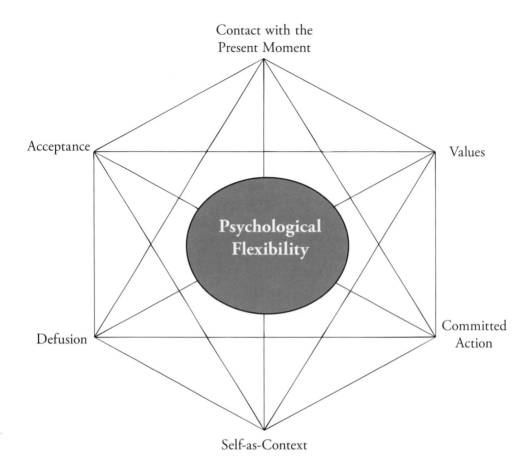

How we deal with discomfort in these situations can either strengthen values-consistent behavior or lead us to engage in behaviors based upon experiential avoidance, fusion, or our conceptualized self. The issue isn't whether we'll have thoughts or feelings about things going awry, but how we relate to those thoughts and feelings. ACT aims to help clients change their relationship to the discomfort that can come from engaging in their values. Defusion and self-as-context work can help clients see that thoughts of failure don't have to be taken literally or guide their behavior, and acceptance work can help them recognize that the discomfort that may come from talking to a boss about getting a raise could be in the service of something that matters. Committed action is about putting valued behavior patterns into action from a defused, accepting stance.

We recommend that values work continue throughout therapy. Early in therapy, before skills in acceptance, defusion, present moment awareness, and self-as-context are built, clients may still be stuck in old patterns. They may remain fused and experientially avoidant and behave in ways that are consistent with protecting themselves from fear, hurt, or abandonment rather than consistent with their values. As clients practice acceptance, defusion, and recognizing their transcendent sense of self, they are more likely to choose values and goals that are effective and reinforcing and that bring an experience of vitality.

Summary

We hope that you have seen and understood the various core processes of the ACT model and are now familiar with the roots of ACT as it affects your work. In this chapter, we also discussed the role of values within ACT work. We have spent time on each of the ACT processes because we want to be clear that ACT is a model and not simply a set of techniques. Further, as we peel back the layers of values work throughout this book, we will discuss the work of values from the perspective of each of these processes. Our techniques and rationale for using them are informed by the model and the work that underlies the model. In chapter 3, we turn our focus to how values develop and how they can become confused, as well as examining the function of values and looking at ways to overcome some common language traps.

CHAPTER 3

Fusion and Potential Language Traps

Now that we have a working definition of values, we will examine how values can get confused. Addressing values confusion is important because, while it would be ideal to have clients get in touch with what matters to them and experience life falling into place, things seldom work quite that easily in practice. Therefore, stripping away confusion around values can pave the way for values clarification more easily than doing in-depth values work early on in therapy. It is common for stumbling blocks to present themselves during the process of identifying and clarifying values. Most often, these stumbling blocks are related to cognitive fusion in some way. As you will recall from the previous chapter, fusion is the process of taking the products of our minds literally. In other words, we become fused with our thoughts, including judgments, evaluations, and rules about ourselves and the world. Fusion is such a central and pervasive problem that we have dedicated this chapter to the myriad ways that different forms of fusion function to keep clients from moving toward their values (or even identifying them in the first place). However, because fusion (and the other processes targeted by ACT) can affect all of us—therapists included—sometimes we will speak to the general human condition and other times we'll target the client. In some cases, we'll suggest that you, the therapist, make use of various ACT strategies. Not only will they enhance your own psychological flexibility, they'll also give you an appreciation of the challenges and nuances involved in the work we ask of our clients.

In terms of values, we think of fusion as "language traps" that keep clients confused about their values. We identify and examine four basic language traps and how they relate to values, and provide hints for dealing with each of them. While there are many reasons why clients aren't living the most valued life possible, language traps play a big role. We hope you will become familiar with each of the traps in the service of planning your interventions accordingly.

Uncovering the Problem: The Effects of Fusion

We've talked about how language is essential for many things, such as problem solving, reasoning, planning, and communicating. But when it comes to values, language can often be more of a barrier than an ally. Consider the case of Rebecca.

Rebecca, a single woman in her midtwenties, was seeking deeper relationships and struggling with anxiety she described as crippling. On initially coming to therapy, she told her therapist, "I've always been and will always be an anxious person. Maybe I'm not capable of being strong and having the kind of relationships I think I want." Despite this explanation for what was possible for her life, Rebecca and her therapist worked together to clarify what mattered to her. However, Rebecca was seldom able to stick to a clear value with regard to relationships. One week she would say, "honesty," and then the next week she would say, "Well, I've been thinking, and too much honesty is a bad thing, you know? If I'm feeling fat, I want someone to tell me I look great, even if they're lying." Subsequently, the session became about the advantages and disadvantages of each value, rather than a chance to explore ways in which she might create those values in her life. Values discussions took this turn each session, with Rebecca consistently tearing down the very qualities she had become deeply and tearfully appreciative of in the session before.

Part of what happened for Rebecca can be explained by some common problems that come from using language. The very process that allowed Rebecca to communicate with her friends, potential romantic partners, and her therapist (all important, valued activities to her) also allowed her to spend a great deal of time predicting, judging, and avoiding feared outcomes in the future. Rebecca became wrapped up in thinking through all of the possibilities of failure and remained convinced that if her fears came true, she wouldn't be able to handle it. She spent so much time weighing the pros and cons of her values that she was unable to move forward with the core process of living consistently with those values. She was trapped by language.

How was Rebecca trapped? She was fused with her thoughts, seemingly in every possible way. She took her thoughts literally, listening to what her mind was telling her rather than choosing to stand up for her values. She spent a great deal of time predicting the future rather than living in the moment. She was fused with the thought that she wouldn't be able to handle the emotional discomfort that would arise if her values-based behaviors didn't work out the way she wanted. She felt it necessary to weigh the pros and cons for valuing interpersonal relationships. A rigid and fused conceptualization of herself as an anxious person meant that Rebecca couldn't even try to do things that might cause anxiety. All of these problems led Rebecca to find ways to avoid her values, escape from uncomfortable situations even if they presented an opportunity to contact her values, and even downplay the importance of values altogether. All in all, Rebecca's life became narrower, less fulfilling, and more oriented toward avoidance.

Fusion can have this life-narrowing effect for many of the clients we see in therapy. Even if clients come to therapy with a clear idea of what a values-based life would look like for them, they usually have language-based barriers to living such a life. Typically, clients believe that they must remove some problem or emotional discomfort before a values-based life is possible. Alternatively, they may be like Rebecca, believing in a static, fused conceptualization of the self that does not have room for values-directed behavior. Either way, fusion is an important problem to attend to in your therapy work. Therefore, we provide ample opportunity for you to learn to recognize each of the ways in which your clients can become fused, leading to a life that is built on avoiding discomfort rather than living a fulfilling, values-driven life.

Now that we have discussed how pervasive fusion can be when it comes to values, let's examine each of the language traps that can lead to values confusion: fusion with the conceptualized self; fusion with thoughts about feelings; fusion with the verbal constructions of reasons and rules; and fusion with outcome.

Language Trap 1: Fusion with the Conceptualized Self

You may recall from the previous chapter our discussion about the three selves from an ACT perspective: self-as-content, self-as-process, and self-as-context. These can be complicated constructs, but we find that understanding them is vitally important to the ACT work. They are important in the present context because they provide a common language with which we can discuss how psychologically different perspectives on the self may impact valuing. To briefly recap, the self-as-content is a perspective involving self-descriptive statements, judgments, and evaluations that are based on our experiential history (for example, "I am thirty years old," "I am generous," or "I am a good person"). The self-as-process is a perspective on our ongoing, changing actions and experiences (for example, "I'm thinking about last summer" or "I'm feeling lonely"). The self-as-context is the overarching perspective from which we describe both ourselves (self-as-content) and our ongoing actions and experiences (self-as-process).

In terms of psychological flexibility, one particularly important contrast is between the self-as-content and the self-as-context. The self-as-context is the most flexible of the three perspectives. It is pure perspective, free of content and therefore maximally flexible with respect to the exploration of values and adoption of values-consistent action. Self-as-content, in contrast, is the least flexible and dynamic of the three. This perspective, as described, includes descriptions, judgments, and evaluations of our lives, including who we are, how we express ourselves, what we like or dislike, and how our values are expressed. Such a description of the self characterizes the behavioral repertoire of every verbal human being. However, ongoing fusion with this concept in which it is taken as literal truth is a problem. Under those circumstances, we understand ourselves in terms of a static conceptualization that can rigidly constrain our future possibilities.

Clients who are fused with the conceptualized self often work very hard to secure this conceptualization throughout life, usually at the expense of values. Humans often seek coherence, as we mentioned in chapter 2, and one way of obtaining it is through behaving consistently with the conceptualized self. Therefore, clients may work hard to maintain the conceptualized self at all costs. One person might be so fused with her identity as a hard worker that she works through a serious illness and doesn't take care of herself. Another might strive for such perfection in all of her relationships that any interpersonal conflict that arises causes her to consider the person with whom she's in conflict unworthy of her friendship, thus leaving her without relationships based on honesty and forgiveness. And though she might profess valuing connections with others, her self-concept might be so dependent on having perfect relationships that she finds herself lonely and unconnected. People can also behave in ways consistent with an explicitly negative self-concept. For example, a client might be so fused with the idea that she's unattractive and unlovable that, although she desperately wants to be in a relationship, she assumes that dating or socializing will be fruitless, and thus avoids it, which ensures the absence of a relationship, and ultimately provides experience that supports her self-concept as unlovable. As you can see, living based upon rigid self-conceptualizations leads to behavioral inflexibility and the narrowing of possibilities, which makes values-consistent behavior less likely.

Fusion with Life Roles

A pervasive problem in therapy is clients' identities being inextricably linked to their role in a particular area of life. Responses to questions about values that reflect the client's career (such as doctor) or life situation (such as mother) suggest that the person believes that such statements are accurate and complete self-descriptions. This indicates fusion with an identity linked to a life role.

Consider the case of Sharon, who comes to therapy to overcome her frustrations with her mother because she feels it is uncharacteristic of a good Christian to be upset at her mother much of the time. Her role in life, for as long as she can remember, was being the caregiver in the family. She babysat for her younger siblings, and when she was old enough, she dropped out of school to care for her ailing mother. When Sharon was asked about her values, her responses were variations on the theme of her role as family caregiver. However, when asked about what was important to her inside her role, she didn't express feeling much joy or reinforcement for doing this job—only duty and responsibility. She frequently stated that it was her lot in life to be selfless and to always put the needs and joys of others before her own. However, she also reported feeling very isolated, lonely, and depressed. Further, she had recently gained a significant amount of weight and doctors were telling her to get more exercise. Sharon complained that because of her role, taking care of herself simply wasn't possible. She wanted help finding ways to let go of her frustrations and feel less lonely.

Although Sharon's case may seem extreme, it's a good example of how fusing with a particular life role can create problems for life and for therapy. Therapy with Sharon need not undermine her role; rather, it can help her identify what she might care about inside the role of caring for others. In cases such as this, the client fails to see that her self-description is simply a limited self-characterization, and that she is actually a whole person who can notice or experience many things from a perspective beyond that of simply acting out whatever role she identifies with.

Fusion with the Current Life Role Obscuring Past Values

Fusion with roles can present an obstacle to valuing in another way. Sometimes a client feels unsure of how to value in particular areas of her life because her current roles preclude living consistently with values she once had. Take Mary, a young professional who came to therapy reporting that she was stressed-out. When asked about social relationships, she told the therapist that they weren't possible for her because as a professional woman she didn't have room for them in her life. However, as therapy progressed, it became clear that Mary had once valued friendships very much. As a child, she had experienced a deep sense of understanding and community with a few very close friends. Mary and her therapist agreed that these qualities of a deeply meaningful relationship were still of value to her. Mary explained that she had put her career first, however, letting old friendships die out. She also stated that new friendships were not a possibility for many years, because she feared she'd lose the respect she believed she earned as she climbed the corporate ladder. For Mary, one barrier to having more meaningful friendships was the presence of thoughts such as "I am a professional woman, and it isn't appropriate to share intimate details of my life with my friends." Mary was very much fused with the role of professional woman and the rules she possessed about the ways a professional woman should act. She could see how she had done what she thought was right at the time, prioritizing her career, and she could also see that it cost her contact with the friendships that were important in her life.

An important element of ACT therapy is the use of metaphor and experiential exercises to introduce the client to the idea that her thinking (relational framing), including thoughts about her self and her values, is simply ongoing behavior (activity of the mind). In ACT the client learns that she can stand back and safely observe the products of this activity (her thoughts) from the perspective of self-as-context without getting entangled or fused with content. From this self-as-context perspective, it is easier for the client to connect with deeply held values that remain constant despite changes in life circumstances. Mary eventually learned that she was able to behave like a professional woman in some contexts, and also to carefully choose with whom she wanted to share more personal information about herself. As she shared more of herself with a few key friends, she found she enjoyed her relationships with these people much more. By defusing from her rigid rules about the ways in which professional women should act, Mary was able to live more consistently with her values regarding friendships. In this example, we see that defusion from rigid conceptualizations of self based upon one's role plays an important role in undermining rigidity with regard to values.

Threats to the Self: When Life Circumstances Change

When the self is tied to what one does, new behaviors or situations (following divorce or a career change, for example) necessitate a new perspective on a person's identity, which can lead to severe disruption of the self. In relation to values-consistent living, this shift in self may lead the client to the idea that because "who she is" has changed, her values must also change or be retooled to fit her new life circumstances. Within rehabilitation medicine, it is often said that a client's prognosis following loss of physical functions depends on her ability to let go of the conceptualized self. A client who has recently lost function of her legs and who is fused with the idea that her self-concept is linked to her ability to walk, run, or play sports will be seriously threatened by this new situation. Such a client is likely to downplay the importance of values linked to intimate relationships, physical activity, or anything she views as linked to physical abilities. She may experience depression and fusion with thoughts that nothing she cares about is possible any longer, and that her life is over. The rehabilitation process will be easier if the client is able to defuse from thoughts about her self-worth being linked to her physical prowess.

Language Trap 2: Fusion with Thoughts About Feelings

The way in which we think and talk about our feelings represents another potential language trap. The human verbal community attempts to teach us to discriminate and describe how we feel. However, unlike teachings about things that are in the environment and publicly observable ("This is a car"), teachings about our covert, felt experience are indirect and must rely on publicly observable concomitants of our feelings rather than the feelings themselves. Parents or caregivers might teach a child to say, "It hurts," when they see the child get a cut or a bruise, for example. However, the stimulus control that is established in the case of covert stimulation cannot be as precise as in the case of overt or publicly observable phenomena. For example, parents can't know if their child really feels pain in the moment they teach them to say, "It hurts," let alone the degree or extent of the pain.

Aside from simply teaching the discrimination of feelings, the socioverbal community also teaches the child to evaluate her feelings as either good or bad, just like many other objects and events in her environment. For example, if a caregiver evaluates a certain feeling as good or bad, the child is likely to learn to evaluate it in the same way.

Thus, the socioverbal community trains the child to discriminate her feelings, albeit imprecisely, and to evaluate those feelings. The result of this training is that the community can find out something about the child's internal state. In addition, the language of feelings can facilitate prediction of behavior. For example, if someone reports feeling anger or sadness, that provides some indication of how she might behave in particular contexts. Although the results of this training in the language of feelings are useful for the community, when combined with fusion with language more generally, this can contribute to problematic behavioral patterns and make values-consistent behavior less likely.

Fusion with Evaluations About Feelings

As a result of the imprecision of language about feelings, there is great variety in how children are taught to express emotions, just as there is great variety in the sensations that they experience. The end result is that we are not always the best at discriminating our feelings, and for some clients in therapy this inability can be quite extreme. Compounding the possible problems that might arise due to this imprecision, we are also taught to evaluate what we feel and to be guided by these evaluations. For example, a child might learn from her parents that the loosely defined set of feelings referred to as "anxiety" is bad, and that she needs to manage this bad emotion by ensuring that it is at low levels before doing anything else. This learned need to manage transitory and ill-defined feelings of anxiety may well take up her time and energy and interfere with values-consistent behavior. In addition, since these feelings can't necessarily be completely managed or eliminated, if she puts other things on hold until they're dealt with, she may remain stuck.

Even those who haven't been taught to evaluate emotions while growing up may begin to evaluate their experiences later in life. For example, Susan found her life fulfilling and meaningful until the loss of her husband, after which she became depressed. She told her therapist she had never known what it was to be depressed, and now that she felt it, she hated her life. She reported trying everything to get rid of her depression, such as sleeping all the time, not talking about her husband, and avoiding sad TV shows and movies. She said that she felt unable to handle her depression. Because she evaluated her experiences as bad and different than before, she was less willing to experience depression. Further, fusing with these evaluations of sadness led her to avoid doing anything that might bring up sadness, narrowly restricting her life. Avoidance is pervasive when clients evaluate their feelings as bad in some way.

The same is true in regard to feeling good. Inherent in evaluating some feelings as bad or undesirable is the idea that other feelings are good or desirable in some way. Once this dichotomy of good versus bad feelings is established and the person fuses with these evaluations, she begins to look for ways to avoid bad feelings and experience good ones. And you don't have to look very far in Western society before you get the message that feeling good is what we all should strive for.

The goal of values-based therapy is to induce clients to live full, vital, values-consistent lives, which is very different from just "feeling good." However, it can be difficult to pursue a values-driven life, along with the difficulties this sometimes entails, when social forces go to such great lengths to convince us that happiness is based on the ability to control or avoid the "bad" feelings. There is nothing wrong with feeling good, but it isn't a value in and of itself. You may feel good when you're engaged in activities in your valued directions, but this is more of a side effect than the goal. You may, for example, feel good after a yoga class and come to associate feeling good with going to that yoga class. But if you go to the yoga class with the intention of feeling good, you will probably miss out on the point of yoga, which is to become mindful of your body in a variety of positions. Actually, most of the positions in yoga don't feel good; they are strenuous, repetitious, and difficult. However, if the pattern of behavior involved in yoga is consistent with your values, you will experience it as vital over the long term no matter how you feel in any given moment.

Another problem is that feeling states are constantly changing. If you were to record all of the emotions you experience in one day, how many times would you notice your feelings changing? In one day you might wake up feeling tired and anxious about the day, feel satisfied with a work presentation during lunch, feel frustrated with your boss in an afternoon meeting, miss your partner on the drive home, feel joy upon seeing your family at home, feel sadness watching the evening news, and then feel tired again before bed. For many of us, it's common to have that many shifts in emotions in a single day—or even within a single minute.

If we wait for our feelings to be good, as if this were a state of being, we are likely to choose only behaviors that get us that quick fix of reinforcement. Many times, people who use drugs report that they don't know how to deal with emotions, so they use alcohol or drugs to eliminate feeling bad and replace it with an immediate reinforcer. Such patterns can create long-term problems. Sometimes when experiences feel good, we tend to want more of the good at all costs, yet this type of obsessive desiring may push us off our mindful, valued path. And when we desire something, it is seldom the object itself that is reinforcing, but rather some short-term positively reinforcing sensation within ourselves. Most of us have experienced how this type of obsessive searching for sensation fulfillment leads to behavior that isn't consistent with our valued directions. Shopping is a common example. You might see that your favorite store is having a sale, which incites you to desire owning more of what you already have. The logical thought might be "If I got pleasure from an outfit from this place, more outfits will give me more pleasure." You might have fantasies about the places you might wear these outfits in the future and how the outfits will make you feel. All of this is a response to an imagined future that takes you away from the here and now. It also reinforces the behavior of craving and increases the probability that you will crave again in the future. In this way, the tendency to seek out a good feeling is, at best, drawing us out of the moment. At worst, it can create the misery of obsessive and addictive behavior.

When we fuse with evaluations of particular emotions as good or bad, we are likely to base our behavior on the goal of avoiding undesirable emotions and seeking pleasurable ones, rather than basing our behavior on living consistently with our values.

Fusion with the Concept of Feelings as Causes

The concept of emotions as causal factors in our behavior is evident in many of our linguistic conventions in English; for example, "I feel like going out to dinner" or "I hit him because I was angry." In the first example, despite the phrasing of the sentence, emotion has little to do with our subsequent behavior. In the second example, there are presumably many variables involved in a person's learning history that might result in her hitting someone. In addition, because we don't *always* hit someone when we feel angry, this supposed explanation is somewhat illusory. Despite their inaccuracy and misleading nature, phrases such as these appear in our language because, as suggested earlier, they are somewhat useful in facilitating prediction of others' behavior, or our own behavior. Furthermore, the fact that such phrases are inaccurate or misleading doesn't impact us very often. However, in certain circumstances, language conventions suggesting that emotions can and do determine behavior can contribute to a lack of behavioral flexibility. This is clearest when we see clients who use emotions as barriers to engaging in valued activities, or as states that must be achieved before they can live a values-consistent life.

For example, consider expressions such as "I'm feeling nervous, so I can't go to school" or "I need to feel safe before I can get emotionally close to you." These statements are like shortcuts that most of us understand clearly. For example, a more accurate way to state, "I'm feeling nervous, so I can't go to school," would be to say, "I'm experiencing nervousness and I choose not to go to school." These two events may occur relatively close in time (feeling nervous and choosing not to go to school), but one does not cause the other. The idea that feeling nervous can literally prevent someone from going somewhere is both inaccurate and widely accepted.

In addition to believing that some feelings prevent behavior, we can also become fused with the idea that we must feel a certain way *before* behaving. This tends to arise because people often use language that indicates that a feeling of readiness or confidence, for example, is the reason that causes or allows us to behave a certain way. When a client comes in highly fused with the idea that she must feel a certain way before she can do something, our experience as therapists tells us that this client is likely to become less active rather than more.

Let's use an example to examine how fusion and use of loose language regarding feelings can be problematic. Imagine you have a client who states, "I would love to have kids, but I need to feel ready for it first." You may think you can understand exactly what your client is struggling with, but ask yourself this: What does feeling "ready" feel like? Is it an emotion or a thought that one is ready? If the word "confidence" came to mind, as is common, consider that in our experience as therapists, "confidence" commonly refers to the evaluation that one is ready (thoughts like "I can do this"), rather than a feeling. Alternatively, one might consider criteria that indicate being "prepared" for having children (a particular income, a house with space for a child, help from family, and so on). Though people tend to talk about feelings as if they are some state that can be achieved or experienced steadily, it is rarely the case that this is so. There may be times that a feeling of calm arises (usually experienced as a lack of anxiety rather than a feeling unto itself), but it rarely lasts for very long. It is human nature for our feelings to change frequently, and calm is likely to be replaced by anxiety in the next instance of engaging in something new. When you think the thought "I'm ready," is all the anxiety about doing something new permanently gone? Usually not.

It's more effective to discuss confidence in terms of overt behavior, rather than either a feeling or an evaluation. We are capable of behaviors whether or not a particular feeling is present. Has there ever been a time when you did something without "feeling" ready? Have there been times when you waited to "feel" ready before talking to someone, and then regretted waiting because you missed your chance? These situations happen frequently for everyone. We hope that recalling the difficulties that you, as a therapist and fellow human being, have encountered in dealing with these entangled emotions will enable you to find compassion for clients when they experience such difficulties.

Language Trap 3: Fusion with the Verbal Constructions of Reasons and Rules

A third language trap involves values confusion that stems from relying on reasons as causes for our behavior. We are creatures who are constantly seeking to explain why we do things, why the world is the way it is, and why we don't have certain things that we want in our lives. In many areas of life, this is a useful strategy. We learn early on that the reasons can be linked to cause, and if there is a cause, we can predict the outcome and possibly even control it. However, when it comes to our feelings, values, and behavior, looking for reasons can be misleading.

To clarify values, it may be useful to look for any internal confusion arising due to statements that have an if-then causal relationship. In our experience, while such statements might provide a framework for predicting the future, when it comes to living consistently with one's values they are often very unhelpful. Here are some examples of internal rules that indicate if some first scenario were fulfilled, a second scenario (related to values) would occur:

- If I felt confident enough, then I would be successful.

- If I lost enough weight, then I could have a relationship.

- If I didn't have to worry about money, my life would be much happier.

- If my pain goes away, then I will be able to go back to work.

The problem here is that there are actually very few instances in human behavior where true cause-and-effect relationships exist. It creates an illusion of simplicity to think in terms of cause and effect because, in human behavior, it is not usually the case that when some first condition is fulfilled, some other condition then changes directly as a result. For example, if a woman thinks her obesity is the cause of her lack of an intimate relationship, she may predict that losing weight will solve the problem and lead her to that desired relationship. However, countless other factors will be influential in determining whether the desired "effect" will take place. This is usually the case when we human beings try to discern cause-and-effect relationships, and, frankly, we're not great at seeing all of those factors clearly. We must remember: Our minds try to help us by simplifying things, but they don't necessarily reflect reality. Given the complex relationships between events, we generally aren't very good at describing the "if" part accurately, and we are never assured of the "then" part, anyway.

If a woman buys the thought that she needs to lose weight as a condition for having an intimate relationship, she is fused with a simple cause-and-effect relation wherein losing weight leads to gaining a relationship. In fact, this woman could have an intimate relationship at her current weight. A more accurate statement of events would be "If I get out there and show people my personality and be open and honest, then I *may* find the relationship I've been looking for." This statement is not as comforting, but it is more accurate. Note that the "if" piece of the statement—"If I get out there"—refers to the person's own actions, not the judgments or actions of another person (someone else's judgment that she is thin enough to be dated). Also notice the caveat "may" in relation to the particular outcome "find a relationship." No one can predict the actions of others, and it can be disheartening and frustrating to try. It is much more values-consistent to behave mindfully and to see what happens. We will discuss the myriad problems with attachment to outcome when we examine language trap 4.

Additionally, problems arise when the conditions set forth in the "if" part of the statement are unlikely to be fulfilled. This effectively keeps us far from the "then" part of the statement. Talk about setting ourselves up for failure! Here's an example: Consider a client who experiences pain and expresses the cause-and-effect relationship "If my pain goes away, then and only then will I be able to go back to work." In this case, being fused with the thought that she needs to rid herself of pain symptoms before she can return to work may result in never return-ing to work, since her pain may never completely go away, and it may not even improve, as is often the case with chronic pain. In this case, it is probably necessary to address confusion regarding cause-and-effect relationships before the client can make further progress.

Relying on Ineffective Rules: Watch for But-Statements

Another variation on this theme is fusion with rules that proscribe certain values, generally stated as "I recognize my valued direction, *but* unless some par-ticular thing happens, I can't choose that value." That this kind of reasoning means, literally, that one thing cannot be true if the other is present. Using but-statements in this way means that something must change or go away before something else can happen in a person's life. This mind-set is generally accompanied by a feeling of being stuck. We use the word "stuck" in this book to mean thoughts and feelings of hopelessness regarding one's options to behave differently or change one's situa-tion. As you'll see in the following examples, this mind-set is similar to some of the other types of fusion we've discussed. The difference here is that the person is able to clearly identify her value:

- ৯ I'd like to have an intimate relationship, *but* first I need to lose a signifi-cant amount of weight.

- ৯ Having a job is a top priority for me, *but* until I get this pain problem solved, that's just not an option for me.

- ৯ I would love to have kids, *but* I need to feel ready for it first.

Each of these but-statements voices an important value and simultaneously diminishes the importance of that value or puts it on hold based on a judgment that there is an obstacle in the way of the value and hence a low probability of living in accord with that value. This judgment serves as an ineffective rule in the context of values. All of the values expressed—wanting an intimate relationship, a job, or children—are perfectly legitimate and not uncommon. However, the narrow, rule-based contingency expressed in each statement tends to subvert the importance of the value. ("I would love X [value], but in order to pursue it, I need Y [perceived obstacle]—and Y is difficult if not impossible to achieve.") This results in nega-tive predictions regarding behavior in these valued directions, as fusion with the resulting rule ("Since Y is difficult if not impossible, then I should give up any hope of pursuing X") will make the pursuit of value X less likely. These sorts of rules transform the functions of a person's situation such that values-consistent behavior becomes less likely. However, feeling that one has no choice about taking steps in a valued direction is not the same as being unable to recognize the value or the importance of the value. In the values work done in ACT, the client is asked to iden-tify a deeply held value and rate its importance, independently of any rules regard-ing the possibility of her being able to act in accordance with that value. To reflect this, clients are asked to shift from using but-statements to using and-statements that reflect the multiple thoughts and feelings that occur in the context of some-thing important. How much more freeing is it to rephrase the previous statements in the following ways?

- I'd like to have an intimate relationship, *and* I have thoughts about needing to lose a significant amount of weight.

- Having a job is a top priority for me, *and* I have been struggling with pain.

- I would love to have kids, *and* I'm not sure if I feel ready.

Note that each example has been reworded to reflect a more accurate descrip-tion of the events (thoughts, feelings, and sensations) associated with these values-consistent behaviors. It can be difficult for any of us to notice that we have used a but-statement to try to escape from the aversive properties of experiences such as evaluating one's physical body as unlovable, sensations of physical pain, and feeling unsure. As we saw with the but-statements, we have difficulty getting rid of these experiences, so we either fight them or resign ourselves to them and spend our lives waiting for them to change before moving toward our values. Except, as we know by now, we have feelings and thoughts (some unpleasant) that are present whether we move toward our values or not. Changing from "but" to "and" is both more accurate and more appetitive; it can allow clients the freedom to choose to move toward their values even if undesirable experiences are present.

But-statements can serve other functions that are worth examining. One func-tion of the type of statements we're examining here might be to block an underly-ing value of importance. To understand why this might happen, let's take a closer look at the statement "I would love to have kids, but I need to feel ready for it first." Having the thought "I need to feel ready for it first" simply reflects normal fear of failure and anticipation of the difficulty in raising children. Wanting to be prepared for such an unfamiliar and highly valued challenge would be commonplace for most of us. Hence, the function of this sort of statement might be to block something the person truly values because she fears failure.

A different hypothesis about this situation is that the client doesn't actually value the activity, but rather is fused with a should-statement that comes from somewhere else, such as family, social community, or identification with cultural stereotypes. In this case, the person may view the statement as a more acceptable way of saying, "I'm not sure I really want X, but I feel like I should because it's what I've been taught." In the case of the woman who says, "I would love to have kids, but I need to feel ready for it first," she might feel pressure to conform to social standards ("I should want to have children"). However, through the process of values clarification, she might come to appreciate that although she may value caring for others, she would rather do so in the context of her career or partnership, or with a pet, rather than by having children.

As you can see, a variety of rules may be operating in statements about values that aren't necessarily clear at the outset. Both therapist and client must have patience in wading through the potential pliance and avoidance to get to the vitality inherent in values clarification. We discussed the concepts of pliance and avoidance in chapter 2 and will cover them in further detail in chapter 4. For now, we'll simply say that these two forms of behavior, which are under aversive control, are often uncovered when working with values.

Language Trap 4: Fusion with Outcome

A fourth language trap is fusion with outcome, in which the person is fused with rules about the need to gain certain types of external rewards, such as money or the esteem of others, at the expense of the intrinsic reinforcement that can come from partaking in genuinely valued activities. This type of focus is made more likely by social training in which the emphasis is on the outcome as opposed to the process, and by familial training in which our interest in certain forms of intrinsic reinforcement is diminished. Finally, one alternative, potentially useful way of conceptualizing this form of fusion is in terms of the confusion of goals and values.

Intrinsic Reinforcement

Intrinsic reinforcement is an important concept in terms of the outcome of our actions, and we'll refer to it often throughout the remainder of the book. In chapter 2, we discussed the idea that values establish reinforcers that are intrinsic in engagement in the valued behavior pattern. Additionally, we explained that since ACT is a functional contextual intervention, we care more about a behavior's function than its form. *Intrinsic reinforcement* essentially means that the reinforcement comes from the activity in which one is engaging rather than some outside source, which we would loosely consider *extrinsic reinforcement*. Here's an example in which function versus form is important. A child might read (the form of the activity) for different reasons (function). She might wish to please her parents or pass an exam (primarily extrinsic reinforcers), or she might read because she enjoys doing so for its own sake (intrinsic reinforcement). We maintain that engagement in intrinsically reinforced activities is a key aspect of valued living.

What activities are intrinsically reinforcing? Activities yielding primary reinforcement (gustatory stimulation, sexual arousal, and so on) might classically be categorized as intrinsically reinforcing, as we are biologically primed to derive reinforcement from these activities. Beyond this, the fact that we are a verbal species means that we find very many other activities, either closely or not so closely associated with sources of primary reinforcement, intrinsically reinforcing as well. Indeed, much of what we find intrinsically reinforcing appears to be relatively abstract and divorced from simple biological reinforcement. Consider, for instance, reading, doing math puzzles, learning, art, or other forms of creativity. These types of activities, while intrinsically reinforcing for many people and certainly relevant in terms of values, are far from being based on simple biological processes. Instead, their capacity for intrinsic reinforcement has its basis in the individual's verbal history and involves reinforcement through transformation of functions, often based to a significant degree on verbal coherence, which, as we suggested in chapter 2, we are trained to find reinforcing. In the case of activities heavily influenced by language and coherence training, the person is particularly likely to describe these intrinsically reinforced activities not just as enjoyable, but as meaningful.

As mentioned, we believe that intrinsically reinforcing activities play a key part in a person's core values. This is because core values must be sustainable in the long term, and activities that are intrinsically reinforcing are more likely to be sustainable. One way of conceptualizing values is in terms of a hierarchy. In such a conception, the top of the hierarchy would include core intrinsically valued activities, while nodes farther down would be activities that offer access to the core valued activities. For example, for the domain of relationship, core valued activities could include physical closeness and sharing experiences, while nodes farther down the hierarchy might include having a job and making money to support oneself and one's partner.

Visualizing values in terms of a hierarchy in this way allows us to conceptualize both healthy and maladaptive patterns of behavior with respect to valued activity. Clearly, engagement in long-term sustainable valued activities at the pinnacle of the hierarchy is psychologically healthy from our perspective, and the more time spent engaging in such activities across a number of life domains, the better. Furthermore, investing time and energy in activity at nodes farther down the hierarchy that allow access to the activities at the top of the hierarchy is also psychologically healthy, and engagement in such activities can also clearly be categorized as valuing. Thus, in the last example, working at a job in order to make money to support one's partner and family may be classified as valuing within the domain of relationships.

These are healthy patterns of behavior because the pinnacle of the hierarchy is intrinsically reinforcing valued behavior. However, imagine now a second hierarchical structure with an activity that isn't intrinsically reinforced, such as gaining money or status, at the pinnacle. Gaining money and gaining status aren't intrinsically reinforcing in themselves. Both are socially constructed pursuits originally intended as means to ends rather than as ends in themselves. However, for various reasons that we shall explore shortly, many people come to be fused with rules prescribing the importance of money and other socially conventional reinforcement and the need to engage in activities that produce such reinforcement. Therefore, they come to invest time and energy in hierarchical structures that have socially conventional reinforcement at their pinnacle rather than intrinsically reinforcing activities that are sustainable in the long term.

This is fusion with outcome, and it can lead to a reduction in activities from which a person might receive intrinsic reinforcement—activities that might provide the basis for long-term sustainable reinforcement. When people focus excessively on seeking extrinsic reinforcement, their values are likely to fall by the wayside. Clients in this situation might speak about money or status as values, or as part of their values. But in reality, this focus on extrinsic activities and secondary reinforcement is neither vitalizing nor sustainable in the long term, and simply means less time for the pursuit of true values, which make life worth living.

The idea of form versus function is important here. Remember, it is not the form of a behavior that determines its psychological health or vitality, but its function. Hence the same activity might be functionally very different depending on the context. Take making money, for example. In the first hierarchical setup, with an intrinsically reinforcing value related to relationships at the pinnacle, making money is functionally healthy and vital because it is a means to the end of participation in a core valued activity. In the second hierarchical setup, however, with socially conventional reinforcement at its pinnacle, making money is functionally problematic because it is seen as an end in itself, time and effort invested in activities with a sole focus on making money have no valued end in sight, and may take precedence over potentially vitalizing valued activities.

Sociocultural Influences

One influence causing people to prize socially constructed over intrinsic reinforcement is sociocultural programming. In the Western world, we are taught throughout the education process as well as in the world of adult life to prize arbitrary secondary reinforcement in such forms as grades, career, money, and status. Once again, the function is of primary importance here. Grades, career, money, or status might be seen as means to a higher end, or they might be viewed as ends in themselves. For some people, fusion with rules concerning the importance of success, social affirmation, and the like may bring them to see these arbitrary markers as ends in themselves.

In school, for example, children learn that they need certain grades in order to progress, and through fusion with rules, getting good grades may become more prized than the potentially intrinsically reinforcing activity of learning. Furthermore, when we receive extrinsic reinforcement for an activity that might otherwise be intrinsically reinforcing, we sometimes begin to categorize it as simply a means to an end, and this in itself can make the activity less enjoyable or vitalizing. In this way, learning and other activities that are potentially intrinsically reinforcing may come to be experienced instead as devitalizing extrinsic activities through fusion with the importance of particular outcomes. Later in life, there are new milestones to reach, new competitions to win, and new quotas to meet. Once again, based on this training, people may fuse with the idea that monetary and other arbitrary results of their work are ends in themselves, and in the meantime they may have relatively less time to determine their own intrinsically valued ends or to learn the persistence required in the face of obstacles encountered while moving in a valued direction.

Shaping the Downplay of Values

The effect of sociocultural influences teaching the importance of extrinsic reinforcement and downplaying the value of intrinsically reinforcing activities can be compounded by the effects of a familial environment in which the expression of interest in intrinsically reinforcing activities is suppressed. A child expressing wants or needs for such activities might under certain circumstances be met with punishing reactions (such as ignoring, ridiculing, or aggression) from parents, siblings, or others. For example, a young girl in a conservative household who expresses interest in a traditionally male activity might be ignored or even ridiculed and as a result may be less likely to express this potential value. In this way, intrinsically reinforced activity and ultimately valuing might be diminished to some degree by the social context.

As young children we all behave to please others (pliance). In some cases, however, particularly in environments in which expressions of the child's own wants and needs are consistently punished, the child never really learns to move past the stage of doing what others tell her to do or acting in line with what others expect of her. If, as in the last example, a child begins to express her wants and needs and those expressions are consistently met with punishing reactions from those around her, she learns to suppress those wants and needs in order to avoid punishment.

Early learning histories in which potential valued directions are frequently associated with pain, punishment, abandonment, and disappointment are particularly likely to result in the diminished expression of values. A physically or sexually abused child is likely to have significant aversive conditioning associated with values. Those who are physically abused are likely to associate violence and the threat of violence with parents, adults, and caregivers. Those who are sexually abused may associate physical closeness and words of love with force and violence. In addition, parents who are intoxicated by alcohol or drugs may ignore the needs and wants of their children.

For clients with this type of abusive learning history, identifying values may take longer than for others. For example, the value of wanting to establish a warm and loving relationship may be present, but there may be a long history of painful experiences associated with relationships to contend with. In fact, it may be the case that aversive conditioning will cause some clients to try to avoid or sabotage the client-therapist relationship, especially as the therapist attempts to get closer to the client. In cases such as these, the therapist might start with values here and now, in the context of the therapeutic relationship. For example, living consistently with values for relationships might be shaped in small steps across many sessions, developing valued living within the context of the therapeutic relationship.

Asking the client to connect to deeply held values may well elicit memories of painful early experiences. If valuing is associated with punishment, this may in part explain why values are diminished and thus effectively avoided. It is important to recognize that this type of learning history isn't the kind of trap it might seem to be. With patience and practice, it is possible for all of us to learn about and live consistently with our values. However, as a therapist, you should be sensitive to the fact that particular learning histories, especially those in which important needs were linked with punishment, may make it more difficult for clients to consider or move in valued directions, as these clients may be more likely to encounter uncomfortable thoughts, feelings, memories, and bodily sensations as they do so.

Mistaking Goals for Values

From a therapeutic perspective, one alternative way of conceptualizing the fusion with outcome described thus far is as a confusion of goals and values. This confusion is all around us in our society, compounding the effects of sociocultural training in which secondary reinforcement is seen as important. Goals such as outcome, achievement, status, income, certain possessions, and physical beauty are not simply held up as important; they are actually marketed as values. For example, in their ad campaigns cosmetics companies include the idea that women should buy their products because doing so is valuing one's self. In order to shape and maintain our consumption behavior, advertising deliberately makes goals look like values.

Consider the following scenario: A client comes to therapy using the language of goals. In behavioral terms, she may say that she has deficits of certain things (for example, self-confidence) that she wants to increase, or excesses of certain things (such as anxiety or pain) that she wants to decrease. She may be unhappy with herself and have the goal of wanting to be more like people who seem to be happy, content, or living full lives. This is the language of goals with no obvious valued direction. In this case goals may mistakenly become equated with values. However, from the current ACT perspective, goals and values are defined very differently. Both are important, and both will be used in therapy in helping the client; however, the difference between them is critically important.

One useful way to illustrate the distinction between values and goals is to use the metaphor of a compass. Taking a valued direction is like navigating by compass. First, once we decide on our direction, we can immediately step exactly in that direction—just the slightest movement can put us right on target. Second, and a more difficult concept for the person who is goal oriented, we never actually get to our direction. This is like traveling east or west by compass; we can travel in either of these directions for as long as we want and never reach a specific end point of east or west. Values are similar: They can never be fully arrived at or achieved, whereas goals can be.

GOALS: NECESSARY BUT NOT SUFFICIENT FOR VALUED LIVING

Goals are different from valued directions. They are waypoints on the set course, and in contrast to valued directions, they are practical and quantifiable and have clear end points. Just like using a landmark as a waypoint as you travel, goals can help you orient yourself in the valued direction you've chosen. Once goals have been reached, however, they lose their value as waypoints and new goals must be set. For example, imagine traveling east starting in San Francisco. You might use Reno, Denver, Cleveland, and New York as successive waypoints. Before you reach each city, it functions to guide you east. After each city has been reached, however, the next city becomes your new waypoint. Notice also that even though you can reach successive waypoints and check them off your itinerary, you can never reach east and check it off.

The purpose of goals is to keep us on track in a valued direction, not to replace the valued direction. They are meant to function as stepping-stones along the path in a vital direction, so they must always support traveling in the identified direction; however, they should not be mistaken for the end point of moving in that valued direction.

When a client confuses goals and directions, she may feel lost, especially if she has fulfilled a particular goal but has lost sight of the underlying value. You can use the following examples to highlight the difference between goals and values by illustrating the value underlying the completed goal:

- Having children doesn't mean you stop caring about your family.

- Getting married doesn't mean you stop caring about being a loving partner.

- Getting a promotion you've been working toward doesn't mean you stop caring about being a hard worker.

These examples are similar to each other in that they illustrate that achieving goals doesn't imply that values are finished or completed. In each example, the achievement involved may entail revising one's values to hone them for the specific circumstance, but the overarching values remain constant. And these core values can remain basically unchanged even if you change your goals.

Summary

In this chapter, we have shown you four different forms of fusion that can cause values to be confused, obscured, or minimized. As a client begins to examine her values, you may recognize some of these language traps. It's important to consider the role of fusion within the client's statements about values and her valued behaviors. Doing so will allow you to form appropriate conceptualizations of the client's difficulty with respect to values. In later chapters, we discuss many ways you can work with defusion, as well as other ACT processes, to loosen up the verbal constraints on valuing and increase patterns of flexible values behavior. In the next chapter, we'll take a close look at the four-step process of teaching clients to contact and pursue their values.

CHAPTER 4

The Process of Valuing in ACT

In the previous chapter we discussed the language traps that people can fall into when they examine their values and make life choices. We examined a number of different forms of fusion with language that can work to prevent clients from contacting their values, specifically fusion with the conceptualized self; fusion with thoughts about feelings; fusion with reasons and rules; and fusion with outcomes. Thus, chapter 3 presented possible obstacles that may prevent clients from contacting and pursuing their values. This sets up the focus of the current chapter, which examines four major steps involved in teaching clients to contact and pursue their values.

There are four major steps involved in the process of valuing as taught using an ACT approach. We usually start values work with values clarification, the process of developing or strengthening values or creating a sense of purpose in chosen life dimensions. Next, we examine the function of clients' behavior and expressed values, looking for patterns that point to vitality rather than avoidance, fusion, or pursuit of the conceptualized self. Then we help clients establish specific goals that are consistent with these chosen values. And finally, we evaluate those goals and work toward maintaining goal-directed behaviors over time.

Step 1: Identifying Core Values

In this section, we explore how to map out core values, a process that involves understanding the function of various life domains for the client and clarifying values in these life domains. Because of the power of core values to illuminate all aspects of life, we think of this process as finding a lighthouse in the dark.

Clarifying Values

The purpose of clarifying clients' core values is to help them find a direction to move in, like studying a map before beginning a trip. When clients find the overarching direction of their values, choosing what they want to do next becomes a simpler task, since core values can provide the basis for making choices, taking steps, and evaluating those steps. In addition, having a clear concept of their values helps clients have greater success in choosing to live consistently with those values, even when difficult situations arise.

Consider, for example, newly separated parents who are seeing a family counselor for guidance in respect to their divorce. The therapist helps the parents establish their common value, "what's best for the kids," as the guide for all of their activities and decisions during the divorce. Once the long-term value of their children's well-being has been established as their common value, both parents should be more aware of it during their interactions with each other. This allows the value to exert more influence on their behavior than the short-term reinforcers of being right, getting more money, or receiving fair treatment. Thus, these angry, disappointed people will be more likely to act effectively in the service of their shared core value. One of the greatest advantages of values clarification in ACT is that it allows this sort of mindful awareness of overarching values, which is very important for keeping on track in difficult emotional situations.

Exploring Values in a Variety of Different Life Domains

One way to clarify core values in ACT is to ask clients to reflect on the qualities of a number of possible life domains that they find important. ACT interventions often present a fairly standardized set of domains, such as intimate relationships, family relationships, friendships and social relationships, career or employment, education or personal growth, recreation and leisure, spirituality, citizenship, and health and physical well-being (e.g., Hayes, Strosahl, & Wilson, 1999). However, there are clearly a variety of ways to conceptualize domains, and this may vary from client to client.

We present a number of different domains to clients for a few different reasons. First, presenting them with a number of possible life domains may prompt and guide clients with respect to possible values. Second, exposing clients to a greater variety of domains is better, since engaging with a greater variety of activities ultimately promotes greater psychological flexibility. Third, by presenting clients with a variety of possible life domains, there is more chance that they will be able to identify and contact a particularly powerfully motivating value within one domain.

Rather than having the client focus on how he wants others to behave toward him in these domains, we have him discuss how he would like to behave. In intimate relationships, for example, the client will need to think of the quality of intimacy for himself and his behaviors regardless of what he might desire from others around him. For many people, this is an unusual way of thinking. During values clarification sometimes clients describe how they would like others to act so that their relationships, work environment, or community would be more enjoyable. However, from an ACT perspective it is important that clients identify how they want to behave, and that they take responsibility for choosing to behave consistently with their values regardless of what others do.

We use the following exercise, which we call "Establishing the Life Compass," to present the client with a number of life domains within which they might identify and clarify their values. We build on the idea of using the compass metaphor to identify and strengthen values in chapter 9, so for now we simply present some possible examples of values-related life domains and how they might be identified and clarified. In this exercise, the client is asked to describe in a few words the essence of his values in each domain. In addition, we explicitly encourage the client to think in terms of lifelong, core values rather than goals that relate to current life situations. In the sample worksheet that follows, we list ten domains that might be used in such an exercise, with a typical client response to each, including a list of potential reinforcing qualities, or functions, that appear to characterize that domain. We find that clients can usually understand, with some help, the idea of reinforcing qualities, but if this is a difficult concept, consider asking the client to examine the value for the qualities that are important to them regardless of the form of activity. For example, the quality of connectedness can be linked to situations with friends or family, and it can also be identified as important even if the client doesn't experience connectedness very often. Providing some examples of the reinforcing qualities of your personal values related to being a therapist (the satisfaction of helping someone else; enjoying the intimacy of the therapeutic relationship; the intellectual satisfaction of solving a therapeutic problem) may be helpful to illustrate what you mean.

The following example of how a client might fill out the worksheet will give you a sense of some of the possible reinforcing qualities in each domain. We recommend that you work through this process with your clients at the pace appropriate to each client and use this worksheet only as a guide.

ESTABLISHING THE LIFE COMPASS

Work	*I want to contribute to work life in a meaningful way with my special talents and capabilities.*
	Reinforcing qualities: *Contributing to the good of the whole community in whatever way possible. Feeling connected to the whole community through this contribution.*
Leisure activity	*I want to give myself time every day to develop my own special interests.*
	Reinforcing qualities: *Engagement in activities in which the goal is simply to enjoy myself; giving myself permission to relax and indulge myself.*
Caregiving	*I want to give myself time to nourish and take care of someone or some living thing regularly in my life. In that relationship I want to be present and dependable.*
	Reinforcing quality: *Taking care of someone or some living thing that is dependent on me, which has an enhancing effect on my own health and well-being.*
Family	*Giving and receiving emotional and practical support.*
	Reinforcing qualities: *Unconditional acceptance and supportive community. Working together to celebrate family milestones and transitions in life.*
Intimate relationships	*I want to be in a relationship where physical and emotional closeness are part of my daily routine. I want to be open and honest with my partner, accepting him for who he is and feeling accepted as well.*
	Reinforcing qualities: *Physical touch, sexual enjoyment, emotional intimacy, and acceptance.*
Community involvement	*I want to actively participate in the community that I live in and share a sense of responsibility for those around me.*
	Reinforcing quality: *Being connected to a community in common efforts directed toward the good of the whole community.*
Spirituality	*I want to give myself a bit of time outdoors every day to reflect on my life and what I am doing.*
	Reinforcing quality: *Experiencing a connection with nature and the meaning of my activities.*

Education and personal development	*I want to keep myself open to the challenge of learning new things every day.* **Reinforcing quality:** *Developing as a human being by being open and curious about new experiences.*
Health	*Every time I eat I want to be aware that I'm nourishing my body and giving it what it needs, including the right amount of sleep and exercise.* **Reinforcing quality:** *Taking care of my physical needs (nutrition needs, hygiene, sleep, exercise), which makes me feel more vital.*
Social network	*Having a small group of friends among whom I feel accepted and accepting, feel open and honest, and have a sense of belonging.* **Reinforcing qualities:** *Feeling connected to a group of people outside of family. Experiencing life's activities, processes, and transitions together with others. Feeling accepted and supported.*

Functions of Domains

One important feature of the domains in the worksheet "Establishing the Life Compass" is that each one has particular reinforcing qualities or psychological functions that are constant regardless of change in life situation. The reinforcing quality of being touched, for example, is functionally the same for an infant as for an elderly person in the final stages of life. Similarly, the reinforcing quality of developing one's own talents and interests is no different functionally whether a person is in prison or lives in a mansion. And as you can see, the examples of core values offered here reflect that quality, being expressed in ways that will remain valid even when life conditions change.

When we work with clients to develop values statements in various domains, we ask questions that encourage them to go beyond the programmed way in which values are usually formulated and expressed in our culture. Thinking about the reinforcing quality of each domain requires stepping away from the content of a value and thinking from a functional perspective. Contemplating the meaning of work, for example, from this perspective, a client may notice that his experience of job satisfaction has been qualitatively the same throughout his life, from the time he got his first job at a local hamburger joint right up to his present-day experience of working as a CEO in a large corporation. The reinforcing qualities or meaning of each domain are probably fairly consistent and transcend changes in the form and content of that domain throughout life. For example, many people describe the functions of working as "being able to contribute to something larger in any way that I am able" or "being useful" or "feeling needed." In this functional sense, acting in a values-consistent manner in regard to work is similar whether the person is a child washing the dishes, a CEO running a corporation, or an elderly resident at a nursing home helping to set the table. Hence, the reinforcing quality of work might not be perceived as higher at higher points on the career ladder.

Step 2: Looking at the Function of Behavior

Once the client has made contact with long-term and overarching valued directions, the next step in therapy is to investigate the function of behavior that might affect movement in that valued direction. In this section, we first consider the concept of awareness of values congruency in behavior. We then examine several "values traps" in which the function of behavior is incongruent with values or otherwise problematic, and subsequently offer an exercise that's useful in determining the function of behavior. Finally, we examine how to help clients establish patterns of long-term values-consistent behavior.

Our behavior affects our proclaimed values. One of the aims in ACT therapy is to help clients become conscious of the function of their chosen patterns of behavior, especially with respect to their values. For example, are particular patterns of behavior congruent with the client's proclaimed values, or do they block or prevent pursuit of those values? In other words, and to ask a question familiar to ACT practitioners: When the client is engaging in an activity, what is that activity in the service of?

Many of the activities we engage in each day are done out of habit rather than being the product of choosing deliberately. For example, a person might flop in front of the TV each evening after work, rather than doing something different, like heading out for a walk. It's not that we think about doing something different and decide not to. In such cases we may not even consider doing anything else. This type of behavior isn't functionally congruent with values because we haven't thought about our values in regard to the activity.

Other activities initially might have been deliberately chosen as steps in a valued direction, but as they become routine they may lose this contact. For example, consider a sister who chooses to help her physically challenged brother on a daily basis. In her mind, she might clearly be taking a step consistent with her valued direction (caring for a dependent loved one). In other words, the function of the behavior might start off being congruent with her values, but as time passes that same activity may become simply another item on her list of chores. She may find herself helping her brother more out of a sense of obligation and as a way to placate her conscience, rather than as a step in valued living. In that way, the function of the behavior may eventually become avoidance of uncomfortable thoughts, such as

"I'm not a good enough sister" or "I'm selfish," rather than living in accordance with the value of caring for her brother.

ACT values exercises such as the values compass (which is examined in great detail in chapter 9) can help both client and therapist see whether the functions of particular patterns of behavior on the part of the client are congruent with his values or not. For example, the values compass exercise might reveal discrepancies between what a client says he values and how he is actually behaving. If, for example, a client says that he values being psychologically present with his children but he drinks heavily each evening, there's a discrepancy between his stated value and his behavior, since he can't really be present with his children while under the influence of alcohol. In this case, it's likely that a major function of his drinking is to avoid or escape difficult emotions. His avoidant behavior doesn't change his stated value, of course; it is simply incongruent with it. The ACT therapist will help the client identify the overarching value in this context and then help him examine the inconsistency between his behavior and his value. If the client sees that his behavior is, in fact, inconsistent with one or more of his values, he may then be more motivated to change it, even though that may involve having to deal with uncomfortable emotions that he's been trying to avoid.

Common Values Traps

Now we'll examine a series of values traps, each of which involves "serving a master" in a way that's arguably inconsistent with long-term valued living. In other words, each values trap is defined by a different behavioral function that's problematic and incongruent with values-based action.

VALUES TRAP 1: LIVING IN SERVICE OF EXPERIENTIAL AVOIDANCE

Preventing, avoiding, or escaping danger and aversive physical conditions is critical to our survival as human beings. We share this capacity to avoid with other animals. But due to the special properties of human language, human beings also attempt to prevent, avoid, and escape *thoughts* about potentially dangerous situations. This tendency to avoid thoughts and other psychologically aversive events does not, generally, seem to be necessary for survival, and in fact, it may trap us in patterns of behavior inconsistent with our values. The activities in this trap may seem to support long-term values, but the functional pattern of avoiding unpleasant feelings, thoughts, memories, or sensations is very different from the functional pattern that defines valuing. For example, a client may quit engaging in meaningful activities once they became more difficult, stating a reason such as "I really value doing a little of everything." In this case, the client's behavior might actually be dictated by trying to avoid looking or feeling like a failure. As engaging in an activity (or getting close to someone else) becomes more important, failure feels that much more painful if it doesn't work out exactly as we had hoped. Escaping from the activity before it becomes too meaningful might reduce the risk of being hurt or experiencing thoughts of failure, but this can come at an immense cost to vitality.

Clients often ask professionals to help them in this endeavor. Think about what your clients commonly say to you when they first start therapy: "Help me take the physical pain away," "Help me overcome my anxiety," "I want to stop feeling so bad about myself," "I need to reduce my stress level," "If I don't lose weight, I'll never find a romantic partner," and so on. However, although clients might successfully avoid pain, stress, or anxiety in the short term, in the long term they will incur serious costs for doing so. For example, in the case of anxiety, using alcohol or drugs can help people feel more relaxed in the short term, while in the case of chronic pain, staying home and being less active can decrease pain levels. However, these avoidance activities can subsequently become a way of life, and engaging in them can have significant costs in many valued areas. In addition, unwanted symptoms such as pain, anxiety, stress, and negative thoughts aren't likely to go away completely or permanently; indeed, research has shown that such symptoms may actually get worse through such avoidance (e.g., Vowles et al., 2007; Feldner et al., 2006; and Feldner, Zvolensky, Eifert, & Spira, 2003). It's also extremely difficult to get rid of the thoughts, fears, memories, and feelings associated with these symptoms, even for a short time. Hence, a client might spend a lot of time and energy trying for the impossible, and in the meantime his valued life directions may be put on hold, since he believes that getting rid of unpleasant psychological phenomena is necessary before he can live his values.

Many clients have a significant history with this strategy of trying to get rid of or solve symptoms first and *then* proceed in valued directions. A key question to ask clients who describe such a scenario is "How has this worked for you?" For most clients, the answer is likely to be that it hasn't worked as an overall strategy in the long term. When life revolves more and more around symptom reduction and less and less around the pursuit of positive values, quality of life is diminished.

However, in such cases it's worth bearing in mind that the client isn't simply choosing a symptom-free life over a life worth living. Let's think about that. The client might say, "I value getting rid of my symptoms." However, why might a person want to avoid symptoms? Usually there is something that the person isn't doing when the symptoms are present, which is, of course, living a valued life. So perhaps if the client thought about it, he would say that he didn't simply want to get rid of his symptoms; he wanted to get rid of his symptoms *in order to get his life back*.

VALUES TRAP 2: STRIVING FOR SECONDARY REINFORCERS

A second values trap involves focusing on activities in the service of expected tangible outcomes. The person may be seeking fulfillment in terms of secondary, socially conditioned reinforcement, such as making money, gaining status, obtaining power, being acknowledged, looking good, being right, or living up to others' expectations. He may strive for years, sacrificing time and energy in primarily extrinsically reinforced activities in the service of conditioned reinforcement, fused with the idea of a promised fulfillment but never actually obtaining it and ultimately feeling empty or disappointed. After years of seeking specific outcomes or secondary reinforcers at the cost of enjoying the process of living, he may even feel fooled. When people focus on extrinsic reinforcers and reinforcement in the future, life in the present becomes simply a means to get there. The vitality of the present moment is sacrificed to an outcome in the future or a socially conditioned reinforcer.

There is often little intrinsic value in socially conditioned reinforcement. Secondary reinforcers such as money, high rank, social success, and so on have no value in themselves but instead are instrumental in creating possibilities for actual reinforcement. Often, however, and as suggested in chapter 3, this instrumental quality of socially conditioned reinforcement gets confused with an actual value. Through processes of fusion, they may come to be seen as ends in themselves rather than as something that may occur within the context of acting in accordance with chosen values. As discussed in chapter 3, function is the deciding factor here. There is nothing wrong with instrumental secondary reinforcers as long as the person's deeper, chosen values are psychologically present as he makes choices about how to behave in regard to achieving these reinforcers. However, a client may describe these types of socially conditioned reinforcers as values rather than as a means of obtaining the intrinsic reinforcement that comes from living consistently with one's values. Such reinforcement is short-term and ultimately unsatisfactory. In the long run, clients will be better off finding ways to live consistently with their values and using money, success, security, and the like to establish values-consistent behaviors.

The first step in the context of this values trap is to help the client see that there might be something worth working for beyond these non-intrinsic, short-term reinforcers. For example, you might ask the client questions along these lines:

- ஃ If you had all the money (success, or whatever) you could possibly want, what would you do with your life then?

- ஃ Say you had that high-ranking position right now. What would you use it for?

- ஃ What would you do if you were suddenly happy and secure?

Through questions like these, clients may begin to see that these non-intrinsic reinforcers are not ends in themselves but rather things that might occur as they behave in accordance with overarching valued directions. Such things as happiness and success are usually instruments for and by-products of living in accordance with our values, rather than being values we can directly strive for. Seeking socially conditioned secondary reinforcers is perfectly consistent with much of our Western culture. Unfortunately, clients may become so focused on these conditioned reinforcers that they lose track of the natural contingencies of long-term valued living. In these cases, clients have confused tangible outcomes with values and are working toward socially conditioned reinforcers rather than long-term valued actions. These achievements could have been functional goals in the service of the greater value, but instead they become ends in themselves. In the absence of contact with larger, core values, however, the conditioned reinforcers that one obtains are likely to feel empty in the long run.

Take the example of Jefferson, who worked very hard to get good grades throughout high school and college and then applied to a top medical school. However, he came to therapy with stress headaches. Although he had been consumed with getting the best grades and getting into the top schools, in therapy he disclosed that it all felt meaningless. He realized that he hadn't been able to hang out with friends or talk to his family because he spent so much time preparing for some distant future. While those around him congratulated him on working so hard, he felt more and more removed from his life. Based on his therapist's intervention, he slowed down a bit and decided to go to a less competitive medical school so that he could devote more time to other aspects of his life, including self-care activities.

We could provide countless other functionally similar examples. A client who values making money may need to reconnect with what he wants to do with the money. A client who values finding a partner may need to identify what quality of an intimate relationship he desires once he finds a partner. In order for secondary reinforcers to sustain our sense of vitality, we must learn to attend to and enjoy the process of engaging in life, not just the things we accomplish along the way, as these typically only satisfy us for a short period of time before we have to seek out yet another short-term fix.

VALUES TRAP 3: KEEPING UP APPEARANCES

Pliance is a type of rule-governed behavior in which the person obeys a rule in order to gain reinforcement from the person who presented the rule. Less technically, pliance might be defined as doing things solely to follow the rules or to please others. Focusing on the short-term reinforcement of conforming and pleasing others is another example of a short-term quick fix. For example, when Susan came to session and began completing the values compass exercise (detailed in chapter 9), she seemed to be trying to say and do all the "right" things. She reported that she wasn't sure what she wanted, but that she did know what others expected of her. In Western cultures, this sort of pliance is common because we are taught that outcomes are important, and we receive reinforcers for behaving in ways that ensure those outcomes. We are programmed to value getting good grades rather than the process of learning, or to value finding the "right" romantic partner rather than the process of becoming intimate. Sometimes we do so because others tell us that wanting these things is important. In this way, conforming or being right can trump figuring out what we want on a deeper, more vital level.

Acting to please others can sometimes appear to be consistent with long-term valued directions, but functionally it is very different. Pliance is complicated, because many of the things we do have some flavor of pliance, and yet over time we may find that the behavior involved becomes intrinsically reinforcing. Consider Hillary, whose brother plays in an orchestra. She attended his concerts even though she didn't enjoy classical music because she felt a sense of duty to her family. Through values clarification, she started to realize how much it mattered to her to show her family that she cared about them. As a result, going to the concerts began to be intrinsically reinforcing. She decided, however, that some of her other behaviors should change. For example, she decided to stop bailing her brother out financially after realizing that the primary function of lending him money was not to show him she cared, but rather to show her family that she was a good daughter, a role trained over many years.

If conforming and pleasing others is the function of a particular behavior or activity, that activity will be under the appetitive control of another person's approval; that is, in the absence of the other person, there's little motivation to perform the behavior and the probability of its occurrence will lessen. This unfortunate feature of pliance has significant implications with respect to the establishment of lasting patterns of values-consistent action. With clients under this form of control, you might ask, "Would you engage in this particular activity even if no one was around to notice?" Such a question may allow the person to more easily discriminate the function of his activity himself.

Examining What We Are Doing and Why

An ACT exercise called "Which Master Do You Serve?" can be useful in helping clients start thinking functionally about how they are behaving in everyday life. The point of this exercise is to help clients discriminate the function of their responding: when they are choosing a value and when they are behaving according to some other functional pattern, whatever the actual form of their behavior might be. The worksheet for this exercise is reproduced in this section. Feel free to photocopy it and use it in session. We find that it's usually helpful to complete part of the exercise with the client in session, helping him look for the function of his own behavior. We also suggest that you do this activity yourself, to examine how much of your own behavior is vital for you. Doing so will also help you see how difficult it can be to examine your own behavior in this way. Even as therapists, we aren't always aware of the functions of our behavior! If you do this exercise yourself, check to see which activities have some form of vitality in them. Where there are imbalances, consider finding ways to increase your vitality.

Note that we've included four columns for the function of behavior. We recognize that there are very few things we do in our lives that have only one function. For example, Shawna goes to work on time partially because she's afraid of losing her job (avoidance of something negative), partially because she wants to share morning coffee with her coworkers (short-term positive reinforcement), partially because it's expected (pliance), and partially because she really enjoys doing her job well (long-term positive reinforcement and vitality). As Shawna practices assessing the function of her behavior using this worksheet, she finds that she sees more nuances in these functions. Sometimes her behavior starts out being pliant, then becomes more values-based as she gets reinforcement from the larger world around her, not simply from the praise of others. As she becomes aware of the reasons for her behavior, she's able to decide whether various behaviors are in line with her values.

WHICH MASTER DO YOU SERVE?

Use this worksheet to record common daily activities, such as eating breakfast, exercising at the gym, or getting to work on time. On the left-hand side, list the time of day and your activity. Use the four columns under "Function" to record what function this activity serves: avoidance (negative reinforcement), a quick fix (short-term positive reinforcement), pliance (doing something because others praise you for it, or because you've learned that it's the appropriate thing to do), or intrinsic reinforcement (long-term positive reinforcement associated with a sense of vitality from living in accordance with a value). You may find that a bit of each is present. Place a check mark in each function column that applies, and use a star to indicate the function that feels like it's primary.

Time of Day	Activity	Function			
		Avoidance, or Negative Reinforcement	Short-Term Positive Reinforcement	Pliance	Intrinsic Positive Reinforcement

Establishing Patterns of Values-Consistent Behavior

If most of a client's activities are driven by avoidance, short-term reinforcement, or pliance, he's likely to experience a lack of vitality or struggle with maladjustment. Your job is to help the client to reconnect with a vital life and thereby increase his willingness to be in the present moment in the service of long-term valued directions. Essentially, valuing entails three important facets: behaving consistently in accordance with an overarching long-term valued direction; willingness to be present and to persist in the face of difficulty when taking steps in that valued direction; and full mindful engagement in valued activities, allowing intrinsic reinforcement.

CONNECTING TO AN OVERARCHING LONG-TERM VALUE

One of the most common questions ACT therapists ask clients is "What do you want your life to be about?" During each and every ACT session, therapists use the client's own chosen, clarified values as the context of therapy.

The skill of noticing how one's behaviors are functioning is useful throughout our lives. It's especially important to be able to recognize how genuine values, free from the values traps discussed earlier in this chapter, may be present over one's lifetime. To reiterate, values are directions, not destinations, and are defined by their function, not their form, so they transcend changes due to varying life conditions (for example, childhood, adolescence, adulthood, and old age). Here are some examples of how the same value can be constant but look different in different stages of life.

Value: Caregiving

Childhood: Caring for my puppy

Adolescence: Caring for my sick grandmother

Adulthood: Caring for my children

Old age: Volunteering in schools and caring for underprivileged children

Value: Education and personal development

Childhood: Being with older kids and learning from them

Adolescence: Studying the subjects I'm most interested in

Adulthood: Learning information and skills I need to be able to play an active, effective role in the working world

Old age: Learning about various topics that interest me, such as art history, now that I have time

These are examples of how the overarching value remains consistent throughout life while the content might vary according to life condition. The value of caring for other human beings or living things stays constant, but the way in which it is expressed changes. The value of learning is constant, but the form of education and personal development varies with age and life stage. In this book we assume that all overarching values are relatively constant over a lifetime. While raising children may be the most important valued action of someone in middle adulthood, caring for friends, neighbors, or the community may become more important valued actions later in life. Still, the overarching value of caregiving is present throughout each phase of life. If you think of values in terms of function rather than content, you may find it easier to see and understand this consistency.

WILLINGNESS TO BE PRESENT AND PERSIST IN THE FACE OF DIFFICULTY

When we live in accordance with our values, we may encounter difficult or unwanted experiences. It is rare that once we choose our values, things fall into place and, voilà, we experience peace and vitality from that point forward. Indeed, the word "vitality," often used in ACT to describe the quality of valued action, doesn't necessarily mean positive affect or feeling. Rather, it means feeling alive, and that may describe a moment of excruciating pain as well as one of joy and happiness.

In fact, for many people the activities related to values can be uncomfortable and sometimes even painful. For this reason, valuing also involves persistence. What helps us persist? When we live in accordance with our values, we increase our ability to contact many sources of intrinsic reinforcement. Too often, we simply focus on negatively evaluated thoughts, feelings, or situations. Persistence over time requires finding intrinsic reinforcement even inside an activity that may indeed have some negative aspects. There are many times in our lives when we make valued choices that we know are likely to bring us pain, such as choosing to put a beloved family pet to sleep after a long illness in order to prevent further suffering, despite sadness at the impending loss.

Let's consider a slightly more difficult example. Consider Annika, who deeply valued open and honest relationships and chose to tell her partner about her recent infidelity. You can imagine the feelings of fear, sadness, and remorse that might arise in that situation. However, mindful awareness of her core values in each moment allowed Annika to notice that despite these painful feelings, she was actually taking steps to live consistently with her stated value of behaving in a genuine manner. By taking steps to live consistently with a core value, such as being genuine, we experience vitality; and while psychological pain doesn't always come with valued choices, sometimes it is inevitable with those choices. In Annika's case, she knew that she was likely to lose her partner, whom she cared for deeply, but she placed her value of being genuine over her fear of losing the relationship.

When faced with difficulties we may feel tempted to avoid, it's important to look at the situation in terms of the overarching value at stake. For example, let's say you value being a caring friend and you find yourself in a situation where you're worried that a friend is doing something that may be harmful to her, such as drinking too much. As you broach the topic of her burgeoning alcoholism, you need to remain mindful of your value and not allow it to be overshadowed by emotions such as shame, embarrassment, fear of confrontation, or fear of unwanted outcomes.

FULL MINDFUL ENGAGEMENT LEADING TO INTRINSIC REINFORCEMENT

At some point in our lives, most of us have experienced what we earlier referred to as intrinsic reinforcement, in which we are fully engaged in an activity and are enjoying it for its own sake rather than for some extrinsic reinforcer, such as money or praise, that we might earn for doing it. In areas of life such as music, dance, art, sex, and sport, many have experienced the "flow" of being one with the activity itself. In such instances, the activity has no purpose other than to be experienced as a chosen activity. The reinforcing quality lies in the process, rather than the outcome. Attending to the present moment allows valued activities to be naturally reinforcing, and doing so requires full mindful engagement with the process as opposed to the outcome. For example, a singer might find that she enjoys the process of singing regardless of whether or not she missed a note or her audience was moved by the song. Further, overthinking or evaluating the process can actually get in the way of some activities. Imagine trying to think through every muscle movement needed to take a dance step or to make a jump shot. While training is helpful, just being present in the moment is required for doing this kind of activity. So, too, can we learn to just be in the moment when engaging our values.

Though engaging fully with valued activities is an intense and often pleasurable experience, not all intense pleasurable experiences count as valued activity, of course. For example, sensation seeking without a valued context cannot in and of itself be considered a value. The kind of rush or high that people report after bungee jumping or shooting up heroin is not what we mean by vitality. Such experiences are characterized by short-term feeling states rather than by the ongoing sense of purpose and vitality produced by long-term intrinsically reinforcing valued activity. Experiencing vitality within the context of values-consistent action gives clients a sense of what to look for in the future. Vitality becomes a reinforcer that supports continuing to make values-consistent choices.

During the process of therapy, you can help clients learn to mindfully engage in a process of understanding the function of their behavior and recognizing when it's in the service of values and when it isn't. You can also help clients learn to be willing to persist and experience discomfort in the service of their values. Each is important in helping clients recognize their potential for living a values-consistent life every moment of every day.

Step 3: Choosing Goals in Service of Values

Recall how we have differentiated between values and goals. Values provide the direction, and goals provide stops along the way that help us live consistently with our values. Without taking action to achieve these goals, we would simply be talking about our values rather than taking steps to live consistently with them. Remember, though, that no matter how many goals we achieve, we always have our values. Consider the example of valuing intimacy in relationships. A typical goal might be getting married. While someone can say, "Yes, I got married," no one can say, "I'm finished being intimate with others." As a value, intimacy in relationships is constant throughout a person's life. If certain kinds of intimacy are important to an individual, he can find ways to build those types of intimacy through specific goals. Working with clients to establish concrete goals in the service of overarching values is a particularly important way to help them live a more vital and fulfilling life.

Taking steps in a valued direction may be seen as a two-step process of moving and then evaluating. After identifying a compass setting—the value we want to move toward—we take what we think might be a step in that direction. After taking that action, we evaluate how well it served the value (which we'll discuss later, as step 4 in the process of valuing). But in truth, it's a bit more complicated. The first part of taking steps, or setting goals, is choosing them, yet there are ways in which even choosing those steps can be difficult and subject to the same fusion, fears, and avoidance involved in the process of clarifying values. We provide some specific strategies and worksheets that will help you guide clients in choosing their goals in chapter 8, so for now, we'll focus on some of the difficulties clients may encounter in setting achievable goals.

When clients begin to live in accordance with their newly clarified values, it isn't uncommon for them to revert back to old patterns of avoidance and fusion. Just as values clarification is a process, so too is learning how to set goals that are consistent with those values.

Biting Off More Than You Can Chew

Sometimes people set the bar too high. For example, if a man values helping others and chooses a goal of going to medical school but he has never passed a science class or completed college, some amount of avoidance may be operating here. Not to say this isn't a possible goal, but applying to several medical schools probably isn't a good place to start. If he's willing to slow down and contact the underlying value, other opportunities may show up, such as researching and signing up for the prerequisite college science classes or choosing a related goal, such as becoming a medical technician. Breaking down the goal into manageable steps is an important process, and one that takes time to learn. It is the clinician's job to help clients choose small steps that together lead toward a larger goal, all under the umbrella of a valued direction.

For example, if someone reports valuing close family relationships and therefore wants to reestablish ties with estranged family members, the best place to start probably isn't moving in with one of those relatives immediately. A better starting point would be small steps such as writing a letter or making a phone call, which may lay the groundwork for building the relationship over time. As the clinician, another part of your job is to help the client be willing to experience the discomfort associated with taking these small steps and expecting some difficulties along the way. Again, helping clients contact the process of valuing as they set their goals is important. It may be that the client who wants to reconnect with family may feel some intrinsic reinforcement from making that first phone call, regardless of whether or not his relative is thrilled about the call. Building patterns of behavior where the process is reinforcing—rather than simply focusing on the outcome—is the key. Also, be aware that in some cases choosing too lofty a goal may be an easy way to avoid moving forward. The inevitable failure or rejection then justifies not moving forward, which can be comforting if that prospect is risky and scary.

Nibbling When You're Hungry

Another common response is to set goals that are exceedingly small to increase feelings of success and reduce the probability of failure. This isn't necessarily a bad idea, as it can help clients, particularly those with a lean reinforcement history, learn that they are, in fact, capable of learning and doing new things that they may experience as vital. However, you may want to help clients be bold and take some risks rather than always playing it safe. Moving outside of their comfort zone in the service of values may increase the opportunity for clients to contact new reinforcers and build increasingly sustainable behavior patterns. Taking small steps can be reinforcing, but if a client has a value of education yet only collects brochures for classes he may want to take several months down the line, there may be some avoidance or fear of failure operating, which is worth discussing in session. Normalizing the difficulty and fear associated with starting something new is important. To that end, it may be worthwhile to help clients choose activities that may be slightly risky but help them get closer to their goals, and ultimately their values.

Step 4: Evaluating Choices and Creating Patterns of Action

Simply taking a step is not enough; clients must be guided to give themselves the time to evaluate each step. Is this goal in alignment with the valued direction? How will the client know? What happens if the goal turns out to be nonvital? Choosing a step in a valued direction is very likely under the influence of the individual's programming: what she has learned about herself and the world through her lifelong exposure to the socioverbal community. Hence, clients need to experiment with many moves and gather experience in order to be able to discriminate between vital and nonvital.

For example, Samuel, a client in his midtwenties, may have established that working toward having an intimate relationship in his life is an important value. He decides that a step in that direction is going out to a nightclub. Taking this step, he's creating opportunities to meet new people, getting himself into the ballpark of intimate relationships. After he has been to the nightclub, he needs to evaluate if this step did in fact bring him closer to the intimate relationship he's looking for. If not, he may need to try other steps and evaluate them. However, by experimenting in these directions he is valuing intimate relationships. He's experimenting and evaluating according to the reference value he has set for himself. This is very different from using mainstream commercial images or what others think as a criterion for what he values. Samuel can choose to persist based on the reinforcement he gets from taking action (often referred to in ACT as "moving one's feet") in the direction of what he values. He can also choose which behaviors seem to serve him best in living his values. Chapter 8 focuses on specific strategies to maintain patterns of valued action.

Looking for the Function of Discomfort

We all know that trying new things often involves fear of failure, fear of evaluation, or some form of discomfort. Many of us can easily recall a time when we started something new and noticed thoughts such as "What if I screw it up?" or "I don't know how well I'll do at this." Each time we step into the unknown, discomfort is bound to show up. When we're evaluating movements in valued directions, the key is to be able to see what type of discomfort is showing up. Sometimes discomfort is a natural part of the process of doing new things, as we just mentioned. But other times there's wisdom in the discomfort we might feel in doing new things.

Let's use the nightclub example again. Since it's rare that people meet their soul mate at a nightclub, it's likely that Samuel doesn't experience any closeness or meet anyone of interest on that one occasion. Coming home, he may feel sad and have thoughts that going to the nightclub was a waste of time. Is this due to the natural discomfort associated with trying new things, or is it because nightclubs just aren't that enjoyable for him? Unless he experienced being in the nightclub as vital in and of itself, even if his goal (meeting new people) wasn't reached, he may not want to go back. Instead, he may want to seek out other, more enjoyable activities where meeting people is possible. But if he enjoyed the activity, he may wish to go back, simply to enjoy meeting new people and dancing.

Simply put, when clients are trying new things, encourage them to ask themselves, "Are my uncomfortable feelings due to the unknown element of this new thing I'm trying, or is it because there's something about this activity that I really don't enjoy?" For all of us, creating opportunities that allow us to behave in ways that are truly reinforcing is part of a vital, values-driven life.

Summary

This chapter has laid out the four steps in the process of valuing: identifying core values, attending to the function of behavior, choosing goals in the service of values, and evaluating the inherent vitality in those goals. In future chapters we'll provide more detailed discussion of techniques you can use to increase the potency of each of these steps as you work with clients; we hope these approaches will revitalize *you* in your work as a clinician. Chapters 7, 8, and 9 all provide concrete steps along these lines. Next, however, we turn to the therapeutic relationship, and how it can be of vital importance for your values work with clients.

CHAPTER 5

Compassion and the Therapeutic Relationship

Forging interpersonal connections in a therapeutic way is both an art and a skill. In ACT (like other therapies) the therapeutic relationship is itself a powerful engine of change—change that takes place right in the therapy room. From a values perspective, both therapist and client, as partners in therapy, are striving together to accomplish a common purpose, and both are struggling with their own history and experiences. The heart of the therapeutic relationship is the perspective of transcendent sense of self (self-as-context), which allows each therapy partner to connect to the shared experience of being human. Obviously, the roles of therapist and client are fairly well established in all psychotherapy traditions, with varying degrees of self-disclosure on the part of the therapist recommended.

From an ACT perspective, the fact that we struggle in the same ways as our clients is one of our biggest allies in therapy. We've found self-disclosure on the part of the therapist allows us to model ACT processes for our clients; it also helps us appreciate how difficult it can be to take some of the steps we ask our clients to take in therapy. However, even for the sake of modeling ACT processes, we caution you to carefully examine the function of self-disclosure, with a supervisor if you can. As a general rule, it often has a big impact if we, as therapists, express that we too have had sticky thoughts, gotten caught up in particular emotions, or gotten off track from important values. If you choose to divulge details, be very careful and deliberate about which details you choose to share. If sharing your fellow human struggle will help the client take steps toward a valued life, we generally recommend it. But self-disclosure shouldn't burden the client in any way, and we caution you to be aware that some types of disclosure might undermine therapy (for example, if therapy starts to become about your struggle as opposed to the client's). Any of your disclosures should serve a twofold purpose: to model acceptance, defusion, mindfulness, self-as-context, values, and committing to valued action for clients; and creating a context for therapy that normalizes struggling and helps clients feel safe in expressing their struggle as they move toward living a more meaningful and valued life.

In summary, the partners in therapy are two conscious human beings struggling together to find a way of relating to human suffering that helps both of them live vital, meaningful lives. The purpose of the therapeutic relationship is not any specific goal but rather the process itself. This process is a valued direction for both partners.

Compassion for yourself and compassion for others is at the heart of the therapeutic relationship. From a values perspective, a powerful therapeutic relationship is created when both partners are conscious of and committed to acting consistently with the six core processes of ACT: presence in the here and now, acceptance, defusion, self-as-context, values, and committed action, all leading to psychological flexibility. Taking a compassionate and defused therapeutic stance provides an open, accepting, safe, and creative space where both therapy partners can try new ways of vital living and leave behind old, nonfunctional behavior patterns.

We will begin this chapter with an ACT and RFT discussion of compassion for self as a prerequisite for compassion for others and therefore necessary in the therapeutic relationship. Next we'll look at the role of values in the therapeutic relationship and discuss how to remain mindful of those values to make the best use of your time in session. Then we'll provide a general introduction to the process and dynamics in this complex relationship, and particularly the role of the client's and therapist's individual histories in the relationship. We'll use some of the core processes of ACT to illustrate how the therapeutic relationship may be improved, complete with examples and dialogues. We provide a template of an ACT therapist's values declaration, which you can use to remain mindful of your values for therapy, and to model the process of valuing for clients. Finally, we discuss how to proceed when therapist and client values clash.

Compassion for Self: A Prerequisite

From an ACT and RFT values perspective, it isn't possible to be genuinely compassionate with another human without being compassionate toward yourself. Psychologically, these two stances are two sides of the same coin. Steven Hayes (2008), a pioneer of the ACT and RFT approach, posits that the roots of compassion and self-compassion both involve:

- Embracing difficult feelings

- Observing one's difficult and judgmental thoughts without entanglement

- 🕊 Connecting with a more spiritual sense of self that transcends this programming

- 🕊 Carrying one's history forward into a life of compassionate engagement of self-validation

Compassion requires the skill of perspective taking. When sufficiently well developed, this skill allows us to operate at the level of self-as-context (or the transcendent self) wherein we are able to take perspective on our experiences as simply parts of being human, as opposed to viewing thoughts, feelings, and memories as experiences that must be avoided, changed, or escaped. As a therapist, it can be difficult to maintain a compassionate stance toward yourself and your clients throughout therapy, especially because your job is to sit with a client's pain (and to sit with your own discomfort as you listen to your clients' pain). At the extreme, lack of compassion can manifest as therapist burnout, which is typically characterized by becoming desensitized and losing empathy for clients' experiences. This is particularly likely among therapists who work with challenging populations, and a common notion is that this is due to the stress of dealing with these populations. However, recent ACT studies indicate that when "burned-out" therapists are trained in self-compassion (taking an accepting, defused perspective on their own difficult experiences), both they and their clients fare much better (e.g., Hayes et al., 2004). It seems that noncompassionate behavior toward oneself is correlated with noncompassionate behavior toward others, while compassion for oneself is correlated with compassion for others. It therefore follows that self-compassion can and should be a part of every therapist's approach.

Relational frame theory can illuminate this relationship between self-compassion and compassion for another. RFT explicates how we can establish this transcendent sense of self through training the deictic (perspective-taking) frames of I-you, here-there, and now-then, described in chapter 2. Compassion can be strengthened by contacting both a transcendent sense of self and a transcendent sense of "other" (recall that the deictic frame of "I" entails "you"). Rather than delve too deeply into this complex idea, we simply point out that we believe we can build empathy by strengthening the perspective on both the self and the other. RFT researchers have been exploring this link, and preliminary data indicate a link between deictic framing and empathy (Vilardaga, Hayes, Levin, & Muto, 2008). The roots of compassion, including self-compassion, assisted in particular by the establishment of a transcendent sense of self, involve taking a mindful, accepting, and loving stance toward yourself and your thoughts and feelings, focusing on what you value and carrying those values flexibly into your life and your involvement with others (Hayes, 2008). Clearly, the ACT therapeutic relationship provides a context in which the therapist can embody, instigate, and support the core processes of ACT in the therapy room. Before we examine in detail how this occurs, let's consider the importance of identifying and clarifying your values as a therapist and bringing these values into your work on a daily basis.

The Role of Values in the Therapeutic Relationship

Think back to the moment when you decided to become a therapist. What was going on for you? Whether you were young or whether you were making a career change later in life, at some point you made a commitment to be a compassionate human being who chooses to sit across from another human being and do your best to help that other person loosen the bonds of suffering and find a more valued path in life.

As therapists, we are usually pretty good at catching when clients are behaving in ways that are ineffective or are likely to derail them from their valued path. However, we also tend to get caught up in our evaluations of clients' struggles. We can find ourselves judging our difficult clients. Even with good supervision and the best intentions, we have all found ourselves, from time to time, having thoughts along these lines:

- If only she would listen to me in therapy! She wouldn't have to make the same mistakes over and over.

- He just can't seem to let go of his past. It's so frustrating to see him view the world as a dangerous place without possibility when he has so many wonderful things and people around him!

- She is the least emotional client I've ever seen. She spends every moment in therapy intellectualizing whatever we talk about. Even the experiential exercises are an opportunity for her to talk about acceptance rather than do it!

Part of our responsibility as therapists is to be aware of our tendencies to get entangled with our evaluations, which moves us off our valued path in working with clients.

Clarifying Your Values as a Therapist

The ACT therapeutic relationship has a special quality that distinguishes it from the relationship in other disciplines of psychotherapy, and in our experience developing that quality requires special attention and training. At first glance, this special quality might seem paradoxical. The ACT therapist relates to the client in a loving, empathetic, and compassionate manner and, at the same time, also practices relating to all thoughts and language expressed in the therapy room in a loose way. In other words, the ACT therapist fully accepts and validates the client and also doesn't buy into the client's verbal formulations about her problems. This entails relating to the client from the other-as-context perspective, which simply means recognizing that the client is more than her experiences. For most of us, this is a very unusual way of communicating; in our socialization process we normally learn to validate fellow human beings via language by taking the words they express literally. This is the reason why supervised attention and training are required to develop the ACT therapeutic stance. This may sound like we're prescribing therapist values. In fact we are not. However, doing ACT work necessarily means that the therapist must value values. In other words, the ACT therapist encourages clients to live meaningful, purposeful lives free from additional suffering, which requires taking an accepting, mindful, defused stance toward clients in the service of this goal. The therapist models the ACT processes for clients by embodying them in the room so that clients may learn to compassionately and boldly live their values from an accepting, mindful, defused stance.

We encourage you to examine your own personal values in relation to your therapy work so that you might model and instigate the ACT processes for your clients to the best of your ability. Notice your reactions to the examples we give, the circumstances in which it would be difficult for you to embody the ACT model in your work with clients, and the way you typically respond to such difficulties. As you do so, check in with yourself: What matters to you most in your work with your clients? Can you commit to finding ways to live consistently with these values even with your most difficult clients? Later in this chapter we provide a list of values that might resonate with your own values for working with clients.

Sharing Your Values in the Therapy Room

To most effectively help a client move forward from the very start of therapy, it can be powerful to make a values declaration at an early stage of the therapeutic interaction. Doing so can model the therapist's accepting, defused, open stance toward the client's pain. Here are a couple of examples that may resonate for you:

- "As you speak about your suffering, I experience how this particular content sends you into a flurry of resistance, negative self-judgment, more pain, and more stiffness. I experience how difficult this narrow space is for you, and I want you and I, just for a moment, to rise above this vicious circle and focus on where you really want to go with therapy."

- "You have given me several examples of what you don't want in your life, and I share that with you. No one wants pain. At the same time, I want to see and experience you beyond that pain. I want us to rise up above the 'don't wants' to what you *do* want, what you truly and deeply care about."

Such values statements allow the therapist to embody the ACT model when working with clients in the service of building a powerful, healing therapeutic relationship. Genuinely and compassionately valuing, accepting, and validating clients while simultaneously not validating the content of the stories they bring to therapy is an art. It seems human beings have a fundamental need to be seen, accepted, and validated in social relationships, and this is at the core of therapeutic relationships in general. It's also at the core of the ACT therapeutic relationship, but acceptance and validation aren't limited to the verbal formulations expressed in the therapy room (self-as-content perspective). Acceptance and validation of clients is far more complex than simply parroting what they have just said. And acceptance and validation aren't the same thing as approval. Acceptance requires a willingness to step into a client's shoes and see the world from her perspective. It requires a willingness to have all the prejudices, discomfort, and evaluations that show up while taking her perspective without allowing those obstacles to overwhelm or distort the process (self-as-context perspective). Validation is the expression of your acceptance of the client in her particular context, not acceptance of her stories about her problems. The therapeutic connection is built as the therapist finds the perfect, competent, and whole human being beyond the verbal entanglement of mind fabrications.

Remaining Connected to Values within the Therapeutic Relationship

As with any valued activity, it's important to remain mindful of values during therapy. In our experience, keeping valued directions close at hand and continuously referring back to them can be a great time-saver. Unfortunately, many therapy hours may be spent ineffectively, especially at the start of therapy, if the client is allowed to repeat well-versed stories, ruminate over past injustices and wrongdoings, and get caught up in mind entanglement. When both therapy partners clarify and connect to deeply rooted core values, it will help keep the therapeutic process on track, just like calibrating and periodically checking a compass can help you stay on course as you travel.

Next we present some questions for you as the therapist and for your clients that might help you both recognize when you're moving away from your valued paths. Taking the time to ask these types of questions may help set the stage for therapy or help get you or the client back on a valued path if either of you wanders off at any point. Although we've split these questions into two categories—questions to ask yourself, as the therapist, and questions to ask the client—we present them side by side to illustrate the parallel processes that happen for therapist and client.

Questions to Ask Yourself Privately	Questions to Ask the Client
Can I make contact with my values regarding why I am a therapist?	Can you make contact with those valued directions you identified at the start of therapy about what you want your life to stand for?
What is the overarching value right here and now in the interaction between me and my client?	What is the overarching value right here and now in the interaction between you and me, as your therapist?
What steps can I take right here and now that are consistent with my over-arching value for therapy?	What steps can you take right here and now that are consistent with those overarching values you want in your life?
If my mind is racing, can I show myself loving-kindness and gently bring myself back to my value for therapy here in this room?	If your mind is racing, can you show yourself loving-kindness and gently bring yourself back to your valued direction here in this room?
When I feel like my buttons are being pushed, can I make room for my own history, notice that it is being activated here and now, and be willing to stay present and continue to work toward my values in therapy?	If and when you feel stuck in negative feelings that come up here, can you see them for what they are, your own history, and be willing to stay present, make room for that history, and stay on your valued track?
In the service of my values in therapy, am I willing to stand by this client unconditionally?	In the service of your values in therapy, are you willing to stand up for yourself, your own vitality, and what you hold to be important, unconditionally?
In my pain and suffering, I can find my values. If I am struggling with this client, feeling the need for her to change, or feeling like I can't help her, can I notice that I value the process of therapy and being with my suffering about this client?	In pain you find your values, and in your values you find your pain. In the service of getting in touch with your deep-seated values, are you willing to have the pain that's inevitable in this process?
If I do what I've always done, I'll get what I've always gotten. Am I willing to let go of unworkable strategies for dealing with difficult moments with clients and do something different?	If you do what you've always done, you'll get what you've always gotten. Are you willing to let go of your usual strategies and do something new with me here?

Here are some examples of when it might be a good time to ask yourself these questions:

- ૐ When you begin therapy with a new client

- ૐ If it seems a client's therapy is no longer moving in a valued direction

- ૐ If therapy starts to feel "mind-y," abstract, or intellectual in nature

- ૐ If you notice that you're starting to defend your ideas, theories, or perspectives

- ૐ If you notice that the client is defending her story

- ૐ If you don't feel connected to the client

The Therapeutic Process: History Meets History

As therapy starts, even despite the best of intentions, the same sorts of difficulties come up for the therapist as for the client. As in a novel with parallel stories going on, we have at least four processes occurring simultaneously: the client, the client's history, the therapist, and the therapist's history.

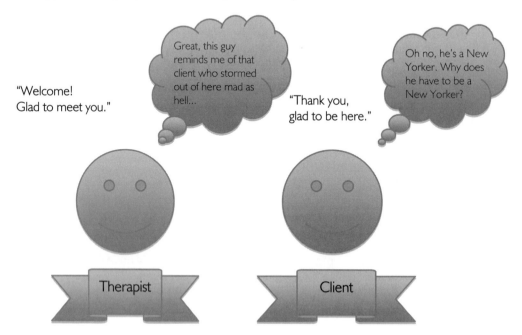

Even though both the therapist and the client come to the therapy room valuing the therapeutic process, each has a history, and particular aspects of this history, unknown to one or to both, are elicited by the mere presence of the other. In addition, both the therapist and the client have tendencies to engage in experiential avoidance. Both will tend to avoid both their own and the other's discomfort and negative emotions. These processes—eliciting one another's history and experiential avoidance—can confound and derail the therapeutic process. Again, core ACT processes such as valuing, contacting the present moment, and a self-as-context perspective can help keep therapy on track.

Confounding Factors: Some Questions to Ask

Here are some questions inspired by functional analytic psychotherapy (Kohlenberg & Tsai, 1991) that can be helpful in revealing these confounding factors in the therapeutic relationship. These questions can be asked outright at any time during the therapeutic processes, even at the outset. It may be especially effective to ask these questions when the client seems to be reacting more to private events than what is going on in the therapy session itself:

- Who do I remind you of?

- What are you thinking of right now?

- Is our way of interacting similar to that of another relationship in your life?

- What would be hard for you to say to me right now?

The client's responses can reveal relevant information for the therapeutic relationship and the therapy process. For example, a client could respond by saying that you remind her of a teacher she had a bad experience with. You can use the elicitation of these negative feelings, along with the client's typical reaction patterns, as a sample behavior and start applying ACT core processes to it in session. Asking the client to express what she's thinking but not saying may provide an opportunity to investigate experiential avoidance. And looking for similarities of ways of interacting in relationships could provide an opportunity to explore issues such as valued qualities or experiential avoidance.

Therapist Reactions to the Client's History

The client's suffering will speak to and likely elicit your own history of suffering. If you aren't mindful when this happens, you're likely to automatically react with your typical patterns of experiential avoidance, and this is likely to get in the way of being a conscious, compassionate therapist. Subsequently, the client may react to your experiential avoidance behavior in her own typical ways right in front of your eyes. Watch carefully how she reacts; this may present a good opportunity to tell the client what's going on with you as a metaphor for or example of experiential avoidance.

Here are some steps to help you to become conscious of the history that both you and the client bring to the therapy room:

1. Be aware of the characteristic content that typically traps you and your client into entanglement. (Note that here, "characteristic" means typical patterns that have repeated themselves during therapy sessions.)

2. Make a functional analysis of an example of this typical entanglement for both your behavior and the client's behavior during the session, considering cues, responses, and impact.

   ❧ **Cues.** What forms and content of verbal expressions of thoughts and feelings or nonverbal expressions of body language typically start this chain of behavior?

   ❧ **Reaction.** Make note of both immediate physical and emotional reactions and secondary reactions or ways of relating to these immediate reactions (typically seen in the form of tendencies toward experiential avoidance).

   ❧ **Impact.** Studying the events following the cues and responses, did this relational chain of behavior bring the therapeutic process closer to or farther away from valued action? What is the plausible function in the short term and in the long term?

Observing examples of in-session entanglement patterns (both yours and the client's) and hypothesizing functional analyses can serve as a primary sample of dysfunctional behavior patterns. Being able to observe, analyze, and intervene directly on behavior is far more valid and reliable than working with subjective and retrospective interpretations of events.

Improving the Therapeutic Relationship

In the remainder of this chapter, we present three core ACT processes—acceptance, cognitive defusion, and self-as-context—and show how an effective therapeutic relationship can be shaped and reinforced by these processes. Each section includes a brief description of the therapeutic posture related to each process, a brief description of the problems that can arise if the therapist behaves in ways that are avoidant or fused, and examples that illustrate how to embody ACT processes in the service of strengthening the therapeutic relationship.

Acceptance

The therapeutic posture of acceptance involves a conscious, empathetic stance and creates an accepting, open, and safe environment for clients where there is an abundance of space for any difficult content. Just as emergency room physicians are willing to deal with anything and everything that shows up on their shift, the psychotherapist must be willing to be present with any and all thoughts or feelings the client chooses to take up.

There is no way of knowing what the client will reveal, even based on a particular diagnosis or referral. Depending on the therapist's particular history, some or most of the client's story will inevitably elicit pain and suffering for the therapist. When this happens, the therapist and client are connecting and sharing a oneness that connects all language-able human beings. This sharing is the vital essence of the ACT therapeutic relationship. If the therapist isn't willing to fully be present with this shared suffering, therapy will likely occur on a more superficial level. In that event, the therapist is actually modeling experiential avoidance. Such avoidance is likely to sabotage an open and empowering relationship as the therapist steers clear of certain topics or changes topics in the service of avoiding personally difficult material. In fact, an emotionally avoidant therapist may not even notice her own feelings that are elicited by the client and the interaction. If the therapist isn't present with herself and conscious of her own emotions, thoughts, and reactions to the client, she will miss out on vitally important clinical information present in the therapy room in the here and now.

A SHARED HISTORY: A MOMENT AS AN AVOIDANT THERAPIST

Let's take a look a dialogue that illustrates a therapist's avoidance moves in response to shared history with her client. To give you some background on the context of this therapeutic interaction, the therapist's history includes growing up with an alcoholic mother who recently died from complications due to alcoholism. The client has a similar history and wants to tell the therapist about some of the history with which she still struggles. The therapist "thought bubbles" convey the therapist's thoughts. These are followed by a functional analysis of those thoughts.

Client: Whenever I try to get into an intimate relationship, I get scared and back away.

Therapist thought bubble:
(Boy do I recognize that, and I hated it when I felt like that!)

Cue. *Uneasy feeling:* Associations and pictures of my own difficulties in this area.

Reaction. *Thoughts:* "I've got the same problem; I can't help her!" and "What is my colleague who referred her going to say when he sees I couldn't help his patient?" *Feeling:* Hopeless. *Behavior:* Squirming in the chair.

Impact. Some relief from uneasiness.

Therapist: You're starting a similar relationship with me, here and now. Can you feel that same scaredness and tendency to back away?

Client: Yes, I feel that scaredness right now.

Therapist: Would you be willing to bring that feeling of being scared into this room, here with me? We would do it in the service of helping you take steps to get into the intimate relationship that you want to be in.

Client: Sounds hard, but okay. I really do want to connect intimately.

Therapist: Okay, good. Please close your eyes and see what pictures pop up that are associated with those scared feelings. (*Thinks, "So far, so good."*)

Client: What comes up now is one where I'm alone in my room crying and feel hopeless about my mother, who is drunk again and I can't help her.

Therapist thought bubble:
(Oh, God, not that. That went right to the gut. I can't feel this and act professionally. I might start crying. I don't know if I can listen to this. What kind of a therapist am I?)

Cue. *Feeling of hopelessness:* Pictures come up of me trying in vain to help my own mother, who is drunk.

Reaction. *Thoughts:* "Get out" and "You can't do this; you can't act professionally. Get out of this place!" *Behavior:* Direct the client to go on, to another place (experiential avoidance).

Impact. Relief from feeling of hopelessness.

Therapist: Let's continue. See if any *other* pictures come up for you.

Client: Okay (*surprised*). Another picture comes up on the same theme. In this one, I'm trying to talk to my mom about her drinking and she tells me she hasn't had anything, but I smell liquor on her breath.

> **Therapist thought bubble:**
> *(Oh shit, that one went right to the core.)*

Cue. Aversive emotions; associations with my own mother drinking and lying; feeling no more worth than a bottle.

Reaction. *Thoughts:* "Escape!" and "Distract yourself" (experiential avoidance). *Behavior:* Make a grocery list (experiential avoidance).

Impact. Try to prevent further pain.

Therapist: *(Speaks with a tense voice.)* Okay, you can just sit with that picture for a few minutes and then come back to this room when you're done.

Client: *(Senses this tenseness, feels something is wrong, and breaks off the exercise.)* This is difficult for me. Maybe we could do it another time.

Therapist: *(Feels relieved.)* Sure, no need to rush through anything.

This example shows how the quality of the therapeutic work can be negatively influenced by the therapist's unwillingness to experience her own pain elicited by the client's suffering. The therapist got entangled with the content of the client's story and reacted as she often reacts in her private life: by escaping and avoiding those feelings. In this example, she let the client down by not proceeding into the most painful parts of those memories—a move made in the service of avoiding her own pain.

THERAPEUTIC BENEFITS OF ACCEPTANCE

The flip side of experiential avoidance is acceptance. In contrast to the last example, acceptance entails being open to what the client is saying and doing and being willing to explore these events fully when clinically relevant. The accepting therapist is fully open to the client's history, along with any feelings and thoughts it produces, and is willing to stand with the wholeness and consciousness of the client. Acceptance increases psychological flexibility by bringing both the therapist and the client into contact with what has been previously avoided, doing so in the safer context of the therapy room.

Therapist acceptance is sometimes referred to as agape love for the client (unselfish, loyal, and benevolent concern), but it also applies to oneself, the therapist. In ACT, when this type of acceptance is directed toward the client, the therapist displays a high degree of flexibility in being open to and embracing all thoughts, feelings, bodily sensations, and memories expressed by the client as valid experiences. When directed toward oneself as therapist, acceptance means creating a space of willingness and flexibility and embracing all thoughts, feelings, bodily sensations, and memories elicited in oneself during the therapy session as valid experiences.

A SHARED HISTORY: A MOMENT AS AN ACCEPTING THERAPIST

Now let's replay the previous interchange, this time with acceptance on the part of the therapist rather than experiential avoidance.

Client: Whenever I try to get into an intimate relationship, I get scared and back away.

Therapist thought bubble:
(Boy do I recognize that! Now, I'm starting to feel uneasy.)

Cue. *Uneasy feeling:* Associations and pictures of my own difficulties in this area.

Reaction. Alert to be extra present, to go into this feeling I share with this client.

Impact. More anxiety. Open up and breathe in this suffering that I share, not only with this client but with so many people. Feel a deep empathy for this client and myself.

Therapist: You are starting a similar relationship with me, here and now. Can you feel that same scaredness and tendency to back away?

Client: Yes, I feel that scaredness right now.

Therapist: Would you be willing to bring that feeling of being scared into this room, here with me? We would do it in the service of helping you take steps to get into the intimate relationship that you want to be in.

Client: Sounds hard, but okay. I really do want to connect intimately.

Therapist: Okay, good. Please close your eyes and see what pictures pop up that are associated with those scared feelings.

Client: What comes up now is one where I'm alone in my room crying and feel hopeless about my mother, who is drunk again and I can't help her.

> **Therapist thought bubble:**
> *(Oh, God, not that. That went right to the gut. I can't feel this and act professionally. I might start crying. I don't know if I can listen to this. What kind of a therapist am I?)*

Acceptance alert. Stay present! Open up, be curious, and be patient with yourself. These pictures come from your learning history. Be kind to yourself and your history, embrace your history, and embrace that little girl who did her best to help her mom. You share this sorrow with your client and with so many other children of alcoholics. Breathe in this hurt and make room for this suffering and hurt, both your own and your client's.

Therapist: I realize that this is a very painful picture for you—maybe one of the most painful you have since it came up first. Can you and I stay in this picture? Is it okay, even knowing this memory hurts, for us to stay here awhile and feel what hurts?

Client: *(Tears streaming, and with strained breathing.)* Everything inside me is telling me to run away and hide from it, but okay, I'll try.

Therapist: Would it be okay if we walked in there, inside that little girl's room and sat there next to her on her bed, where she's sitting and crying? You next to her and me next to you?

Client: Okay, I can try, but I think she's ashamed. I think she wants to be alone; she doesn't want anyone to know.

Therapist: That's okay. Could we just sit near her and let her feel what she's feeling? Whatever she's feeling is okay.

In this second example, the same negative feelings and memories were elicited, but the therapist valued relating to the client's suffering, and her own suffering, with acceptance. Together with her client, she made room for those negative emotions and helped herself and her client see them for what they are: history offering reminders of hurtful events. By making room for these memories and allowing them to hurt, both client and therapist are accepting their history. It will still hurt, but they will experience far less suffering, which is caused by the resistance and avoidance.

PRACTICING ACCEPTANCE

Since the client has come to the therapist for help in changing something, the concept of acceptance may seem contradictory. It probably isn't immediately apparent to the client why she should accept a symptom she has struggled with for so long. An accepting therapist can help the client learn that any difficult private event is acceptable and can be brought into the present. Accepting what has been and what is now doesn't mean change is irrelevant. The role of the therapist is to support the client in changing any overt behavior or situation that is unhealthy. Acceptance means the client learns to be open and willing to experience any and all thoughts, feelings, bodily sensations, and memories as valid experiences. It also means that the client takes a loving and kind stance toward herself. In the therapy room, the therapist will have many opportunities to see the client express accepting or nonaccepting behavior toward herself, and to model and shape acceptance as a loving relationship toward oneself and others.

ACT applied in the therapeutic interaction involves acceptance of the elicited negative emotions and a commitment to relate to this discomfort in ways consistent with the valued direction. Going back to the sample therapist-client interaction, each of the partners would use the ACT core processes to become mindful or present with the initial discomfort, make room for and accept these feelings, and watch for learned tendencies to avoid, control, or escape these negative emotions, along with any accompanying thoughts. Each of the partners would be conscious of the feelings and the tendency toward experiential avoidance and choose to relate to all this in a way that allows continued movement in vital, valued directions.

Defusion

The therapeutic stance related to defusion includes being creative and playful with language in the service of keeping a healthy distance from verbally expressed content. This cognitive defusion helps both the therapist and the client increase contact with the process of thinking and decrease the power of thoughts, the products of thinking. The therapist can model changing the relationship to verbal behavior and encourage the client to do the same. If acceptance in the therapeutic relationship is characterized by loving-kindness, defusion will be characterized by playfulness, flexibility, and creativity.

THERAPIST DEFUSION

In our experience, therapists may need to learn to defuse from any of their own verbal constructions that aren't helpful to the therapeutic relationship or to therapy itself. Most of us have a long and expensive education behind our certification, and it's tempting to be cognitively fused with a particular school of thought. Viewing these theories of human behavior as tools for making a difference rather than truths is likely to be more conducive to therapy. There is nothing to be right or wrong about and nothing to defend. Verbal constructions that are held lightly help us reap the benefit of psychological know-how while maintaining psychological flexibility. The defused therapist climbs down from the pedestal of being the expert and embodies a more equal and vulnerable position in the therapist-client relationship.

CLIENT DEFUSION

Just like therapists, clients also come to therapy with stories and formulations about themselves that are invariably a reduction of the complicated human beings they are. Fusion with these formulations leads to inflexibility and is usually seen in the therapy room as expressions of bitterness or resistance to the therapist's perspectives. Defusion helps clients move away from this stuckness about being right or wrong and move toward what works.

Self-as-Context

As described earlier, self-as-context is the idea of self as a pure locus of perspective that's consistent throughout one's life. Our private thoughts and feelings are essentially in a state of constant dynamic flux, and even apparently immutable self-descriptions can change under particular circumstances. However, the sense of self as pure perspective is always with us. Hence, this sense of self provides us with a stability that supports long-term values-consistent behavior even in the face of the kind of aversive psychological content that can sometimes accompany such behavior. When self-as-content, the flip side of self-as-context, shows up in the therapy room, this can interfere with the effectiveness of therapy. It's very easy for either therapist or client to view the other narrowly in terms of a particular role or history, rather than to interact with each other with an appreciation for the other in an open, unfolding, moment-to-moment interaction.

SEEING THE CLIENT IN TERMS OF CONTENT

Fostering a transcendent sense of self that supports a particular kind of relating to oneself and one's clients is an important posture for the therapist. As alluded to previously, most of us are taught to view our clients in terms of their content. Clients are categorized in terms of symptoms using categories indicating varying degrees of dysfunction as derived from guidelines such as those in the *Diagnostic and Statistical Manual of Mental Disorders* (American Psychiatric Association, 2000). Clients are labeled accordingly with descriptive nouns such as "social phobics," "epileptics," or "obsessive-compulsives." This type of labeling encourages professionals to see the syndrome or symptoms as the problem. Once we have these simplified labels, we are also likely to become fused with masses of content about these labels. It isn't uncommon to hear statements such as "A social phobic typically behaves like this" or "Epileptics have a certain type of personality." These labels, along with all of our associated prejudices, are sitting with us as we meet the actual client in all her complexity as a human being. Viewing clients in terms of their content can undermine effective ACT therapy.

Similarly, a self-as-content perspective on the part of the client can create psychological rigidity. For example, the client might attach herself to a story in which she has been victimized by people in positions of power. As a result, she might be more likely to engage in behavior in the service of avoidance of victimization and less likely to engage in behavior that would help move her toward valued ends. For example, she might continue to assert that her position is right, rather than opening up and showing her vulnerability in the therapy room.

Those of us trained in behavioral therapy are taught to make functional analyses based on the self-as-content perspective. The traditional functional analysis looks at the presenting problem as the client describes it, rather than as the therapist sees it with her own eyes in the therapy room. If a client comes to therapy with a complaint of anxiety, the traditional functional analysis would focus on mapping out the behavioral chain of events: antecedents, response, and consequence. For example, in what situations do you have anxiety, how do you behave in response to that anxiety, and what are the consequences of the anxiety? Typically the client is asked about what this chain looks like in the natural environment, an approach that relies on the client's memory and interpretation. This is functional analysis from a self-as-content perspective, as it takes the client's verbal construction of the problem literally and as seen from the client's perspective. The problem with this is that the therapist is then operating from the perspective of the client's content, which often becomes a dead-end street. If the client's perspective or the story she fabricated about the problem had been workable, the problem would have been solved.

CONNECTING VIA THE TRANSCENDENT SENSE OF SELF

In contrast to the self-as-content perspective, self-as-context involves taking a transcendent point of view, which entails valuing a looser connection with all verbal constructs describing the predicament at hand. Being conscious and empathetic toward the client means seeing the world through her eyes but from a transcendent viewpoint—with the awareness that this is a perspective rather than the truth. The connection between the therapist and the client is made and shared on this level of human consciousness rather than via words. This sense of oneness, which lies at the core of an effective therapeutic relationship, is found in the transcendent sense of self.

Creating a functional analysis from this transcendent point of view means watching from outside the language system rather than from within. This is never entirely possible, since even deciding on a different focus requires verbal processing. We can never totally escape using the mind to look at the mind. Generally, clients go to a therapist with a ready-made agenda: "I have this problem, this is the story about how it came to be, and this is what I've tried. Nothing has helped, so can you help me?" From a transcendent self-perspective, the ACT therapist consciously and compassionately watches how the client brings her suffering into the room while speaking about the problem, and subsequently observes how she relates to her suffering, now in the room. The ACT therapist then begins to make a functional analysis of the problem that generates hypotheses about what happens outside the room based on what's seen in the therapy room.

This is not to say that it isn't necessary to talk about events taking place outside the room or to do analyses of those events. Clients are interviewed about their lives and problems occurring outside the therapy room. But typically, those problems also show up in the therapy room, and the only experiential work that can be done takes place in the here and now, in the room. Most often, the real work of ACT is done by focusing on the current therapy process. Partners in therapy need not talk about problems like experiential avoidance or cognitive fusion in day-to-day life; they can experience and analyze those problems in the here and now in the therapy room.

A Declaration of Therapist Values

Earlier in this chapter, we encouraged you to examine your personal values related to therapy. You may find that your values for being a therapist are somewhat specific to each of your clients, and they may differ based upon what is occurring in each session with a given client. Here, we offer a values declaration that reflects one possible stance in the therapist's delicate movement between compassionate empathy for the client and a functional perspective that might seem unempathetic. Given the importance of embodying the ACT processes during therapy, this sample values declaration incorporates each of the ACT processes. You may use this declaration, or something similar, as simply an ACT type of creed to remind yourself of now and again while doing therapy, or you may actually say parts of it aloud to clients when appropriate.

I commit, throughout our work together, to do the following:

ॐ I will value your vitality and what is important to you in your life. I also am conscious that you may not, at this moment, be aware of what is actually important to you in your life.

ॐ I will see the you beyond the story you have come with regarding the cause of your suffering. I also honor the unique learning history that brought you here today.

ॐ I will value the you beyond your stuckness with your stories. I also empathize and share with you this inevitable tendency to fuse with and get stuck in the stories fabricated by the mind, especially stories regarding the "causes" of human suffering.

    I will value the you beyond the symptoms you are suffering from. I also empathize with the reality of that human suffering, a condition we all share.

    I will value the you beyond the countless solutions you've tried in the service of lessening your suffering, including coming to me now. I also empathize and share with you this hopeless tendency we all have to want to solve the unsolvable suffering inside the skin.

    I will value the you who, on a deeper level, recognizes your own vitality and vital direction and knows which steps you can take to get back on that path at this point in time. I also empathize with and share with you the tendency to consistently avoid this vital direction, despite knowing what is possible.

    I will value the you who has the courage now to show me glimpses of what you know to be possible, taking the risk I will see, recognize, and validate this and hold it as a guiding light in our work, causing you even more anxiety. I also empathize with and share with you the habitual tendency to run away from this vital path into familiar hiding places.

    I will stand by your side as you commit to and take your first difficult steps consistent with your vital direction. I also empathize and share with you the inevitable fear that these steps will initially elicit.

    I will value and feel inspired by your willingness to embrace your pain and suffering in the service of living a conscious, vital, and meaningful life. I commit to embracing my own difficulties as we work together to build a conscious, vital, and meaningful therapeutic relationship in the service of helping you find your own vital path outside of this room.

As this declaration illustrates, the ACT therapist can bring all parts of the ACT model into the room. From the ACT therapeutic posture, the therapist may honor the client beyond her story while honoring her unique historical context (self-as-context), and share the tendency to get verbally entangled (fusion) even while attempting to see the client beyond this entanglement. The therapist works to see the client beyond her symptoms and at the same time empathizes with the suffering due to those same symptoms (acceptance and self-as-context). Empathy for the hopelessness of repeated attempts to solve the unsolvable can be combined with seeing the client engaged in the process of valuing beyond all of those attempts (acceptance and defusion from barriers to engaging in values work). Knowing what one cares about is only the first step toward living in that direction, and bringing about changes in behavior can be difficult for both therapist and client (committed action and acceptance). Finally, the therapist can honor the client's willingness to experience pain during the therapeutic process and pledges that same willingness to experience her own pain as it shows up in this context (acceptance, defusion, and values). In short, clarifying your values as a therapist and examining your own history surrounding living consistently with your values (including your own barriers, roadblocks, and self-judgments) can help you take perspective on how difficult it can be for clients to do the same. Staying true to your values as a therapist may require you to come back to your values declaration repeatedly, whatever it may be, especially when you encounter a difficult client.

When Client and Therapist Values Clash

One final issue to consider when working with clients is the fact that there may be important differences between your values and clients' values. Reflecting upon one's values is a key concern for values-based ACT therapists, and it will certainly be critical in preparing for this type of situation. In most cases, it's important for the values of therapist and client to be congruent, as this allows the therapist to be more easily engaged in the client's valued activities and able to sensitively and enthusiastically reinforce those valued activities. If the values of the therapist and client don't match, it might be difficult for the therapist to genuinely and enthusiastically guide and reinforce the client's valued behavior, which would ultimately mean that the therapist wouldn't be able to do the best job with that client. In such cases, the best course would be to refer the client to another therapist.

Consider the following example: A nonwhite therapist with a history of racist violence against him as a child is referred a client who's been in jail for racist violence. This isn't necessarily a situation in which the therapist and client couldn't find a way to work together. In fact, there might even be advantages for the therapist, who has certain insights into the cost of racist violence that he may be able to communicate to the client. However, the therapist might also decide that, based on his values, he can't work with this client and therefore refer him to another therapist.

In general, when a client presents with a history and values that indicate a possible conflict with your values, you might make the decision before therapy begins that it's against your values to work with this client and choose to refer the client. Alternatively, you may find that a values clash occurs further down the therapeutic course, after a number of sessions in which the client's values have been explored. Subsequently, the client may later proffer values you're unwilling to work with. It is arguably rare that such a thing might happen, but to go back to the last example, perhaps the client would later maintain that racism is a deeply held value. The first step in such a situation is to seek supervision. Ultimately, however, a values clash such as this may lead to serious problems in the therapeutic process. Your final decision should be based upon your values, both as a therapist and as a human being with a personal history. Therefore, it is of the utmost importance for you as a values-based therapist to consider your own values carefully so that you can mindfully choose whether you can fully commit to working with a specific client.

Summary

The therapeutic relationship is a powerful engine of change, and a loving, compassionate therapeutic relationship that embodies the core ACT processes will empower the clinical work of ACT. And remember, bringing compassion to this relationship entails developing self-compassion. In this chapter we've presented the special qualities of the ACT therapeutic relationship and have shown how the core processes of ACT can be used to assess and improve the therapeutic interaction. We haven't necessarily differentiated the roles of the therapist and the client. The core processes of ACT draw the client and the therapist into one coherent system. With the next chapter, we begin to take a closer look at the practical side of values work, starting with case conceptualization. Specifically, we'll look at the role values play in some common presenting problems: depression, anxiety, coping with trauma, substance abuse, and chronic pain or medical problems.

CHAPTER 6

Values-Based Case Conceptualization and Assessment

As you have seen so far, part of your job as a therapist is to artfully link clients' struggles to something that matters to them throughout therapy. By intervening with skill and sensitivity at moments when you see something painful occurring, across sessions you will support them in behaving more mindfully and flexibly, not just in therapy but in their lives more generally. This type of intervention obviously doesn't involve telling clients what their values are; rather, it means asking, looking, instigating, and modeling ACT processes as they relate to even the simplest forms of values.

In this chapter, we provide some guidelines for case conceptualization and assessment in the service of helping you work this way with your clients. We point out how values are related to common presenting problems and assess the relationships between values and the different areas in which clients struggle. We provide you with tools for clinical case conceptualization in relation to values, as well as a detailed example of a values-based assessment instrument. In addition, we provide some examples that will help you learn how to use yourself as an assessment instrument, both at the start of therapy and throughout your work with your clients. In chapter 5 we discussed how you may recognize your own tendencies to avoid or become entangled with your own experiences when working with clients, and this awareness will help you recognize similar processes in your clients' behavior.

Values and Common Presenting Problems

Case conceptualization should be based on both verbal and nonverbal behavior, roughly translatable in this context as what the client says as well as what he doesn't say. Traditionally, therapists ask about the presenting problem in order to find out about it, make some guesses about how the problem is affecting the client, and thus develop a case conceptualization. Before that, however, a lot of information can be gleaned from simply observing the manner in which a client behaves (for example, shuffling his feet when walking, fidgeting in the chair, shaking a foot when sitting, speaking very slowly or very rapidly, or mumbling). These observations can provide much information for case conceptualization and also suggest possible opening questions in session. As you formulate a general ACT conceptualization, you may discover what the client values through the therapeutic interaction, the obstacles to engaging in his valued actions, and how the client relates to those obstacles.

In the first part of this chapter, we'll give you some examples of presenting problems linked to some common problem areas. After each, we'll show you how you can investigate and conceptualize such cases by interacting with clients in the moment.

Depression: Withdrawal from Values-Based Action

Depression is one of the most common psychological disorders we see in treatment. Most current treatments for depression target both cognitive and emotional factors (for example, negative views of the self and the world) as well as withdrawal from activities such as work, relationships, and recreation. Depressive withdrawal often means that clients reduce their engagement in values-based action, which in turn can maintain or exacerbate depression. There are many hypothetical routes to withdrawal. A client who is highly fused with thoughts about the inevitability of failure may have difficulty stating values or moving toward valued directions in therapy. Consider Paula, who values social interaction but is fused with the thought "If I leave the house, I have to have a positive experience with people, or else I really am a failure and I'm not worth being around." If she then goes to a party and has a poor interaction with someone, she may be less likely to engage in similar valued activities again. If Paula wasn't fused with thoughts about her failure, she might notice positive things at the party in addition to this one negative experience, such as a friend bringing her some food without being asked, or a conversation about something that interests her. Acceptance and defusion work can help clients examine what really matters to them and attend to the process of living consistently with their values, regardless of the outcome.

RFT analysis suggests a number of important ways in which language processes can contribute to depression. Transformation of functions through relational frames can exacerbate the aversive qualities of an aversive event. For example, if a person who fails an exam responds in accordance with the rule "People who fail exams are losers," then through transformation of function, he is a loser and all of the aversive qualities verbally associated with this term are transferred to his conceptualized self. Therefore, it is not just that he has failed an exam; it is that he is fundamentally flawed. RFT also explains particular symptoms of depression. For example, in the case of rumination, in which the person spends a long period of time attending to a negative train of thought, three factors combine to give rise to this thinking pattern: the frequency and relentlessness of the strongly established operant of derived relational responding (that is, as verbal humans we are constantly thinking); the established reinforcing nature of language coherence (based on our history of language training, we find sense making extremely reinforcing); and the reinforcing effect of using language to problem solve under certain circumstances.

For example, consider a woman who suffers from depression being scolded by her fiancé: Thoughts about this aversive emotional event may reoccur afterward. She may derive relations about what has happened and what has gone wrong with her relationship which, though aversive to a certain degree, are coherent with respect to what happened. ("He scolded me because I wanted to stay at home rather than go out. He's annoyed that I don't want to do things. These arguments are happening more and more often.") Thinking about what has gone wrong may be further reinforced by implicit though inaccurate rules about problem solving, such as "If I spend time thinking about this, I can figure out what to do." The outcome of this sort of depressive pattern is that the person spends more time attending to a train of thought with aversive (painful or unwanted) functions and less time engaging with her immediate environment in accordance with her values. Thus, ACT and RFT suggest that depressive patterns of behavior can be maintained and exacerbated by the way in which the depressed person responds to her own feelings and thoughts, and this behavior means less values-consistent engagement with life.

Depressed clients sometimes report values in the form of rigid rules that have aversive functions for them. For example, a client may believe that he has to endure a harsh work environment because it's the only way to get by in the world, and thus his behavior at work is likely in service of avoiding negative consequences rather than living consistently with an intrinsic value related to working. Hopefully values clarification would help such a client move away from behavior under aversive control, choose behavior more in line with his values instead, and thereafter track the intrinsic reinforcement involved in behaving consistently with those values.

INVESTIGATING DEPRESSION IN THE ROOM

It's likely that a clinician will see examples of depressed behavior in the therapy room. For example, Sally sits on the edge of her chair and looks down at her hands as she rubs them together. As the session begins, Sally's eyes are welling with tears and she looks down at her hands, rubbing them together and seemingly unaware of the room or the therapist. The therapist notices that Sally appears to be focused on uncomfortable private events as opposed to the potential reinforcers around her. The intensity of Sally's distress may be a cue that something important is missing in Sally's life, most likely linked to his values. The therapist also sees evidence of avoidance behavior in the room. Rubbing her hands and looking away probably distracts Sally from her emotional pain, and looking away helps her avoid sharing her pain with her therapist.

Following these observations, the therapist asks Sally about how she's feeling in the present moment. At first Sally responds by looking away, tears still welling up, but then she confides that she's been working very hard to keep from crying. She says she doesn't like others to see that she's suffering because she's embarrassed to be feeling depressed when, on the surface, her life is going well. She says she doesn't want to burden her friends with her suffering. Now the therapist has more information about Sally's presenting problem. From both Sally's verbal report and the therapist's observations, he makes the following early case conceptualization: "Sally attempts to control her inner experiences by avoiding meeting people, avoiding eye contact and other interactions with people she does meet, avoiding showing what she feels, and distracting herself and controlling unacceptable feelings in public by rubbing her hands and focusing on keeping her feelings from showing. These strategies are preventing her from gaining reinforcement from engaging with others, a potential value of Sally's. Therapy will likely begin with encouraging Sally to practice interacting with others, even if she's feeling depressed."

Anxiety: Avoidance and Values Constriction

In the case of anxiety disorders, a client might find that he has restricted his life immensely to avoid feeling anxious. Typically, a client might know what he cares about and deeply desire to live more a values-consistent life but be fused with the idea that anxiety must be removed in order to live that life. Hence, he might seek to avoid any circumstances where anxiety is likely to be experienced and might thus find his life quite restricted.

For some clients, even if a value is present, behavior in relation to that value might be under aversive control. Chris, for example, says that intimate relationships are the most important thing in her life. However, she lives in fear that her boyfriend will leave her and spends most of her time trying to predict his needs and seeking assurance from him. She has stopped doing most other things that matter to her in the service of always being available to him. If she continues this way, she will constrict the possible range of reinforcers available to her. While she gets short-term relief from fear of losing the relationship, she gets little intrinsic reinforcement either from the relationship or from other areas in her life. Furthermore, she may be hastening the end of the relationship because her partner is unlikely to find her constant reassurance seeking reinforcing.

INVESTIGATING ANXIETY IN THE ROOM

Anxiety is usually quite easy to see. For example, Mike is standing in the waiting room ten minutes ahead of schedule and is looking anxiously at his watch when the therapist meets him and comments that he's early for the appointment. Mike seems jumpy and tense and is continuously talking at the therapist without waiting for her to respond. When the therapist finally asks a question, Mike interrupts to ask for a drink of water. It appears that starting new relationships elicits high anxiety for Mike and that he attempts to control these feelings by talking continuously. These are clues that social relationships and possibly intimate, one-on-one relationships are valuable to Mike. Following this hypothesis, the therapist asks Mike about the kinds of relationships he has in his life. Mike responds that he has very few, saying he feels too anxious to get close to others. He says he gets so embarrassed by his overt signs of anxiety when he meets people that he withdraws. For Mike, therapy is likely to focus on helping him strengthen the mindfulness processes of ACT (acceptance, defusion, self-as-context, and contact with the present moment) in the service of building intimate relationships.

Surviving Trauma: Recovering Personal Values

When we face experiences that violate our assumptions about the relative stability of the world around us, it can shape us and our subsequent responses to the world. People who have experienced interpersonal traumas are particularly at risk for having problems in the values arena. Long-term or ongoing interpersonal traumas, such as childhood sexual or physical abuse, can leave people quite unsure of how to approach relationships. Sense of self and the limits to one's personal boundaries can become unclear when the person has learned to try to predict others' moods and behavior and to suppress his own wants in order to prevent potential perpetrators from harming him. In such cases, valuing becomes difficult to separate from pliant or avoidant behaviors. In extreme cases, a client may have experienced environments in which his personal needs and wants were actively punished.

INVESTIGATING TRAUMA IN THE ROOM

According to RFT, traumatic thoughts and feelings can and will be carried everywhere, including the therapy room. Often the suffering is maintained not by the trauma itself, as painful as it was, but by the unwillingness to experience trauma-related private events, such as thoughts, feelings, and memories. Vanessa, who has been diagnosed with PTSD, reports that leaving the house is difficult for her. She is nervous and hypervigilant and says that her fears make it difficult to have meaningful relationships. She believes that it's impossible for her to have a romantic relationship because intimate physical contact reminds her of her childhood abuse, and this realization saddens and angers her. In the therapy room, Vanessa frequently changes topics, lashes out at the therapist, and appears to dissociate when emotional topics arise. Her therapist concludes that Vanessa finds interpersonal connection and emotion threatening, and though Vanessa wants to build relationships, she has difficulty staying psychologically present enough to be an engaging partner. Therapy is likely to focus on grounding mindfulness activity to help Vanessa stay present and learn to cope with her emotions in the moment. Rather than do formal values clarification, the therapist will help Vanessa contact reinforcement from the healthy therapeutic relationship in the service of building a willingness to engage others in relationships of any kind.

Recovering from Substance Abuse: Choosing Long-Term Values

Substance abuse is a pervasive problem. For most clients who use substances, it provides a powerful short-term reinforcer, but it can have long-term negative consequences such as major health problems and loss of money, employment, relationships, or housing. Upon entering recovery, clients may experience shame and fusion with the narrow concept of themselves as users. Further, they may have difficulty coping with or identifying emotions, as substances may have been used to control or avoid emotions. All of these issues can lead to difficulty regarding values. Particularly challenging is the fact that for many, no valued activity in and of itself feels nearly as good as using. Even so, values work can happen early in therapy by finding ways to engage in small valued activities and practicing tracking small amounts of reinforcement or paying attention to moments that have a sense of vitality. Examples include taking a walk, playing with a pet, greeting people on the way to work, watching a favorite movie, playing a musical instrument, or cooking a meal. More long-term values can be introduced and worked toward step by step as therapy progresses. Together with ACT mindfulness work, slowly building up a values-consistent life can become more reinforcing in the long term than using drugs or alcohol was in the short term.

INVESTIGATING SUBSTANCE USE IN THE ROOM

One of the personal costs of substance abuse is typically loss of relationships. Thus, building up trusting, honest, and open relationships is fundamental for rehabilitation. Consider the case of Carrie, a client in recovery who's entering the therapy room for the first time. As she gazes at the picture of children on the therapist's desk, her posture stiffens and she brashly asks if they are the therapist's children. Without thinking the therapist replies that yes, they are her joys and that the picture was taken on a camping trip, something the family loves to do frequently. Carrie retorts that it's probably better for everyone that she never had children. She then begins a thirty-minute monologue conveying the details of what seems like a rehearsed story about why she is the way she is. She frequently denigrates herself, laughing and stating that she is probably permanently screwed up because she's been using for so many years. She says that she's committed to recovery, but she also isn't convinced that it will work for her.

The therapist views Carrie's dedication to treatment as an indicator that she cares very deeply about her recovery. Her self-deprecating humor may indicate that she cares deeply what others think of her, and it may be a subtle way to avoid feeling shame by putting herself down first. She is also clearly fused with a conceptualization of herself as someone with little worth. When she responds to these fused thoughts and avoids contacting her values for intimate relationships, she's moving away from actually becoming close to others. Therapy with Carrie will focus on helping her accept the pain of longing that is likely to arise when she's asked to examine her values in regard to intimate relationships, and to help her move slowly and mindfully in that direction.

Chronic Medical Conditions or Pain That Constricts Values

Clients struggling to cope with a chronic physical condition, such as diabetes or pain, may find that life narrows due to efforts to manage the condition. For example, a diabetic may find that he stays home to manage his diet better and becomes depressed or angry that he's unable to live as freely as he might like. Likewise, chronic pain is likely to lead to greatly reduced physical and social functioning as the person cuts out more and more activities to reduce the possibility of feeling pain.

INVESTIGATING COPING WITH CHRONIC CONDITIONS

ACT systematically examines the workability of the client's attempts to control physical symptoms such as pain in the context of deeply held values. In the case of chronic pain, a client will typically reveal that his life has been on hold for a very long time in the service of getting rid of the pain. Clients struggling with other chronic conditions may report that they ignore taking care of themselves or don't adhere to their medical regimen. These clients have not yet found successful strategies for dealing with the wealth of difficult emotions (such as fear) and thoughts (for example, "It isn't fair") that arise in coping with chronic medical conditions. Instead, they might try to avoid thinking about the problem by avoiding their medical treatments. The general case conceptualization is that attempts at ignoring symptoms or trying to get rid of them have moved the client farther away from his valued directions. Therapy focuses on helping clients become more mindfully aware of all of their experience so that they may notice other things besides their pain and also notice that the pain itself typically ebbs and flows over the course of any given day. These mindfulness and acceptance skills will be helpful in moving clients toward their valued activities. In the case of other chronic conditions, helping the client become more flexible in regard to how he acts on or expresses his values will be a key part of therapy.

Values Assessment Questions Linked to ACT Processes

Now we explore several questions you can ask directly to discover more information either early in therapy or whenever you wish to engage in values work. These questions are designed to help you open the client up to discussing values and help you get more information regarding the client's presenting problem and how it impacts his life. These are simply examples; we hope that you generate others that fit your particular clients and your therapeutic style. Some questions are general, and some are linked to particular presenting problems discussed previously. After each question is a brief description of what you might be looking for in terms of ACT processes, and then potential ACT targets, depending on the answers the client provides.

Question. What would you do if what you're struggling with [insert presenting problem] was no longer a problem for you?

Aim. To examine engagement in values-based activities, which avoidance may be functioning to prevent.

Possible responses and targets. If the client responds with particularly lofty goals, this may indicate that he sees values as particularly distant, and the seemingly hard-to-reach goals he brings up may serve an avoidance function. If the client has difficulty answering this question at all, consider the role of cognitive fusion (such as fusion with feared outcomes or fusion with rules about the self as incompetent) in preventing the client from stating a desired direction.

Question. What kind of life do you see yourself living in five years?

Aim. To assess the client's ability to generate goals for the future even if distant.

Possible responses and targets. If a client has difficulty generating future-oriented goals, assess the barriers to doing so, looking particularly for rigidity in rule following, a rigid sense of self dictating what is possible (or not possible), or fusion around the futility of looking forward. If a client generates grandiose ideals for the future, note this as a possible pliant, protective, or avoidant move (for example, "Everyone tells me I should want great things," "When I win the lottery I'll be able to do whatever I want," or "I can easily *talk* about big plans, but I'm not so good at following through"). Alternatively, a grandiose ideal could be quite values-directed, but the client might need some help establishing smaller steps toward these larger goals.

Question. Is there something you care about that your mind says just isn't possible?

Aim. To assess possible fusion targets around values statements.

Possible responses and targets. Look for fusion with unworkable rules that focus on the fulfillment of some criteria before a valued action can happen (for example, "I'd love to go out on dates, but I need to lose weight"). Look for self-statements that might indicate fusion with a particular self-conceptualization that seems to prevent flexible behavior with regard to values (for example, "I'd love to have more friends, but I'm not interesting enough"). Specific fused statements can be used in defusion exercises and metaphors to enhance the effectiveness and personal relevance of these interventions.

Question. What has this problem stopped you from doing in the past week?

Aim. To get at how the client is functioning on a daily basis by assessing more recent valued actions negatively affected by avoidance.

Possible responses and targets. A client may respond in a variety of different ways. He may be disconnected from areas of life that have been constricted slowly over time due to anxiety, depression, or other problems, and in this case, it may be useful to return to valued activities following defusion and self-as-context work. A client may also be acutely aware of what activities his problem has made "impossible" in his daily routine, in which case acceptance work may be useful in allowing the client to move toward a place where valued activities are possible.

Question. What life goals have you given up to avoid creating more suffering?

Aim. To assess larger areas of life avoided in the service of reducing psychological pain (uncomfortable thoughts, sadness, fear, uncomfortable memories, and so on).

Possible responses and targets. Sometimes a client takes certain life goals off the table due to unwanted thoughts and feelings. Discussing the link between values and psychological pain may be a useful intervention; rather than simply seeking out safe values, the client might be guided to work on willingness to experience fear of failure or loss while acting in accordance with important values.

Question. Are there things you find anxiety provoking but you've been successful at doing anyway?

Aim. To assess potential for values-driven psychological flexibility in the face of anxiety.

Possible responses and targets. When a client is in touch with certain values, he may be more willing to experience anxiety or anxiety-related thoughts. For example, a client may face a fear of flying to visit a dying relative one last time or a mother may deal with fears of social evaluation to attend her daughter's baseball game. While these activities may be achieved due to "white-knuckling" it through, doing so does show some flexibility of action from which broader patterns of values-based activity can be built. If there are very few activities or the situation must be dire for the client to engage in anxiety-provoking valued behaviors, therapy should focus on flexibility, acceptance, and defusion.

Question. How do you see yourself now versus how you were before you were suffering as you are now (or if a trauma survivor, before the trauma)? Is there anything that seemed possible then that doesn't seem possible now?

Aim. To assess for changes in self-concept that may function as psychological barriers to engaging in valued actions that were important before the client's struggles (or traumatic experiences). This question also assesses valued activities in which engagement may seem impossible given the client's history.

Possible responses and targets. If the client reports feeling very different from who he was before his problems arose, consider working to enhance a transcendent sense of self (self-as-context) that is stable beyond his experiences. If a trauma survivor reports feeling "broken," "dirty," or otherwise unhealthily changed, consider strengthening self-as-context before engaging in values work.

Question. Is there anything in your life that you wish could feel as good as using drugs or alcohol?

Aim. To assess for valued activities already present in the client's life in which the client doesn't experience much vitality.

Possible responses and targets. If the client endorses some areas that he wishes were more vital, consider using these values areas as a measure for progress in therapy and build reinforcement in these areas through acceptance, defusion, present moment awareness, and self-as-context work. If the client doesn't endorse anything specific that matters within some life domains, consider basic activities and commitments to get him engaged in activities loosely related to his overarching values (for example, "I just don't want to use anymore" or "I just want to keep a job for more than a month").

Establishing the Life Line: An Experiential Metaphor

The life line exercise, described in detail in this section, is an experiential metaphor. Metaphor is considered an extremely useful intervention in ACT. From an RFT perspective, metaphor involves the coordination of relational networks, allowing a transformation of functions such that newly insightful behavior becomes more likely (e.g., Stewart & Barnes-Holmes, 2001). This pattern is the centrally defining feature of metaphor in ACT. Another feature is particularly important in the context of experiential therapeutic metaphors such as the values compass: In successful metaphors that actually contribute to a change in behavior, there is often an awareness of physical similarity between two contexts that increases the likelihood of a transformation of important functions of the target context involving the client's behavior.

Consider using a metaphor likening struggling with anxiety to the futility of struggling in quicksand. This classic ACT metaphor offers a relational network involving equivalence or coordination between relational networks, each of which includes a causal relation involving self-defeating struggle. Furthermore, this similarity in relational networks might allow an awareness of the physical similarity between the two situations described by these causal relations, namely, a feeling of suffocation resulting from the self-defeating struggle. This physical similarity can then act as a further contextual cue for the derivation of coordination relations, further facilitating transformation of response functions so that the client is more likely to accept future feelings of anxiety.

Thus, awareness of physical similarity across contexts may be an important factor in behaviorally efficacious metaphors. This may be one reason for the particular effectiveness of experiential metaphors in which the client can engage in physical role-playing. This allows the client to become aware of actual physical behaviors and experiences during the role-play that are similar to physical aspects of the client's behavior and experience in his everyday life outside therapy. In the life line exercise, there are several such physical experiences. One is stepping off the life line and into a dead end. In addition to understanding the metaphor at an intellectual level, the client may perceive a physical similarity between some of his own values-relevant behavior patterns in real life and the role-play experience of moving at a tangent from a chosen direction and getting stuck in a dead end. Another physical experience is having his arm tugged by the therapist as he tries to move forward, analogous to the real-life experience of having nagging thoughts and feelings as he moves in a values-consistent direction. In the case of these types of experiences during the metaphorical role-play, the awareness of similarity may be an important factor in transforming the functions of values-relevant situations in life outside of the therapy session such that the client is more likely to recognize values-inconsistent behavior and take steps to stay on his valued path instead.

In our practical experience, the life line exercise is particularly useful because it can be employed early in therapy and replace much talk about the problem or how it came about. In that respect, this exercise is a time-saver. It is also flexible, with many variations possible depending on the client and the situation. We will provide a couple of examples; hopefully these will inspire you to explore more variations.

Instructions

To do the life line exercise in session, you'll need an open space about ten feet long and a few props: sticky notes (for writing events, feelings, and reactions to be tacked to the life line), a few full-size pieces of paper (for writing values and barriers), tape, regular and thicker writing pens, and a long scarf, piece of rope, or belt.

We recommend spending time in session generating the events and reactions to be used in the exercise (as described next). In our experience, doing this work in session together can be more powerful; however, the exercise can be expedited by giving a homework exercise in a prior session. In general, the client is asked to reflect on and write down significant examples of difficult episodes in her life. She is asked about both the situations or events themselves and how she reacted to them. Next you'll find an example of how to prepare the client for this exercise. You can give the client these instructions and ask her to record her responses on a blank sheet of paper. Be aware that if you assign this as homework, you may miss some moment-to-moment reactions that could provide important information for you, but it may save time for working toward values in session. Consider using this example or the alternative approach described a little later in this chapter as a foundation for the exercise.

1. **Significant losses.** List up to five significant losses you've experienced in your lifetime.

    a. Describe each loss in a couple of words, along with the date. (Example: Father died, 1981.)

    b. Describe your feelings about each loss in a couple of words.

    c. Describe how you reacted or coped with these feelings.

2. **Things going wrong.** List up to five instances when things just didn't go the way you wanted or planned for.

    a. Describe each instance in a couple of words, along with the date. (Example: Fight at work, 2001.)

    b. Describe your feelings about each event in a couple of words.

    c. Describe how you reacted or coped with these feelings.

3. **Off track.** List up to five instances where, despite your best intentions, you felt that you got off track from the life you wanted.

    a.   Describe each event in a couple of words, along with the date. (Example: Broke up with boyfriend, 2006.)

    b.   Describe your feelings about each event in a couple of words.

    c.   Describe how you reacted or coped with these feelings.

4. **Hanging on to good feelings.** List up to five instances where you felt something wonderful and tried to cling to that feeling.

    a.   Describe each event in a couple of words, along with the date. (Example: Fell in love and got obsessive about the person, 2003.)

    b.   Describe your feelings about each event in a couple of words.

    c.   Describe how you reacted or coped with these feelings.

In a subsequent session, ask the client for her completed homework, then lay the scarf in a line on the floor and say, "In this exercise we're going to try to both re-create and experience your life. We'll start off by identifying some important directions that have been constant for you throughout your life. This valued direction will be symbolized by this scarf on the floor." Ask the client to stand at one end of the scarf with a foot on either side of the scarf. You stand in a similar manner at the other end of the scarf, face to face with the client. Here's an example of how this exercise might proceed. In this example, all of the losses the client wrote about in her homework were about relationships.

As the therapist and client stand at opposite ends of the scarf, the therapist asks the client to establish a reference point by stating how she wants to behave in a relationship when it is at its best. The client answers that she wants to be open, honest, loving, and caring. The therapist writes down these words on one of the full-size pieces of paper, repeats them, and places them at the end of the line or on a wall facing the line; now the scarf symbolizes the value of being open, honest, caring, and loving. The therapist asks the client for a commitment in this valued direction, and the client answers that she strives to behave in this way in all of her relationships.

Standing side by side with the client, the therapist asks what the first loss of important relationships was, and the client answers that her mom died when she was fourteen years old. The therapist writes this event on a sticky note and bends down and places it on the life line. The therapist asks if the client is willing to step into this event and gently encourages her to step onto the paper with this loss written on it. The therapist says, "I want you to step into the shoes of this fourteen-year-old who had just lost her mom. Are you willing to do that? You might want to shut your eyes and just feel what this young girl is feeling right now." The client closes her eyes and says she feels desperate as the fourteen-year-old girl on the day she lost her mom. The therapist writes this word on another sticky note and places it in front of the loss event on the life line, then asks if the client is willing to step into this feeling of desperation. The client does so and shows clearly that she is feeling desperate now.

The therapist asks if the client can see how the young girl coped with these strong feelings of loss and desperation. She answers quickly, saying the young girl acted bravely, that she took good care of her dad and sisters. The therapist writes this coping behavior on another sticky note and asks the client if this behavior is consistent or inconsistent with the valued direction she just committed to: being open and honest in her relationships. The client sees that this shutting down of her own feelings wasn't consistent with being open and honest. As she says this, the therapist places the sticky note to the side of the life line and gently pulls the client off the life line and her value into a detour they label "avoidance of negative feelings." The therapist asks the client if the fourteen-year-old still wants to be open and honest. As the client nods, she gently pulls her back onto the valued direction.

The therapist says, "As the fourteen-year-old moves forward in her life, she is now changed. She has learned some important lessons that she is now carrying with her to new situations in life. First, she now knows that bad or unpleasant things that are beyond our control just happen to us. People we love can and do die, relationships end, accidents happen. This fourteen-year-old now knows that she is not the choreographer of her life. Second, she has learned that when these awful things happen, she will feel awful. And so far, we are just talking about all that happens in regard to the single value represented by this life line. Life itself contains all kinds of events and surprises, and our feelings go up and down like a roller coaster. That's life. But this young woman has learned something else as well. She has learned that she can get short-term control or protection from these awful feelings by shutting herself down. This is a type of learning that isn't like the other two. Those events and her natural reaction are just things that happen, but how she relates to those events and feelings requires her to take action. These actions, which for her are caring for others, drinking, and cleaning, all gave her a feeling that she was controlling that awful feeling, but the cost is that she got off her valued path in a way that hurt only her. We can call this her learned tendencies. As we continue down the life line, I'll show you your learned tendencies by tugging on your arm as if trying to suck you into those familiar detours. You will feel pulled by me, your learned tendencies, but you decide each and every step yourself. Now the fourteen-year-old you gets back on her life line again. What was the next experience we can place on the line?"

This exercise can continue in the same way with additional experiences generated in session or from the life line homework sheet. We recommend choosing those that still impact the client the most. This can take a long time, so if necessary consider repeating the exercise in another session. Each chain of events is dismantled into the form of a functional analysis: the event and the natural reaction on the life line, followed by the active response to the discomfort. The client is gently pulled off the line when she chooses action in relation to the discomfort that isn't consistent with her valued direction. The exercise ends as the client is "here and now," carrying all of her learning history in the form of verbal rules of behavior and resisting old tendencies to get off course and get pulled into her typical detours. She is ultimately asked to commit to staying on the valued line, conscious that new events and the subsequent, inevitable discomfort will follow, and knowing that her learned habits may tug her off of her path. The life line exercise may be used throughout therapy in every session.

An Alternative Approach to Using the Life Line Exercise

Here's another example of how the life line exercise can be used, in this case for the common problem in therapy in which the client hasn't done homework exercises. The therapist responds to the client's statement of not having done the homework, saying, "This makes a great opportunity for both of us to investigate and experience what happens to you on your life line. Is it okay that we step up on the life line again and see what happened?" Once the client is on his life line, the therapist asks questions that help the client consider his overall life direction, obstacles, and detours:

1. **Valued direction.** Discussing the purpose of the homework exercise, the therapist asks, "In which of your life domains was this exercise a step for you to take?" The therapist writes down this valued direction and puts it at the end of the line (for example: getting healthy and strong).

2. **Commitment.** Standing at the end of the life line, the therapist asks the client if he still stands for this value or if he now wants to set it aside.

3. **Obstacles.** The therapist stands side by side with the client and reenacts the situation last week when the client left the therapy room intending to take a step in his valued direction. They can role-play the client's mind ("I wanted to do this, but then I got home and things were just too crazy") or other barriers to get a greater understanding of what happened that prevented him from taking that step (for example, perhaps the client had a deadline to meet).

4. **Event-reaction-response detour.** The client describes the disturbing event (the obstacle), and the therapist writes this down on a sticky note and places it on the line, along with the client's immediate reaction on a second slip, also still on the line. But for the third event, where the client makes the move to avoid the homework and the discomfort associated with it, the therapist gently pulls the client off course and onto his familiar detour (for example, avoidance).

5. **Conceptualization.** The client is asked to conceptualize if this behavior fits into avoidant or other off-track patterns or whether the behavior is more in line with what he wants his life to be about.

6. **Commitment.** The client is asked to commit to his valued direction again and identify steps he will take, knowing that this history with its habitual "tugging" tendencies will occur again.

The life line exercise is essentially an experiential metaphor in functional analysis that incorporates all of the ACT core processes. It is useful anytime clients appear to be getting off track away from their valued direction. It provides a fast and effective means for gaining perspective on one's behavior.

Case Conceptualization Summary

We've shown you several ways to critically think about a client's presenting problems in terms of the impact they have on areas of the client's life that matter. We also provided an intensive experiential exercise to help establish a values-based case conceptualization of your client's struggles early in therapy. We hope that one or more of these techniques will appeal to you. As ACT therapists, we strive to use both critical thinking and experiential exercises in our clinical work as needed. The information we have provided so far is best used in the following ways:

1. Framing what the client might be experiencing in terms of values difficulties, which can allow you to plan how to work together more efficiently.

2. Generating conversation with your clients about their difficulties. The questions provided in the first part of this chapter can be used to start a conversation about values, especially when clients have difficulty bringing up their values or understanding how they relate to their presenting problems. Don't forget, your client's experiences are the ultimate guide!

Assessing Your Client's Values Using the Bull's-Eye

Now that we've discussed the possible ways values can become constricted, ignored, pushed aside, or otherwise avoided, let's move on to using this information with clients directly. ACT clinical researchers have developed several instruments to measure values and the client's reported psychological barriers to living those values. Many of these instruments, which are still being validated, can be found at www.contextualpsychology.org. We present one here—the Bull's-Eye Worksheet (Lundgren, Dahl, & Melin, 2007)—which we provide as an example of how to use a valued living worksheet as a clinical tool. Feel free to photocopy it and use it with your clients.

BULL'S-EYE WORKSHEET

The dartboard in this exercise is divided into four domains, or areas of living, that are important in people's lives: work and education, leisure, relationships, and personal growth and health.

1. Work and education refers to your career aims, your values in regard to improving your education and knowledge, and generally feeling of use to those close to you or to your community (volunteering, overseeing your household, and so on).

2. Leisure refers to how you play in your life, how you enjoy yourself, and your hobbies or other activities you do during your free time (gardening, sewing, coaching a children's soccer team, fishing, playing sports, and so on).

3. Relationships refers to intimacy in your life in a variety of forms: relationships with your partner, your children, your family of origin, and your friends and social contacts in the community.

4. Personal growth and health refers to your spiritual life, either in organized religion or personal expressions of spirituality, along with exercise, nutrition, and addressing health risks like drinking, drug use, smoking, and weight.

In this exercise, you'll take a close look at your personal values in each of these domains and write them out. Then you'll evaluate how close you are to living your life in keeping with your values. You'll also identify the barriers or obstacles that stand between you and the kind of life you want to live. Don't rush through this exercise; just take your time.

Part A: Identify Your Values

Start by describing your values within each of the four domains. Think about each domain in terms of your dreams and imagine your wishes could be completely fulfilled. What are the qualities that you'd like to get out of each area, and what are your expectations from these areas of your life? Your values shouldn't be a specific goal, but instead should reflect how you'd like to live your life over time. For example, getting married might be a goal you have in life, but it would be just one action in the service of a value of being an affectionate, honest, and loving partner. To accompany your son to a baseball game might be a goal; to be an involved and interested parent could be the value it reveals. And most important, remember that your personal values are what's important in this exercise. Don't choose your values based on what you think is expected of you. Now write your core value in each domain in the space that follows.

Work and education: _____

_____

Leisure: _____

_____

Relationships: _____

_____

Personal growth and health: _____

_____

Part B: The Bull's-Eye Dartboard

Now take another look at the values you wrote down. Think of your value as a bull's-eye (the middle of the dartboard). Bull's-eye is exactly how you want your life to be, a direct hit, where you're living your life in a way that's consistent with your value. Now, make an X on the dartboard in each area that best represents where you stand in regard to that value, thinking about your behavior this past week. An X in the bull's-eye means that you're living completely in keeping with your value for that domain. The farther your X is from the bull's-eye, the farther off the mark your life is in terms of how you're living your value.

Since there are four areas of valued living, you should mark four Xs on the dartboard. Be sure to fill out the dartboard before you go to part C of this exercise.

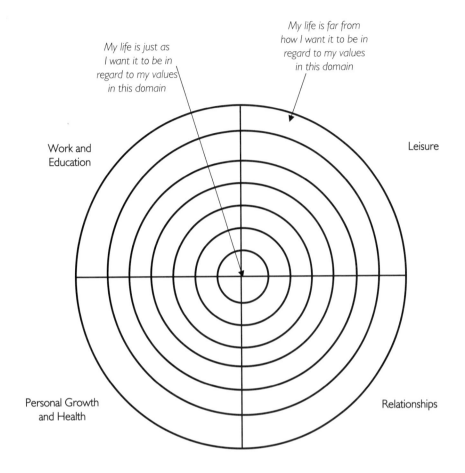

My life is just as I want it to be in regard to my values in this domain

My life is far from how I want it to be in regard to my values in this domain

Work and Education

Leisure

Personal Growth and Health

Relationships

Part C: Identify Your Obstacles

Now write down what stands between you and living your life as you want to, as described in your values statements for each domain. When you think of the life you want to live and the values you'd like to put in play, what gets in the way of living that kind of life? Describe any obstacles have been in your life during the past week.

_____

_____

_____

_____

_____

Now estimate to what extent the obstacles you just described prevent you from living your life in a way that's in keeping with your values. Circle the number below that best describes how powerful these obstacles have been in your life during the past week.

1	2	3	4	5	6	7

Doesn't prevent me at all   Prevents me completely

Part D: Your Valued Action Plan

Think about actions you can take in your daily life that would tell you that you're zeroing in on the bull's-eye in each of these four domains. These actions could be small steps toward a particular goal, or they could just be actions that reflect what you want to be about as a person. Taking a valued step usually includes being willing to encounter the obstacles you identified earlier and taking the action anyway. Try to identify at least one values-based action you're willing to take in each of the four domains listed next.

Work and education: _____

_____

Leisure: _____

_____

Relationships: _____

_____

Personal growth and health: _____

_____

The bull's-eye was designed to gather information in the context of behavioral therapy. It can be used for three purposes: as a therapeutic tool, as an outcome measure, and as a process measure. Here we'll describe how to use the bull's-eye as a tool for in-session work. We won't describe the psychometric properties of the instrument (see Lundgren et al., 2007, for this information). The therapeutic aims of the Bull's-Eye Worksheet are to help clients qualify their values in therapy and quantify how often their actions are consistent with their values, and to examine barriers to valued living and stimulate taking valued actions. We will also discuss how the Bull's-Eye Worksheet can help clients detect the value in their actions.

The Bull's-Eye Worksheet consists of four parts: A, which describes values; B, examining how well clients' actions coincide with their values; C, examining barriers to moving in valued directions; and D, creating a plan for valued action. We will present parts A through C in this chapter and examine part D in detail in chapter 8. As you'll see in the following example, the worksheet includes one or more graphic dartboards. The client is asked to put an X on the dartboard where it best represents how well he has lived according to his valued direction within the last week or two weeks (or whatever time line is appropriate to his therapy). An X in the bull's-eye represents perfect consistency between action and the stated value, with successive outer circles representing living increasingly inconsistently with the value. The outer circle represents living the farthest away from the value in that domain.

We'll use an extended example to show how the bull's-eye can be utilized in the first session to help set values as the context of therapy. The following interaction, which focuses directly on the bull's-eye work, takes place after the therapist has offered some introductory information regarding therapy. Frank is new to therapy and has only stated that he's unhappy in his life. His therapist asked him what he would like to be different in his life, and Frank replied "being a better father and husband." His therapist asks Frank what gets in the way of doing so. Let's take a look at Frank's response and see how the therapist brings the bull's-eye into the work of the session.

Frank: (*Bursts into tears.*) It's my stomach. I have the worst stomach! I'm always afraid that I won't be able to get to the bathroom quickly enough. Doctors have said it's lactose intolerance or an allergy and have had me cut all kinds of foods out of my diet, but nothing has worked. It's been like this for about fifteen years, and it's not getting any better. It's embarrassing because I need to be close to a toilet. I can't go anywhere if I don't know where the toilets are, and I can't go to a restaurant or to a parent-teacher conference because the toilets might be occupied. I can't take my kids to the circus, soccer practice, or anything like that! Hell, I can't even have sex with my wife without being worried that I'll have to go!

Therapist: Frank, I can see that this is really important and causes a lot of pain for you. Let's say that the bull's-eye of this dartboard represents being the father you want to be—a present, loving, caring father who is active in your children's lives—and that the ring farthest from the bull's-eye represents that you are very far from being the father you described. What would best represent your behavior during the past week? Put an X on the dartboard that represents how well you have been living according to your values during this past week.

Frank: I would probably miss the whole dartboard! I don't even think I'd hit the wall where the dartboard hangs. (*Marks an X in the outermost ring.*)

Therapist: Can you do one more dartboard, about your intimate relationship with your wife? It sounded like there's a pretty high discrepancy between how you want that relationship to be and how it is in your life at the moment.

Frank: Yes, it really sucks. I love her to pieces but… (*Frank marks the second dartboard just like he did the first.*)

Therapist: Frank, should our time together be about getting closer to the bull's-eye in your life?

Frank: Yeah, very much! I have lost so many things because of my stomach and the pain and the worry from that.

You'll notice that the therapist didn't let Frank tell too many stories about his stomach pain or problems because he knew that Frank had gone through a lot of medical treatments and that the doctors had done their best. Instead, the therapist set values as the context for their time together by focusing on the impact Frank's problems had on valued areas of his life. With his therapist's help, Frank identified vitality and meaning for his life in the domains of parenting and intimate relationships by expressing his intention and direction. Importantly, early in the session the therapist assessed what Frank perceived as the barriers that got in the way of being the father and husband he wanted to be. In the course of this interaction, Frank's valued direction has been established. Next, the therapist will help Frank take a closer look at how effective his behavior is for getting him closer to this valued life.

With this background established, let's look at what using the Bull's-Eye Worksheet looks like, based on an extract from Frank's completed worksheet.

FRANK'S BULL'S-EYE WORKSHEET

Part A: Identify Your Values

Relationships: *I would like to be a present, loving, caring father. I would like to be there when my kids need me, and I would like to be a person my children can come to when they're either happy or sad.*

Part B: The Bull's-Eye Dartboard

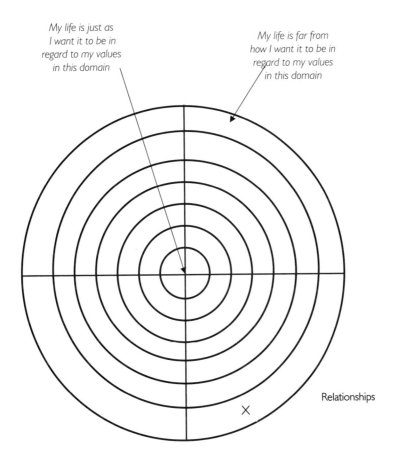

My life is just as I want it to be in regard to my values in this domain

My life is far from how I want it to be in regard to my values in this domain

Relationships

Part C: Identify Your Obstacles

My stomach. I'm fed up with it. I'm afraid of everything because of my stomach. I'm afraid I'll poop in my pants if I go out with my kids or play with them. There are so many thoughts and feelings that bother me.

Now estimate to what extent the obstacles you just described prevent you from living your life in a way that's in keeping with your values. Circle the number that best describes how powerful these obstacles are in your life.

1	2	3	4	5	6	7

Doesn't prevent me at all   Prevents me completely

Measurement of Values Congruency Using the Bull's-Eye

As you've seen in Frank's bull's-eye, the dartboard in part B of the Bull's-Eye Worksheets creates two possibilities for measurement. First, the dartboard provides a visual metaphor for what it means to live a valued, vital, and meaningful life: a bull's-eye life. It also provides a number that represents the discrepancy between how clients live and how they want to live. An X in the bull's-eye is given a 7, the next ring a 6, the next a 5, and so on down to the outermost ring, which is given a 1. This way, both therapist and client have a concrete but visual way to measure therapeutic success. The bull's-eye is intended to be used repeatedly. At each meaningful interval (for example, each session, once a month, or before, during, and after therapy) the client can place an X on the bull's-eye to represent how consistent his current behavior is with his value in that domain. Over time, these Xs provide a quantitative way of evaluating if the therapist and client are taking important steps in therapy. The change in the distance from the bull's-eye from before treatment to after has been correlated with meaningful changes in therapy (e.g., Dahl & Lundgren, 2007).

In terms of Frank's therapy, part D of the Bull's Eye Worksheet (which we'll discuss in detail in chapter 8) helped Frank get closer to living the life he wanted. For example, Frank made a commitment to attend his daughter's soccer game one week, and the next week he made time to help his son with his homework. Each time he came into session, he placed an X on the dartboard showing where he felt he was that week. Sometimes he felt farther away than the previous week, but overall Frank and his therapist were able to see and chart Frank's progress on very specific core values.

Assessing Barriers to Valued Living

Believability of barriers is measured using a simple scale of 1 to 7. Believability is one way to talk about cognitive fusion, which is a very important issue to address in relation to values. If the believability of barriers is very high, a close examination of internal and external barriers may be required (see chapter 8). Where internal barriers are present, defusion will be particularly important to help clients engage their values and move closer to a bull's-eye life. Where there are external barriers, concrete plans to deal with them can be put into place.

Discriminating the Vitality of Living in Bull's-Eye Territory

What does living a bull's-eye life mean? Living in bull's-eye territory means acting in accordance with one's values, fully present and mindful, without defense or attempts to control private experiences such as thoughts and emotions. It also means embracing the moment and everything that comes along with it, whether pain, happiness, sadness, or joy. However, the very practice of attending to the process of living one's values (discussed in chapter 4) can be reinforcing in and of itself. The vitality experienced from choosing to act in the service of one's values increases the likelihood that a person will continue to behave consistently with those chosen directions. Sometimes, though, clients don't know what their values are at the beginning of therapy. Their values might be intertwined with a lot of painful experiences, and it might take some work with acceptance, defusion, self-as-context, and mindfulness to make room for values work in therapy. In such cases, the Bull's-Eye Worksheet can be used to help the client start the process of discriminating what he considers to be meaningful action in his life.

Therapeutic Pitfalls When Using Values Assessments

There are pitfalls that therapists can fall into when working with clients on values, whether it be with the bull's-eye or other formal assessments. It is important for both therapist and client to recognize that values and valued actions can change over time and not get particularly caught up in the fixedness or "rightness" of the client's values. There is always a risk of pliance in this process, which is something you may need to assess directly with your clients. In particular, watch out for values that clients state simply to please others, which point to the possibility of pliance but may or may not be. For example, some religious or ethnic groups may endorse duty, honor, or obeying; in these types of situations we recommend examining the personal value within a seemingly external value, or the reinforcement coming from such values statements.

Next, we provide tips for avoiding several common pitfalls when working with the bull's-eye in particular and discussing valued living in general. In the spirit of examining your own barriers, take a couple of minutes to reflect on some of the pitfalls that you've noticed in your work or that you might predict for yourself, then make a list of those pitfalls. Once you've done so, consider the following tips for avoiding some of the more common pitfalls.

> ❧ Be present and mindful of the client's needs when you do the bull's-eye. Don't get stuck following the instrument to the letter. Be flexible and present to whatever shows up in the room. Be aware of the two

simple questions this worksheet is built on: What do you want? What are you afraid of?

   ❧   Notice any tendency on your part to state the client's values or declare what is intrinsically reinforcing for him. It can be all too easy to state values for the client, particularly with those who aren't very forthcoming or have difficulty expressing their values in words. If you notice this happening, tell the client about it and talk to him about your desire to help him live a more fulfilling life, then explain that you'll back off from trying to tell him what that might look like. Here's one suggestion for clients who have difficulty verbalizing: Try asking your client to express in a posture, image, or movement what living a bull's-eye life would look like and, conversely, what not living close to the bull's-eye looks like. You can use this posture or movement as a way to assess values throughout therapy and practice converting that to bull's-eye numbers in session. Further, your job is to help clients learn to discriminate what they find intrinsically reinforcing as they engage in values-consistent action.

   ❧   Watch for a tendency to push the client too fast or to sit back and wait for the client to engage in values-consistent action completely on his own. On one hand, it can be easy to push the client to commit to a valued action plan before he's ready. On the other hand, it can be very easy to sit back and let a client struggle with values on his own. Neither approach is very flexible or open to the client's struggles. If you see resistance in the therapy room, you can use that as an opportunity to assess and validate how hard it can be to think about change, and how talking about and planning valued actions can create fear. Slow movement in valued directions can be the result of rigid rules, fusion, or experiential avoidance, and your attention to these areas will be very important for promoting movement. Finding the balance between pushing too much and not enough will take practice.

Creating the Context for Committing to a Valued Path

You can help clients start pursuing valued directions even after the first session of values work. You can ask them, "What steps are you willing to take now, in this moment, in the direction of the life you have described as your valued life?" They may not have very much success in living their values right away, but you're still providing important assistance in establishing a new way of being that brings clients' values into the present, even if they "fail" at a particular goal.

Summary

In this chapter we have provided you with detailed information about how values can play a role in some common presenting problems and have described some tools for getting at a case conceptualization of your client's presenting problems in terms of values. In chapter 7, we discuss the steps of ACT interventions that will support valued living, targeting ACT's mindfulness processes (defusion, cultivating present moment awareness, cultivating self-as-context, and acceptance).

CHAPTER 7

ACT Core Processes and Values

Having discussed the importance of the therapeutic relationship and provided some strategies for assessing clients in the early sessions of therapy, in this chapter we present a detailed examination of the four ACT mindfulness intervention strategies—defusion, present moment awareness, self-as-context, and acceptance—as they bear upon values. As you'll recall from previous chapters, each of the ACT intervention strategies is a component of the ACT model. In this chapter we provide examples of metaphors, exercises, and client-therapist interactions related to each of the four ACT mindfulness processes and their relation to values, and for each process we provide lists of indicators of the extent to which the client is engaging in that process.

For the purposes of this book, we mainly focus on intervention strategies related to values. Our hope is that we cover enough of the basics that you'll feel comfortable trying ACT techniques as you're reading this book. It would be impossible to reiterate the literally hundreds of ACT intervention strategies that we have created, learned, and used with clients. Many standard exercises can be found in other texts, and we do recommend that you read more on ACT. If you're interested in a more in-depth understanding of the model, more ACT intervention strategies, or workbooks to use with your clients, visit www.contextualpsychology.org. As you work with ACT, we hope that you'll create your own metaphors and experiential exercises in line with the goals you and your clients have for therapy.

As a reminder, we wish to reiterate that the ACT model is not six independent processes; rather, each process builds on and supports the others. So as each intervention strategy is presented, you may notice significant overlap with other processes. For example, in order to cultivate self-as-context, clients must be able to track the process of thinking and feeling in the moment, be relatively defused from the idea that thoughts and feelings cause behavior, and practice willingness to experience their thoughts and feelings as they engage in values-based activity.

The intervention strategies listed for a particular process generally involve other processes, and we encourage you to consider the ways in which other processes are involved in each intervention strategy.

As we walk through each of the intervention strategies, keep this important point in mind: The goal of ACT is flexibility, so watch out for becoming rigidly attached to doing ACT in a particular way or expecting a particular outcome when working with a client. For example, when we're discussing acceptance, we don't suggest that you encourage the client to accept all of her experiences all of the time. Rather, your job as a therapist is to recognize avoidant behavior and help the client examine whether, in that particular instance, avoidance functions as a barrier to living a valued life. A similar level of flexibility is also appropriate with each of the other processes. To further promote flexibility, ACT work involves using many different modalities to help clients develop new skills and new approaches to old problems. In many cases, clients have a long history of engaging in unworkable strategies for coping with their experiences, so you will need to provide many examples, metaphors, and stories, and many opportunities for your clients to practice new skills. In most cases, clients don't start behaving in an accepting manner toward all of their experiences after exposure to just one metaphor about acceptance, for example. So when you find that a client isn't particularly accepting, compassionately notice any frustration you feel and consider offering additional examples of acceptance, defusion, or self-as-context that might help the client experience a new way of living with her experiences.

Defusion: Letting Go of Literality

Cognitive fusion refers to the tendency to be controlled by our verbal experiences. In RFT terms, it is the domination of behavioral regulation by verbal events. As you'll recall from chapters 2 and 3, we've talked about fusion a good deal already. By now, you know that ACT views fusion as a common process that comes from the fact that most of us grow up within environments that promote literality, reason giving, problem solving, and evaluation. But we also know that language isn't necessarily harmful. In fact, if we look at our human environment, it's difficult to find anything that hasn't been made possible in some way by language (problem solving, evaluation, or creating and following rules). The problem arises when fusion becomes overextended—when we begin to take our thoughts literally and behave based upon those thoughts without noticing that we're doing so, or without even noticing the process of thinking itself. This creates problems because it can limit behavior and keep us from behaving consistently with our values.

Defusion exercises can help clients recognize that they are thinking and when they are taking their thoughts seriously, automatically responding to those thoughts, or otherwise buying into them. Defusion requires an awareness of the process of thinking—essentially catching the word-generating machine in flight. From there, it's easier to see the possibility that thoughts don't have to determine behavior. Then we can start to create an alternative. This alternative is values.

Strategies for Undermining Excessive Rule Dominance

Fusion with certain types of rules tends to prevent values-based behavior. Our minds are very good at creating rules for our behavior—both adaptive and non-adaptive rules. Adaptive rules are those that indicate that we should take steps to go to work, take care of our bodies, and avoid danger in order to live a valued life. As mentioned earlier in the book, following rules, solving problems, and evaluating are all extremely useful for helping us stay safe from physical harm and make decisions for our overall well-being. Following a rule to avoid eating food that is moldy can prevent you from getting sick, and problem solving to find a new driving route when your usual route is under construction will get you to work. However, we tend to overgeneralize and apply particular rules in ways that prevent us from behaving very flexibly. Have you ever had the experience of being so caught up in thinking about how you should act in a situation that you felt disconnected from the moment or actually missed out on something that happened? We can easily get so focused on a particular kind of experience (a thought, feeling, or rule) that we don't see other things around us. Excessive reliance on rules based upon experiential avoidance and self-as-content can be especially problematic because they can narrow our behaviors, including values-consistent behavior, quite extensively. For example, a client who is fused with rules about what is possible for her life ("The world is an unfair place, so I won't try very hard") is likely to exhibit very few valued behaviors. Thus fusion can be highly problematic in the context of valued living.

LOOKING FOR THE VALUE INSIDE THE "SHOULDS"

In ACT we spend much of our time undermining problematic aspects of language. A key indicator of potential problems is linguistic form. For example, one sign that a client is particularly fused in relation to her values is frequent use of the word "should." It's very common that when discussing values, the first thing that comes to mind is a big old "should." Typical examples of "shoulds" often heard early on in therapy are "I should be happy, but I'm not," "I should be helping my parents more," or "I should be taking better care of myself, but I'm just so busy."

Sometimes clients use the word "should" because they're responding to a rule rather than the deeper value behind it. In doing so, they may be attempting to reduce the anxiety caused by the discrepancy between their stated values and their actual behavior. However, performing a duty or activity solely as a means of reducing anxiety doesn't qualify as moving in a valued direction. This very same behavior may at one time have been consistent with a valued direction and it may look the same, but now its function is to reduce a negative feeling rather than be present to the underlying value. In these instances, the client doesn't need to change the behavior; she needs to reidentify the underlying value within this "should." If she doesn't, she can actually be contaminating valuable and meaningful behavior patterns with aversive conditioning from the "should." Here are two common examples:

- A couple who enjoyed spontaneous, passionate sexual relations together before they were married lose interest when sex becomes an expected routine.

- A woman who has longed to spend more time with her son commits to going to his sports events to watch him play; however, seeing this subsequently as an obligation, she finds herself physically sitting in the bleachers but mentally still at work.

In both of these examples, the original behaviors were clearly chosen in alignment with valued dimensions in life. But as soon as these behaviors are performed in reaction to a "should," they become a fairly meaningless ritual with little or no connection to the original value. How do we move away from behaving based on "shoulds"? By clarifying values and being more present with them in the moment. Doing so requires us to broaden our attention so that we can be in contact with our values, notice our own experiences (from a defused, accepting stance), and notice what's going on around us. We'll provide some examples of exercises to help clients reconnect with their values and their experiences a bit later in this chapter.

Ways to Undermine Literality: A Values Perspective

One important way to pull the power out of the words we use and the thoughts we have is to weaken their literality. We know from RFT research (and our own clinical experience) that we can't directly change our thoughts very effectively. But we may be able to reduce the dominance of certain aspects of language. How? Many books on ACT describe numerous defusion exercises in detail, such as thanking your mind for a thought, singing or using a funny voice to say a particularly undesirable thought, or writing the thoughts on cards (e.g., Hayes et al., 1999). ACT therapists are creating new defusion exercises every day, and we encourage you to create your own metaphors, to pay attention to those created by your clients, and to play with these exercises and make them your own. As long as you're attending to the function of undermining literality and being respectful of your client (albeit a little irreverent), then anything is fair game. In this book we focus on providing examples and exercises that we've found to be useful in working with clients on values.

CHANGING THE WAY YOU SPEAK: CATCHING THE PROCESS OF THINKING OR EVALUATING

Reformulating language conventions can be a powerful tool for getting us away from taking our thoughts so literally, as it helps us note the process of thinking. One way to do this is for both therapist and client to practice noting thoughts as they occur in session, along with when the thoughts are taken seriously or, more colloquially, have "hooked" the client. The client may initiate this process by saying something like "I'm noticing the thought that I'm a bad person" or "I got really hooked by that one; I beat myself up over that thought that I'm no good for days." Likewise, the therapist may comment on the process by saying something like "And here's another thought that your mind has generated" or "It seems like you easily get hooked by thoughts about how others have let you down." The therapist can reframe client statements to promote some distance from particularly unwanted thoughts by saying things like "So you're noticing that you're having the thought that you're a failure because you didn't do your homework perfectly." Repeatedly responding to thoughts simply as thoughts, regardless of whether their content can be evaluated as unwanted or uncomfortable, is a way to practice putting some space between the client and her thoughts and reducing the literality of those thoughts.

Another common ACT intervention is to ask clients to notice when they're speaking in terms of "but" and to move from "but" to "and." As you'll recall from chapter 3, "but" actually means that something cannot be true in the presence of something else. With clients, changing from using the word "but" to the word "and" can reveal how language sets us up to create barriers for ourselves. For example, consider an anxious client stating, "My friends asked me to go to a party last weekend, but I was too anxious." The use of the word "but" connotes that going to the party can't be true if anxiety is present. What ACT tells us, however, is that anxiety can be present even as a person takes action. Using a values context, the client can learn to reconnect to her valued direction in this situation. If seeing her friends and meeting people is important in her life, this may be an overarching valued direction for her. Even though taking steps on that path is likely to elicit anxiety, in light of the valued direction the question is whether the client is willing to have more anxiety in the service of walking in her valued direction. Changing the previous statement to "My friends asked me to go to a party, and I was anxious" can change the function of the statement and may create some flexibility on the part of the client. She may start to see that behaving consistently with her values is possible just by changing the way in which she speaks about her own behavior.

LOOKING FOR WHEN THE LOGICAL MIND LIMITS VALUED LIVING

We spend so much time listening to our minds that it becomes easy to think it has all the answers and knows how to do everything. It convinces us that we need to predict the future, that we must plan, feel a certain way, or have a clear understanding of things before we can do anything. The problem is, when we live in accordance with our values, we seldom know the outcome. While some planning and predicting is useful to keep us safe and to make careful choices, some things can't be planned for, predicted, or carefully judged, and values are in this category. Further, it is easy to spend a lifetime planning rather than actually living. Therefore, in ACT it can be important to point out how the mind's ability to predict and plan can become overextended. This sort of "mindiness" can get in the way of actually doing what needs to be done for our values, such as moving in the direction of our values rather than simply planning for doing so. Consider the following metaphor.

Imagine you've never swum before, and then I tell you how to swim—in detail. Could you learn how to be an Olympic swimmer from my description of swimming? Imagine I said to you, someone who's never swum in your life, "First you move your arms in a circular motion, and then you kick your legs up and down. Then you keep moving across the pool and turn around." Could you swim flawlessly the first time? Probably not, right? Why not? Because there are some things our minds cannot do on their own. Picking out paint colors, designing a building, sure, but something as complicated and fluid as swimming? It would be ridiculous to believe that we could think our way into learning how to swim without actually practicing and doing it. What if values are like swimming? We can talk about values because that helps us identify a direction. But talking about your values is only useful to help you get closer to living consistently with them, similar to how finding out the directions to the pool or asking about the hours when the pool is open only gets you closer to swimming; it doesn't get you in the water. Talking about values is not the same as living consistently with them. Contrary to what your mind says, you cannot think your way into your values.

This example suggests that the mind tries very hard to convince us that we can learn how to do something just by thinking about it hard enough. Here's another example, one that's often particularly relevant to young adults or anyone whose therapy goal is to find and cultivate a romantic relationship. Some dating websites are set up with the explicit assumption that if you enter the appropriate information into a computer program, you can find the perfect partner. The applicant generally provides a self-description and checks off preferred qualities in a potential partner. The dating site then matches criteria and produces potential partners based on logic. But despite these complicated statistical matches, most people find that choosing a partner seems to have little to do with logic, reason, or judgment. Logic might bring two people together, but what maintains a relationship is more complicated than logic. Physical attraction, chemistry, timing, and any number of other factors play a role in whether two people choose to try out being in a relationship.

Have you ever made a list of pros and cons for deciding between two things? Perhaps even whether or not you should stay in a romantic relationship? Though you might have found the list to be of some use, did you find it adequate for making your final decision, or was there something else that helped you in that? There are some decisions in which logic and reason are very useful, such as which route to take to work, which outfit to wear to a job interview, or what flight to take to visit a relative. However, when it comes to values, decisions that are solely based upon logic are rarely fruitful and fulfilling. For instance, Arnold explained to his therapist that he had many "good" reasons for seeking a divorce from his wife, but that after some consideration, he realized he still loved her dearly. He stated that while she could be condescending and rude at times, many other times she was caring and understood him better than anyone else. Therefore, he was willing to work on his relationship with her and share his value for their relationship.

WALKING WITH THE BARRIERS ON A VALUED PATH

Walking with the barriers on a valued path is an exercise in which you work with the client to identify a difficult life situation and a related value, and then practice walking the valued path in session. Ask your client to describe a situation in which she's struggling, and then work with her to identify why she's struggling in relation to her values. For instance, if she's having difficulty working with a colleague who is domineering, ask her about her value surrounding her behavior at work. If she were to imagine she could take steps in her valued direction, right now, even though nothing has changed—not her confidence, not anyone else's behavior—what might she do? Consider together what might get in the way of her being able to live consistently with that value, such as fear that her colleague will be rude to her, that she might not be correct in her opinion if she stands up to her colleague, and so on. Have the client write down the barriers, then ask her if she would be willing to put this piece of paper in her pocket and see if she can take a step in her valued direction with this thought about the apparent barriers in her pocket.

For example, Anna found it difficult to take time for herself at home. She preferred to sit and read in the evening, but her husband wanted her to watch television with him. She sat with him not because she wanted to but because she was afraid of creating a conflict. In session, Anna identified the overarching value here as giving herself her own time and space in her daily life. When imagining taking this step, she wrote down the barrier as the thought "Creating conflicts can lead to a divorce." Anna wrote this thought on a piece of paper, put it in her pocket, and practiced standing up for her value at home that evening. She expressed to her husband what she wanted for herself while carrying this thought in her pocket. This experiential exercise shows that our behavior doesn't have to be dictated by belief, and no matter what our minds say, we can still move in a valued direction. Whether or not we believe we can do something, we are able to move our feet and behave as though we can.

The point of this type of exercise is simply that there are some things our minds don't know how to do. Values are simply things we care about and need not be overthought, predicted, judged, or reasoned.

Watching Out for Judgment and Evaluation

Our minds tend to judge what is right and what is wrong all the time. Sometimes this can be vitally important, but when it comes to values it can create problems. Judging our values as good or bad, right or wrong, as we might judge a piece of fruit in the supermarket, is not so helpful. One problem is that many of us often find ourselves judging others. We wish people would act differently, and when it comes to our interpersonal values (in regard to friends, family, coworkers, and others), these judgments can get in the way of living our values. Have you ever felt judgmental about someone you cared about? Did you notice that your behavior toward this person changed? Did you become closer, or did you find that you were moving farther away from this person?

An important distinction to make with clients is the difference between description and evaluation. Description is listing formal properties of the object or event that cannot be argued, whereas evaluation is judgments we make based on our individual experience and history. Why is this important? It relates directly to our values. It becomes very easy to overextend our evaluations about the world to our values. There are many ACT metaphors that get at this concept in simple ways. You can practice this with your clients by asking them to evaluate an object in the room with statements such as "That's ugly" or "It looks cheap," and then simply describe it in terms such as "It's made of wood" or "It's three feet tall." Similarly, you may practice this skill with thoughts and feelings by labeling "evaluation" when it arises in relation to values and then practicing describing values or valued actions without evaluation. Here's an example: If a client says, "I'm not good at living the value of connection with others in an honest way; it never works out right," you might consider helping the client tag the evaluation and then restate the situation a bit more descriptively (for example, "I notice having an evaluation of not being good enough when things don't work out the way I would like in living my values.")

MOVING BEYOND RIGHT AND WRONG

When we're having judgments, we tend to use them as guides for our behavior. When they're negative, we tend to pull away, act out, or do things that aren't in line with our values. Sometimes, however, a focus on certain positive judgments can also lead us to behave inconsistently with our values. For example, if Laticia judges a potential partner as appropriate for her because he has a lot of money and is physically attractive, but she doesn't assess for other qualities that she values in a romantic relationship, then she might end up in a relationship devoid of those other valued qualities. Therefore, it's important to look out for judgments of any kind.

Right versus wrong is a particularly strong judgment that we've all had at some point. We'll use an example to illustrate how to help a client move beyond such judgments, even when the client feels cheated, harmed, left out, or otherwise wronged by another person. The following transcript is from a session with Carlos, a thirty-five-year-old man who recently found out about his wife's infidelity. He had been coming to therapy regularly for a month when he found out his wife was pregnant with the other man's child. Following this discovery, Carlos stopped doing many of the things he valued in his life—going to the gym, eating well, and taking an interest in his friends—and instead had been sleeping a great deal, missing meals, and alienating his close friends because all he could talk about was his wife's infidelity. He was miserable not just because of the situation with his wife, but also because he felt completely alone and angry all the time. In this session, the therapist improvised with a stack of index cards.

Carlos: I've thought about it over and over and I still just cannot believe that she could do this to me! I always wanted to have children with her and now... Oh my God! It's someone else who will get to raise her child. I hate her right now! I really do.

Therapist: I can see that this is hard for you. Do you mind if we try something here? We've talked about this issue for a few sessions now and I'm feeling a little stuck. Are you? (Carlos nods emphatically.) Okay, great. (The therapist takes an index card from the pile and holds it up.) Let's use these cards to take a fresh look at your situation. Would that be alright?

Carlos: Sure. Anything to help me feel better about this.

Therapist: Okay. So, what we know so far is this: You've been wronged—big time. (Places an index card on the client's left knee.)

Carlos: Yes! Exactly. She's such a... I'm so angry! I wish we'd never met. I feel like I've lost every chance I had at happiness and having a family.

Therapist: You're right. You'd never have been hurt this way if you'd never met. (Places another index card on the client's left knee.)

Carlos: I mean, I did everything for her. I always was respectful, and I supported her career and her wishes about where we should live. We planned everything together. I can't believe I wasted so much energy on her. I am such a fool.

Therapist: You're right! What a waste of energy! (Places another index card on the client's left knee.)

Carlos: But I suppose I could have done things differently. I know I was gone a lot, working, and then I got so moody when my business got hectic. It's probably my fault, too.

Therapist: Yes—you were wrong. (This time the therapist places an index card on the client's right knee.)

Carlos: Wait a minute, though! *She* took it too far! Why didn't she just talk to me? If I had known how much she was hurting, I wouldn't have let things get so screwed up. At least I always worked hard for our relationship.

Therapist: You're right! She shouldn't have done it, no matter what you did first. (*Places another index card on the client's left knee.*)

Carlos: (*Crying.*) Augh. I can't stand myself. I feel like I'm not a man anymore... so weak and alone.

Therapist: (*Pauses briefly, then speaks compassionately.*) So here you are, hurt and alone. I can see that this is painful for you... And I want to ask you something really important: What have you got to show for all of this pain and suffering?

Carlos: (*Looks up, confused.*) What do you mean?

Therapist: Well, let's think about this. Look at the cards on your knees. Let's say that your left knee represents the "You're Right" pile and your right knee represents the "You're Wrong" pile. Which has more cards?

Carlos: The left.

Therapist: Exactly. You're right! The cards say so! And I bet if we asked everyone you both know who was in the wrong, they'd all pick your wife.
             By a show of hands and according to these cards, you are in the right... But what then?

Carlos: I don't know what you mean.

Therapist: When you first came to therapy, we talked about what mattered to you more than anything. Inside all of this anger and hurt, I can hear it. Do you remember what you said?

Carlos: I said I wanted to be about love. But now I don't know.

Therapist: Exactly. Now let's look at these two piles. What happened to love when we were talking about these cards?

Carlos: It's gone.

Therapist: Exactly—even though I, your friends, maybe even your wife, would say that you're in the right. But now what? What do you have now that you're right? All you have left is what you care about—your behavior, your values, and, yes, your pain. Do you want to spend your time being right or do you want to live your life with love? What if you could have your pain, honor that you were hurt, and still choose to attend to what matters to you? Not to let her off the hook, not to forget, but to continue your life and do what matters to you.

Carlos: I guess. So, even though this painful, horrible thing happened, I don't have to stay stuck in it... That's what you're saying?

Therapist: Maybe. It's so easy to get stuck... I'm not blaming you here. I've done this very thing, too. It feels good to stay powerful and "right" when someone else is "wrong." But it takes an awful lot of energy and it has a cost. You've told me that you've pretty much withdrawn from your life.

Carlos: Yeah. So I should stop feeling bad about what she did to me and just move on, you know, pushing ahead and things?

Therapist: Yeah, so even now, your mind is saying that's the only way to move on. That's not it either. This pain seems like it might stick around for a little while, and I'm not suggesting that you let it go or ignore it, but rather that you see if you could still live your life in ways that you care about deeply. What if you could continue to live your values—maybe in a new way that you aren't used to—*with* the pain you have from being hurt?

Carlos: I guess I could try, but I'm not exactly sure how.

Therapist: Yeah, me neither. Would you be willing to work together to move toward living with love, even in the face of this horrible upset and pain?

Carlos: Yeah. I think I'd like that.

We don't recommend that everyone should do this exercise with every client. However, if done skillfully, it can provide a powerful illustration of how, even in the darkest of moments, living one's values can still be possible. This exercise is best done when a client is highly fused with righteousness due to being wronged, such that it prevents her from living her values, and when you have a good rapport with the client. If you choose to make this kind of move, we recommend that you practice compassion and awareness of your values as a therapist throughout the process. Exercises like these can push clients in a way that might feel invalidating if the therapist isn't genuinely compassionate with the client's pain. It requires willingness on your part to sit with the client's pain in such a way as to communicate the deep caring that comes from compassionately pushing past difficult emotions in the service of helping your client become unstuck. Also, we recommend mindfulness on your part in regard to the possibility of being overly fused with the idea that all clients *must* be more open, accepting, and effective in the face of their difficult experiences. Can you be flexible enough to choose to push a client to examine the overall effectiveness of her behavior and also let it be completely okay if she doesn't make this move?

Undermining Reason Giving: Choice vs. Decision

We know from previous chapters that reasons are powerfully seductive in speaking about our behavior. We like reasons for doing things and reasons against doing other things, and when we don't know exactly why we did something, we're really good at making up reasons for why we did it. In essence, our minds can be reason-generating machines. In defusion work, we want to increase the client's ability to move beyond reasons and get into her valued behaviors. One way we highlight this distinction in relation to values is by making a distinction between choices and decisions. Choices are selections we make freely, without rules, avoidance, or regard for social consequences. Decisions, on the other hand, are carefully considered selections made with reasons. Reasons are not all bad, but there are times to make decisions and times when it is more effective or desirable to make free choices. Values and values-based actions are choices, not decisions.

We highlight the importance of free choice in therapy because we find that many clients are focused on making the "right" decision or have fears that making an incorrect or poor decision will have catastrophic consequences. Some clients may become paralyzed when faced with a choice or need to reason out every choice before making it (transforming it into a decision). In these cases, you may want to help clients practice making small choices in session, such as taking very small valued steps and noting the consequences. In the next chapter, we provide an exercise for freely choosing a valued direction called "Ten Steps to Trying On a Value." It's particularly helpful when clients are stuck in patterns of looking for the "right" choice or the "right" value.

Recognizing Fusion and Defusion in Session

Given how pervasive fusion is, it's very common to see it happening in the moment, in session, and not just on the part of the client. It isn't uncommon for us as therapists to be fused with the way we think therapy should go or how a client should react to us or to an exercise. Defused responses on our part involve a willingness to let go of the "right" way to do things. We may also tend to judge clients' behavior, their in-session responses, or their lack of progress. Watching for these moments can be very helpful in avoiding unnecessary conflict between you and your clients. Here are some possible indicators that fusion or defusion is occurring in the moment—for both you and your client:

Fusion Indicators

- Making statements like "Yes, but..." or trying to convince the other of one's opinion

- Repetition of a story about why life isn't going as planned

- ❧ Frequently talking about the problem and providing interpretations about its cause

- ❧ Entanglement with reasons, causes, self-judgment, or bitterness

- ❧ Rigid adherence to unworkable rules

- ❧ Adherence to one's own perspective as right

- ❧ Seeking approval for one's interpretations

- ❧ Judging the other's experiences, difficulties, or lack of progress in therapy

- ❧ Seeking fairness or justice, or wanting to be right when it's unworkable or outside the scope of therapy (for example, frequently asking the therapist to agree that the client has been wronged, or seeking advice about how to get revenge or punish someone else)

- ❧ Mindiness or intellectual and abstract discussions

- ❧ Looking for the "right" way to respond to exercises, or expressions of failure in regard to exercises or homework activities

Defusion Indicators

- ❧ Awareness of the thought process itself and its inferred function

- ❧ Making statements regarding the process of thinking, such as "I'm having the thought that…"

- ❧ Catching fusion in the moment verbally ("Wow, I just got hooked by that thought") or nonverbally (pausing during discussion of an old story, smiling when a particularly fused thought is expressed, and so on)

- ❧ Awareness that thoughts and rigid rules don't reflect the "truth" and need not always be followed

- ❧ Ability to choose to behave in a certain way even when contradictory thoughts are present (for example, having thoughts that one is incapable of living consistently with one's value and taking steps in that direction anyway)

- ❧ Expressions of tiredness, boredom, or that some response to a difficult experience is old, familiar, or unworkable in some way (for example, "I'm so tired of thinking that I have to put my life on the back burner; it's really not what I want to do")

ৰ৶ Spontaneous playfulness with regard to one's own process of thinking (for example, singing one's thoughts unprompted or making chattering noises in response to one's own thoughts)

ৰ৶ Creating new metaphors to describe an experience, perspective, event, or reaction

Present Moment Awareness: Cultivating Openness to Experience

A key component of the ACT model is contact with the present moment. Present moment awareness allows a fluid, moment-to-moment connection to ourselves and the world around us. The ability to notice the things both around and inside ourselves (including our sensations, feelings, and thoughts) from moment to moment is vitally important. Yet many of us spend a good deal of time out of the present moment, either ruminating about the past or predicting or planning for the future. In addition, anytime we narrowly fixate on private experiences such as thinking or feeling in an attempt to manage or change them, we tend to overlook the constant shifts of our experience in relation to the world around us. Many spiritual traditions have focused on contacting the present moment and all of its changing experiences through practices such as mindfulness and transcendental or Zen meditation. While contact with the present moment in ACT is similar to these approaches on the level of technique, the theory underlying it is deeply embedded in our theoretical model. Many of the ACT books, articles, and protocols present detailed exercises for contact with the present moment, often referred to as mindfulness, so we will simply point out their importance and their link to values. The ability to notice the world around us, and to observe our thoughts, feelings, sensations, and memories as they come and go on a moment-to-moment basis, is vitally important in allowing us to contact the reinforcement from living consistently with our values.

Contact with the present moment can be cultivated like a skill and is useful throughout values-based therapy. The goal for clients is not to achieve a particular state of mind before they can choose to take valued actions, but rather to become better at observing their experiences so that fused, evaluative, and undesired private experiences such as thoughts or feelings exert less influence on behavior. Cultivating mindful awareness helps clients broaden their awareness of the environment (instead of focusing solely on fear or fused thoughts) as they engage in valued behaviors. Becoming aware of their own experiences can help them see what is reinforcing for them in the moment and thus help maintain valued actions over time.

Learning to Track Reinforcement in the Moment

Clients are not often very good at tracking the in-the-moment consequences for values-consistent behavior, so your clients may need a lot of practice in this. Consider an overweight client, Oliver, who chooses to commit to walking for twenty minutes each morning before work in the service of his value of being healthy. Oliver originally chose to make the commitment as a pliance move because a doctor told him that he should walk. However, with his therapist's help, Oliver started to notice he felt more alive, awake, strong, and capable of exercising after walking for a few weeks in a row. Further, he started to notice and appreciate more of the environment around him, such as the woods around his house and the children waiting for the bus in his neighborhood. Being able to notice these things increased the possibility of Oliver continuing to walk. His therapy homework assignments included writing down everything he noticed before, during, and after engaging in his walk. The therapist's job was to help Oliver start to notice other things beyond the previously dominant, usually aversive experiences that were present as Oliver tried to start walking regularly: the physical discomfort of starting an exercise program and having to get up earlier to walk, thoughts about how useless it is just to walk, fears about his health, and so on. Eventually, walking in the morning became reinforcing as Oliver became adept at tracking feeling sleepier, weaker, and not as connected to his surroundings when he skipped his daily walk. These moment-to-moment consequences are often the most important for building valued behavior patterns.

Recognizing Present Moment Awareness and Lack of Awareness in Session

A powerful therapeutic relationship should feel vital and be based in present moment awareness for both parties. How do you know whether a client is struggling with being present in the moment? And how do you know when you aren't really present with a client? These are important questions. The context of going to therapy will likely predispose clients to be less present with what's happening in the moment. Clients typically come to therapy thinking they're supposed to tell their stories about the past and worries about the future in order to "explain" their presenting problem. You also are predisposed, by nature, socialization, and education, to spend a great deal of time examining the past or anticipating the future rather than being present in the here and now. It's easy to become preoccupied with previous events of the day, other clients, or worries about future events. This makes it all the more important to be aware of your own tendencies to get caught up in the past or the future, in addition to looking for when your client is doing so. Here are some in-session behaviors that may indicate either lack of contact with the present moment or present moment awareness, most of them relevant to both you and your clients:

Lack of Present Moment Awareness Indicators

- Getting lost in one's mind (ruminating, thinking, not speaking for long periods of time, not paying attention to what is said because one is thinking rather than listening, and so on)

- Poor tracking of what's happening in the environment (including the therapeutic relationship)

- Inability to maintain focus, or insensitivity to changes in topic during therapy

- Weak awareness of moment-to-moment changes in thoughts, feelings, and bodily sensations

- Being unaware of the fact that a particular response in therapy is more due to one's history than to what is really happening in the moment (for example, repeating old stories or speaking in monologues that feel rehearsed or repetitive or don't take into account the particulars of the therapy interaction)

- Being preoccupied with past events, memories, or worries about the future

Present Moment Awareness Indicators

- Mindful awareness of the external and internal environments

- Mindful awareness of reactions in therapy that are actually based upon history (for example, a client saying something like "Wow, just look at me; I got all sweaty and started breathing fast just at the thought of how to answer your question, and that's typically how I react to demands made on me")

- Sensitivity to the fact that the therapist and client are building a new relationship rather than being focused on the way one has behaved in past relationships

- Flexible attention to the process of therapy, being able to either maintain focus or change focus when appropriate

- Demonstration of presence and awareness of one's thoughts, feelings, bodily sensations, and memories

- Willingness to be present with whatever comes up in the therapy room (on the part of the client, being willing to express difficult experiences with the therapist as they occur; on the part of the therapist, willingness to experience one's own psychological or physical suffering that might arise when clients share painful experiences, struggle with new ways of relating to the therapist or others, or express intense emotion in the room)

Cultivating Self-as-Context: The Self That Transcends Experiences

Developing self-as-context awareness can be one of the more difficult ACT processes to understand and to cultivate with clients, but it is vital for creating patterns of values-consistent action. You will recall from previous chapters that attachment to the conceptualized self can lead to stagnation and restrict flexible, values-based actions. Our goal is to help clients gain perspective on their experiences in the service of building flexible patterns of behavior linked to values. Self-as-context involves many of the other ACT processes, which is why many of us choose to do major self-as-context interventions later in therapy. In order to be able to take perspective on their experiences, clients must be able to track the process of thinking and feeling in the moment, be relatively defused from the idea that thoughts and feelings cause behavior, and practice willingness to experience their thoughts and feelings as they engage in values-based activity. We do believe that it is possible to practice earlier on in therapy, however, by consistently and subtly promoting a sense of awareness or perspective on one's experiences throughout exercises with a primary focus on acceptance, defusion, and present moment awareness. In this section, though, we wish to present a few formal and in-depth (and, in our experience, powerful) self-as-context exercises that we find useful in addition to the many that can be found in other ACT books (e.g., Hayes et al., 1999; Luoma, Walser, & Hayes, 2007).

Becoming Aware of Self-Concepts That Function as Barriers to Valued Living

There are many ways to practice awareness of self-concept, and particularly awareness of self-concepts that function as barriers to valued living. Clients often have difficulty noticing the rules they've learned about what is possible for them—rules that are serving to keep them from living the life they want. Such clients may list myriad reasons why they are "screwed up," "broken," or "defective" and cannot do something in line with their values. One way to help clients look for ineffective self-rules based upon a rigid conceptualized self may be to practice tagging them in session. For example, consider writing down all of the client's statements about the self that appear to present barriers. Doing this may cultivate some distance from those thoughts, feelings, and stories as "truth."

There are many other ways to cultivate a nonthreatening, observer perspective with your clients, ranging from short activities to in-depth experiential exercises, including eyes-closed exercises. For example, there is a lengthy eyes-closed exercise called the "File Drawer Exercise." One of the authors (JD) has used this exercise with a number of clients with great success, and a therapist-client role-play in which she enacts this wonderful exercise is available on the *Values and Action* disc of the ACT in Action DVD series (Hayes, 2007). Rather than try to convey the subtleties of this exercise via written narrative, we offer several other in-session exercises with a similar aim of taking perspective on one's experiences. In addition to learning about and using these exercises, we recommend that you design your own or look for other exercises that fit your therapeutic style.

Contacting the Cost of Living in Old Stories

Because clients often have difficulty moving past the conceptualized self, you might notice that a client seems distant and caught up in her old patterns. You may feel less connected to her in session, instead feeling like a spectator to the inner world of your client's conceptualized self. In the following dialogue, a therapist uses an exercise with sticky notes with a client to help him see how his old stories and conceptualizations of himself cut him off from possible sources of support from others. Ethan is a thirty-year-old recovering alcoholic who has come to therapy seeking direction for his life now that he's sober. Ethan struggles with many different rules about what's possible for his life due to his alcoholism. He frequently states that he is a screw-up and is not worthy of the love of his friends or family, and therefore has turned away from cultivating intimate relationships with them even though doing so causes him great suffering and loneliness.

Therapist:	(*Writes on a sticky note.*) Okay, Ethan. So you have this thought "I am a screw-up." (*Holds the sticky note up between herself and Ethan.*) So, what does this sticky note tell you to do?
Ethan:	(*Looks confusedly at the note.*) Um, I guess it tells me that it's not possible to fix things with my family even though I want to.
Therapist:	Great! Sure, so it kind of hangs out here. (*Waves the sticky note in front of Ethan.*) But how can this little piece of paper keep you from talking to your family? Or caring about your friends? Is it that powerful?
Ethan:	No, I guess not. But, I've screwed up too much to deserve their support anymore.
Therapist:	(*Sticks the first sticky note to her shoulder.*) Oh! Okay, here's another one: "I don't deserve good relationships." (*Writes on another sticky note and holds it*

up to Ethan's face.) So this one gets in your way, telling you that you're not worthy of relationships.

Ethan: (*Annoyed, moves his head to look past the sticky note at the therapist.*) Um, well, it just seems impossible for me to do anything right. I borrowed so much money and then spent it on booze. I sold their stuff sometimes and abused their trust.

Therapist: So this sticky note is getting in the way between us now. It's keeping us from really talking about what you care about. I'm not blaming you; this is just a thought that you've picked up from your history, and it seems that you're experiencing some suffering as we even bring up these thoughts. (*Ethan nods, and the therapist places the second sticky note on her other shoulder.*) I want you to know that I'm in here for you, and that what I care about most is supporting you in living your life the way you want. My intent isn't to hurt you by bringing up these thoughts. In the service of what you most care about, maybe we can practice just noticing these "yucky" sticky notes. These thoughts just seem to show up and tell you who you are and what you can do, but they are just that—words written on sticky notes. Let's imagine for a moment that you could do what you wanted—not what this sticky note says is possible for you. Would you be willing to practice looking at me, working with me on what is possible for you, even if these thoughts are still here, in your line of sight? (*Points to the sticky notes on each shoulder.*)

Ethan: I think so… But they're pretty distracting.

Therapist: Yup, just like they normally are when they show up for you, right? So, let's take a minute and try something. Sometimes these stories about you are pretty rude, huh? I'm going to write, "I'm not worthy of my therapist's attention" and put it here. (*Sticks the note to her forehead.*) Your job is to look only at this note while I'm talking. (*Both laugh, then Ethan agrees and looks at the note as his therapist speaks.*)

Therapist: So, Ethan, you were telling me that caring about your family is very important to you, and that you are in a lot of pain about not feeling like you can share your caring with them because you are a "screw-up." I feel really sad when I hear that, because I know you care for them deeply and these rules about yourself and what is possible are really putting up roadblocks for you. I don't know what your family would really do if you were to share your caring with them, but the first step might be to share it openly with me. Let's just sit here for a minute and contemplate the possibility of being willing to have that value of being close with the people you care about here in this room.

Ethan: (*Stares at the sticky note, then starts to get tears in his eyes.*)

Therapist: (*After a bit of a pause*) Ethan, now you can look at me... What do you see?

Ethan: I see you looking at me, not caring that I'm a screw-up.

Therapist: Yeah, and what did you see when you were looking at the sticky note?

Ethan: Just that—that I'm not worthy.

Therapist: So, when you attend only to your story about who you are, you're missing out on a lot of things around you—in this case, me caring for you. There was a real cost here, and I noticed that when you were looking only at this sticky note, you weren't really here with me. I'd much rather be here with *you* even if these sticky notes are here, too. Our job will be to watch out for when these stories about you get in the way of living your values. We'll have a sense of when that's happening when they start to become barriers to us doing what you came here for—looking for what you really care about and choosing how *you* want to live. Would you be willing to look out for these patterns in the service of creating new ones?

Ethan: Yeah, I think I can do that.

In this interaction, the therapist and client work together to examine the function of his stories about his life. In essence, the therapist is showing Ethan that when he lives his life within the confines of what his self-concept says is possible, he's cutting himself off from opportunities to live his values. The simple act of writing out Ethan's self-as-content thoughts is a subtle defusion move, designed to help Ethan see them as just thoughts. Placing them between her and the client illustrates—concretely, powerfully, and in the moment—that these thoughts are functioning as a barrier to Ethan living his values and connecting with others. She does so to help Ethan contact the cost of holding on to his old stories so that he might choose to live consistently with his values even if the story is present.

Recognizing Self-as-Content and Self-as-Context in Session

Of all of the ACT processes, it can take the most practice to identify self-as-context in the moment. Self-as-context is a perspective, and most of us don't have much experience talking about our "observer self" or the ability to transcend our experiences. It can be especially difficult for clients to describe this perspective to us, so we look for other signs. First, we look for signs that the client is taking perspective on (or observing) her own experiences as simply events that take place within her but that are not her. Second, we look for the ability to take another's perspective, as doing so involves the frames of you-there-now (for interactions happening in the now between therapist and client, for example) and you-there-then (for other interactions in the past). The following indicators will help you identify moments when either your client or you are behaving from the perspective of self-as-content or self-as-context:

Self-as-Content Indicators

- Adherence to a concept of self related only to roles or judgments about one's self, particularly evaluations such as "I am a depressive" or "I'm a bad person"

- Excessive reliance on what others say to define one's self (statements like "Everyone always said I was so sensitive that I'd never be strong enough to be on my own, and I think they're right" or "I've always been seen as the go-getter so that's what I do!")

- Expressions of fear or feeling threatened by a perspective of the self beyond one's roles (for example, "I don't know who I am if I'm not just a mom," or becoming confused, angry, or withdrawn in session when discussing what the person might really want to be about outside of being a parent, child, wife, and so on)

- Discussing one's life circumstances as fixed, unchanging, or otherwise permanent, or feeling threatened by a change in any circumstance (for example, facing a divorce and fearing losing a standard of living tied to self-concept as part of a rich married couple)

- Holding on to explanations for why one cannot behave any differently due to historical factors (for example, "I can't do that because of my PTSD," "I'm like this because I was abused," or "I will always be an anxious person")

- Expressing little ability to talk about the self in general or making statements like "I don't know who I am" or "I have no self"

- Expressing fear or evaluation about viewing the self as constantly changing

Self-as-Context Indicators

- Expressions indicating an ability to see rules and stories about one's life as just verbal formulations that have some use but do not determine one's life choices (for example, "I noticed that I started believing again that because I'd been abused I wasn't capable of being healthy in a relationship, but I know my abuse doesn't define me or what I am capable of" or "I never even thought about the possibility of changing jobs because I always thought of myself just as an engineer, but now I'm realizing that I really love being more creative artistically and want to try to do something else")

ક Flexibility with regard to perspective taking and easily taking the perspective of others (for example, "I can see now that my mother is really trying her hardest, even though it drives me crazy sometimes" or, to the therapist, "You seem so at peace with listening to all the things that have happened to me")

ક Flexibility with regard to observing one's own experiences and easily catching when old rules begin to arise or one is hooked by thoughts about the self (for example, smiling when discussing old patterns; saying things like "I just noticed that the old thought 'You're not a person who tries new things' showed up when you said that"; or using the word "have" instead of "am" with regard to one's experiences, as in "I have depressive thoughts" or "I'm having the thought that I'm a bad person")

ક An ability to dispassionately examine patterns of thinking or other experiences that have functioned to keep one from behaving with respect to one's values in the past

ક Recognizing that even though one has a history that might bring with it particular difficulties, new behaviors and valued choices are possible (for example, "I know I have PTSD, but I'm willing to work at not getting too scared to live my life")

ક Flexibly relating to multiple conceptualizations of self depending on the context, with a stable perspective present throughout all of these different roles and conceptualizations

---

Acceptance and Willingness: Living a Valued Life When Psychological Pain Is Present

In this section, we explore the interconnectedness of pain, values, and acceptance. When people seek therapy, what they're struggling with most is often related to what they care about most. What would be possible in our work if instead of simply helping the client defuse from a statement such as "I'm too afraid to do that," we also focused on the value inside the statement? What value might lie inside such a statement? With some exploration, you might uncover that the client cares deeply about being open and honest when interacting with others. What if sabotaging a new relationship indicates something very important that the client is avoiding, or a link to the pain of having lost valuable relationships in the past? A paralyzing fear of making a mistake on the job may be linked to caring about how one contributes at work. Pain, suffering, fear, and hurt may be indicators that something the person is doing (or isn't doing) is of value to her. Out of fear, she may disavow, actively sabotage, or avoid what matters most. In the service of our values, then, we must learn to accept all of the experiences that arise as we make valued choices. Indeed, for many of us, we would not consider opening ourselves to the potential hurt and psychological pain that comes with caring deeply about people, relationships, or other important aspects of life if these experiences weren't tied to our most precious values.

When a client's psychological pain is linked to what matters most to her, she is more likely to be accepting of her private experiences. Acceptance work can be done moment to moment, in small ways, throughout therapy. In our experience, acceptance is most powerful when the pain to be accepted is inextricably linked with a value. In this section, we present ways to cultivate acceptance by linking a client's discomfort to what she cares about most.

Examining Experience to See How It Gets in the Way of Valuing

A client may report that her emotions get in the way of living a valued life. Yet when pressed, she may not have a good sense of the internal experiences with which she struggles. Clients who have difficulty identifying their private experiences often find they become overwhelmed by them and stop moving toward their values. In such cases, acceptance becomes difficult because internal experiences appear to be big, scary, unpredictable events. As a result, such clients may avoid situations that might produce undesired experiences. Having no tools for acceptance, they may miss opportunities for taking valued actions.

An exercise involving naming the parts of experience can help clients break down their experience into smaller chunks that are easier to recognize and whose function (such as avoidance) is easier to discern. It can be useful to do this exercise when a client becomes avoidant of or overwhelmed by emotion in the room, or when a client reports that she's currently struggling with a lot of private experiences in regard to a recent situation or event. The exercise essentially involves slowing the client down as she tells you about her experiences and asking her to label each aspect of the experiences as "thought," "sensation," "memory," or "emotion." Willingness can be built by slowly breaking down the parts of an unwanted experience and creating psychological space for each part of the experience. This is always done in the service of the client's values. Consider the case of Markus, who struggled with overwhelming fear and other emotions upon leaving his house. He had difficulty seeing how he could ever overcome his fear unless he was able to stop feeling it. Markus also reported that what mattered to him most was his six-year-old son. However, he had immense difficulty going to his son's Little League baseball games even though his son desperately wanted him there. In session, his therapist worked with him to practice acceptance of the physiological sensations in his body, the thoughts and evaluations he had about those sensations, and the fear he felt. As they named each part of the experience, Markus practiced noticing each one and cultivating willingness to allow those internal experiences to be present as he left the house in the service of doing things that mattered for his relationship with his son.

WHAT WOULD YOU HAVE TO GIVE UP?

Many clients who come to therapy somehow minimize their values, particularly in relation to other people. Expressions of pain, sadness, fear, withdrawing from others, and minimizing one's own needs can often be indicators that pain is masking what's really important to the client. For example, Loretta came to therapy frustrated and angry at her husband for being distant, moody, and disrespectful. She spent many sessions fuming about his disrespectful behavior and sharing stories about his latest "mistake." For some time, Loretta didn't endorse any personal values with regard to intimate relationships. She simply stated that she didn't want her husband to be a jerk, and otherwise she just wanted to live in peace. However, following some defusion and acceptance work, and with some trepidation and embarrassment, Loretta reported feeling sad when her husband treated her poorly. It became clear to both her therapist and Loretta that her anger was a way to escape from the feelings that came up when she interacted with her husband. She said she thought if her husband would just change, she might feel better. Further, Loretta said that she was very unwilling to have these feelings of sadness, loneliness, and frustration at her husband—she wished they would go away. As the session continued with the dialogue that follows, the therapist guided Loretta to the value underlying her psychological pain.

Therapist: So, you notice that these feelings come up and you aren't very fond of them. What would you have to lose to get rid of these feelings?

Loretta: (*Laughs sarcastically.*) Him! Well, in all seriousness, I guess the relationship.

Therapist: Not only the relationship, but in order to never feel lonely or sad again, you'd also have to give up caring about whether any other relationships you have will work out. And how could you stop caring about them?

Loretta: Well, I could pretend that nothing mattered. But I've done that...for many years. And it wasn't fun.

Therapist: So, if you couldn't stop caring on command, you'd probably have to give up all relationships. Would you be willing to give up all future relationships, including the one with your husband—and even those with your daughter and your sister—so that you'd never feel sad again?

Loretta: No! I'd hate that. Especially my daughter and sister. I love them and I couldn't live without them in my life.

Therapist: It's like "relationships" are on one side of this index card here, and "sadness and loneliness" are on the other. So, as painful as it is, in order to give up sadness, you'd have to give up caring about your relationships, whoever they're with. You'd have to throw away this whole card—you can't just erase one side of it and move on.

Loretta: Wow, I never thought about it that way. I've always thought, "Change Earl and you'll feel better." But you're right. I'd have to live all by myself until I get old and die to stop caring about people.

Therapist: Would you be willing to make room for the possibility that something matters to you in your relationships that you can work toward every day? I'm not saying fix Earl. But what if you could allow yourself to choose how you want to behave based on the fact that you care about your relationships?

Loretta: Sure, I will. I'm not sure how much it'll help with Earl, but I'm willing to try.

Looking compassionately with the client at the cost of behaving out of line with her values (in this case, angrily) will set the stage for working on more effective, values-based patterns of behavior and interaction. For Loretta, staying true to her values helped her consider the best way to approach her relationship problems with her husband.

VALUES PROVIDE THE CONTEXT FOR ACCEPTANCE

Just as the pain of caring about relationships was masked by Loretta's anger, sometimes clients come to therapy discussing how the pain of caring feels overwhelming. Linking this kind of pain to a value provides a context in which acceptance is possible. Anastasia, a forty-year-old mother, came to therapy for anxiety problems following a recent divorce. She was so afraid of losing important relationships that she pulled away from those she felt close to in order to avoid the possibility of feeling hurt or abandoned later on.

Anastasia and her therapist examined her values in regard to closeness with others in detail. They uncovered previous patterns in which she had disengaged from relationships when she perceived that she had behaved in a way that others would find irredeemable. Missing a breakfast meeting with a close friend because she felt too depressed to get out of bed fell into this category. Her worst fear was that if she attempted to apologize, her friend wouldn't forgive her. Rather than try to make amends, she chose to end relationships prematurely, which allowed her to avoid the discomfort of apologizing, the fear of others being angry at her, and the disappointment of doing her best and still being rejected. Recognizing the value revealed by the pain of disconnecting from her friends, Anastasia was willing to practice acceptance of her fear and also to live her values. She practiced this by calling her friend, asking for forgiveness, sharing her appreciation for the friendship, and rescheduling the breakfast.

Recognizing Acceptance and Avoidance in Session

Acceptance in the therapeutic relationship means that you behave with compassion for yourself and your clients. As discussed in chapter 5, it can be difficult for therapists to sit with clients' pain and suffering, and as a result, we may become avoidant of topics related to their pain. Noticing that you're pulling back or avoiding particularly emotional topics due to your discomfort is important. Sometimes you may do so because you feel that the therapeutic alliance isn't strong enough for you to delve into the pain deeply; alternatively, you may simply find it uncomfortable to allow this pain into the room. In the latter case, it's useful to remember that human suffering is what brings a client to therapy, and to recall your values related to being a therapist. As suffering and pain enter the therapy space, habitual patterns of experiential avoidance may arise for both you and your clients. The same practice we cultivate with clients—compassionately noticing avoidant behavior that conflicts with a personal value and coming back to a practice of acceptance in service of that value—is also applicable to us as therapists when we notice patterns of avoidance that are in conflict with our values for therapy. Cues to watch for will generally be avoidance of external or private events and rigid behavior patterns—on the part of both therapy partners. More specifically, the following indicators will help you identify moments when either therapy partner is engaging in avoidance or acceptance:

Avoidance Indicators

- Resistance to discussing or maintaining a discussion of uncomfortable experiences

- Long periods of silence in response to being asked to explain or share a painful experience (particularly those moments that function to keep therapy from progressing, as opposed to moments when the client is practicing acceptance of private experiences)

- Body language such as averting eye contact, squirming in the chair, fidgeting, or rigid or shrinking body postures (particularly during discussion of painful experiences)

- Changing the subject or a marked increase or decrease in the amount or rate of talking when painful experiences are about to be discussed or are being discussed

- Frequent or suspicious tardiness to session or skipping sessions, particularly following a previous difficult therapy session

- Not complying with exercises in or outside of session (in which case therapy is likely to feel strained, with both partners acting rigidly and with a narrowed repertoire of behavior)

Acceptance Indicators

- Verbal expressions of kindness toward oneself or one's therapy partner

- Verbal expressions of acceptance of self and one's therapy partner

- Verbal expressions of willingness, flexibility, or compassion toward experiences, memories, or historical events associated with discomfort (for example, playful expressions in response to difficult experiences, such as "Oh, here's Mr. Upset again; welcome back")

- Nonverbal expressions of willingness, flexibility, or compassion toward experiences, memories, or historical events associated with discomfort (smiling, nodding, open posture, slowing down and allowing emotion to be present, allowing crying without needing to rush or end the experience, and so on)

- Willingness to see things from another's perspective (particularly the therapist seeing the client's perspective)

- Willingness to experience and witness the other's discomfort

Summary

In this chapter we've presented various intervention strategies designed to help you move past fusion, the dominance of self-as-content, and avoidance so that your clients can begin to cultivate valued living. We focused on four of the ACT processes in this chapter, sometimes called the "mindfulness processes," to show you how each of these processes are related to values. In the next chapter, we'll show you how to develop another core ACT process—committed action—to create and maintain patterns of values-based behavior.

CHAPTER 8

Developing and Maintaining Committed Action

Though values were the focus for all interventions in chapter 7, we have not yet discussed committed action, the ACT process that is key in maintaining behavior in valued directions. In this chapter we will combine many of the concepts and approaches discussed so far, focusing on ways to cultivate long-term values-directed behavior patterns, or committed actions. The aims of this chapter are to increase your knowledge about committed actions, teach you how to maintain valued behavior, and guide you in applying these skills to your own behavior as well as your clients' behavior. Case examples, worksheets, and metaphors will broaden your knowledge of how to create patterns of committed actions. We will also follow Frank, from chapter 6, as he continues his work with the Bull's-Eye Worksheet. In chapter 6, Frank identified some of his values, and in this chapter, he will move to the last part of the worksheet and use it to build a valued action plan.

As a reminder, valued actions are simply vital, meaningful behaviors linked to valued directions, taken while embracing all emotions, thoughts, and sensations that arise. If you contact your values and act in the service of them, the likelihood that you will act in a similar way again increases (this is the basic principle of reinforcement). In this chapter, we will examine how committed action work can be conducted at different stages in the therapeutic process. As we do so, we return to the most important aim of ACT, flexibility. We have discussed flexibility previously in the book, but because this concept is so important in relation to valued action in particular, we think it's appropriate at this point to reiterate some points regarding both.

Flexibility: A Key Element in Valued Actions

Flexibility and valued living are the overarching goals of ACT. Flexibility plays an important role in relation to committed action. As clients choose committed actions based upon values, they may begin to do so with some rigidity. Obviously, some consistency is important, but it's all too easy to hold tightly to one's values as a rigid set of rules. Again, we look for function. Has there been a time in your life when you committed to something (for example, exercising daily no matter what) as a rigid rule and then sometime afterward failed to keep the commitment? If so, how soon did you begin to break your own rule and come up with excuses for why you couldn't keep the commitment? Has there been a time when you committed to a very similar behavior under very different circumstances? For example, consider this commitment statement: "I choose to exercise as much as I can in a week because I feel better when I do it. I commit to making exercise a priority even when other things take me away from exercising, and I also commit to continuing the commitment, even when I fail." We would say that the same behavior (committing to exercising) is under aversive control in the first instance, but under flexible, appetitive control in the second.

A related point is that commitments are not about sticking to a course staunchly; they should involve willingness to continue a commitment *and* be open to reassessing the course frequently. For example, if a client committed to exercising every day but then started to notice that he missed his girlfriend immensely because he was spending so much time at the gym after work, he would demonstrate flexibility by getting up earlier and going to the gym before work some days, spending a longer time at the gym fewer days per week, or finding physical activities he and his girlfriend would enjoy doing together, such as bike riding, hiking, and running. Commitments are about sticking to a course, but they shouldn't be so rigid as to prevent changing course if appropriate. Changing the form of the behavior doesn't mean the underlying value has changed. It's important to examine values and commitments for function. Flexibly applying our values to a course that's workable and gets us closer to our values-based goals allows us to maintain patterns of valued behavior for long periods of time. It's helpful and adaptive to make small corrections to the course based upon our experiences regarding what works for us, applying the mindfulness skills from chapter 7 each step of the way.

So where does committed action start? In the next section, we describe how we help clients try on committed actions driven by stated values.

Trying On a Value

In order to experience the reinforcing qualities of values, clients must begin to take steps toward their values. However, when talking about choice and starting to act in valued directions, clients commonly respond with something like "But I don't know how to choose. I don't know what's best for me!" This doesn't mean making a choice isn't possible for the client. It only means that he's fused with the thought that it isn't possible to choose. We've discussed reason giving and how easy it is to get stuck in our heads, trying to solve emotional and cognitive "problems" instead of starting to move toward what we really care about.

At this point, we introduce a brief exercise that can help clients get in contact with the reinforcing qualities of values. The aim of the exercise is to help clients who are stuck get going and thereby hopefully come into contact with positive reinforcement. "Trying on a value" means that the client is encouraged to choose a value and then behave as if he knew how to take a step in that direction—to act like someone who knows how to act according to his values. It's important to encourage clients to be mindful and to use all the processes that they have learned so far while doing this exercise. Before you ask a client to do this exercise, we encourage you to at least touch upon the processes of acceptance, defusion, and present moment awareness, and related skills, in order to prepare him for both taking the step and experiencing the reinforcing qualities of the valued move. This will help the client recognize whether particular committed actions work for him. Furthermore, in this exercise the client should be encouraged to evaluate the chosen value, and the steps in that direction, only after some time has passed, not based upon what his mind says in the moment.

An important part of this exercise is watching out for judgments. Ask the client to not engage in evaluating whether the chosen value is "good" or "bad" or whether that value fits him until after an agreed-upon period of time. Rather than evaluating the value, his job during this period should be to simply notice consequences (the way other people behave toward him, the way he feels about others or a life domain such as work or recreation, and so on) and continue to behave as he has committed himself to behave. During this process, the client is asked to use everything that he has been taught in therapy prior to the session. Here's a step-by-step worksheet that you can use as a guide in session or assign as homework. We provide some brief instructions for the client so that you may easily hand this out as a worksheet or homework assignment.

TEN STEPS TO TRYING ON A VALUE

The purpose of this exercise is to commit to trying out a value, whatever it may be, for a certain period of time (a week, two weeks, a month) and simply notice all that you notice during this time. This is not about right or wrong or finding the perfect value; it's about practicing committing to a value and noticing the results. You may find that you need to do this exercise more than once, with the same value or with other values, to develop a sense of what works for you and what doesn't. Any and every experience you have while doing this is important information for therapy.

1. **Choose a value.** Choose one value that you're willing to practice for at least a week. This should be a value that *you* can enact and a value that you care about. This is not a time to try to change others or manipulate them into changing.

2. **Notice reactions.** Notice anything that comes up about whether or not this is a good value, or whether you really care about this value. Just notice all of your related thoughts for what they are. Remember that your mind's job is to create thoughts. Let your mind do that while you stay on the exercise.

3. **Make a list of behaviors consistent with the value.** Take a moment to list a few behaviors that are consistent with the value you chose.

4. **Choose one or more behaviors.** From this list, choose one behavior or set of behaviors that you can commit to doing between now and the next session (or several sessions ahead).

5. **Notice judgments.** Notice anything that comes up about whether or not this is a "good" behavior, whether you will enjoy it, or whether you can actually do this action you're committing to.

6. **Make a plan.** Write down a detailed description of how you will go about enacting this value in the very near future (today, tomorrow, this coming weekend, at the next meeting with your supervisor, and so on). Consider anything you need to plan or get in order to take this action (calling someone, cleaning the house, making an appointment—whatever). Then choose when to do that (the sooner the better).

7. **Just behave; don't share the assignment.** Even if this behavior involves other people, *don't tell them what you're doing.* See what you can notice if you enact this value without telling others that you're doing this as an experiment or assignment.

8. **Commit.** Commit to following your plan every day until an agreed-upon session. Notice anything that shows up as you do so.

9. **Keep a daily diary of what happens.** Things to look for and record in your diary include other people's reactions to you, any thoughts, feelings, or bodily sensations that occur before, during, or after the behavior, and how you feel doing it for the first, second, fifth, tenth, or hundredth time. Watch for evaluations that this activity, value, or valued direction was good or bad. Watch for judgments about others, or about yourself in relation to living this value. Gently thank your mind for those thoughts, and see if you can choose to not buy into its evaluations or judgments about the activity or the value.

10. **Reflect.** Bring your daily diary to the agreed-upon session.

To illustrate how this can be used in session, we turn to a depressed client, Anna, who spends most of her time in bed. Intellectually she understands that it isn't working for her to stay in bed all day and night. She realizes that it makes her more depressed and understands that she won't get her life back as long as she is lying in bed. Nevertheless, while Anna is lying in bed she has the thought that she can't get up and out of the bed, and she believes that thought, so she simply stays in bed. Her therapist uses the preceding exercise to encourage Anna to act even though her thoughts present a barrier to doing so. Here are Anna's responses as she reads through the exercise in session:

1. **Choose a value.** *I want to take care of my health and be active with my friends.*

2. **Notice reactions.** *"Everything feels impossible" is one thought that pops up immediately, but alright, I'll let it be there for now...*

3. **Make a list of behaviors consistent with the value.** *Get out of bed every morning and take a shower. Text my friend Patty and ask her to grab a coffee with me at the coffee shop around the corner. Get a haircut.*

4. **Choose one or more behaviors.** *Maybe I'll wait on the haircut but go ahead and do all the rest.*

5. **Notice judgments.** *I'll do that for now, but it feels strange that you're asking me to do it. It feels strange to commit to doing this even though I know I can't. Well, guess that's a thought too... I will observe them...*

6. **Make a plan.** *I'll text Patty tomorrow at ten in the morning. I'll do it from my kitchen table, which means I'll have to get up and put some coffee on around nine.*

7. **Just behave; don't share the assignment.** *Sure, I can do that even though Patty and I try to talk about everything. I have a couple of other things I want to talk to her about, so that's okay. I might tell her later though.*

8. **Commit.** *Well, I'll get up and take a shower every morning till next time I see you. I will for now, but after that we'll see.*

9. **Keep a daily diary of what happens.** *Writing about it each day will probably help me remember. I'll try my best to keep track of everything.*

10. **Reflect.** *Sure, I can bring that with me to the next session. I'm actually a little nervous about this, and I'm up for the task of sticking to my commitment.*

Now that you've seen how you might introduce the exercise to a client, consider the length of time for which to assign the exercise. One week is usually a good starting point. During the agreed-upon session, check in with the client about his reactions. Ask him about his overall impression of how the experiment went—an impression free from fusion with judgments. See what the client noticed. What was surprising? Did anything get harder or easier during the experiment? Did he notice any evaluations showing up? How was it to commit to doing something for a certain period of time (a week or two weeks)? How did others behave in reaction to his behavior related to this value? Any of these questions can start the conversation. Also, ask your client about his private reactions. What feelings arose? Were there times when engaging in the valued behavior was difficult due to thoughts or feelings? What happened when the client bought into the thought or feeling or didn't buy into it? Asking the client how things went is a way to help him practice noticing his own experiences, and hopefully notice that he can behave because he committed, even when his mind didn't necessarily agree that this behavior was reasonable, right, good, or useful (or whatever).

Doing this exercise with a client who has evaluations about his chosen values or who doesn't think that he knows how to choose may be helpful, especially if you do it more than once. Have the client try on a value for a week or two and then try another, and then another. The goal is to help the client flexibly choose, commit, and find his own personal way of evaluating valued behaviors based on his experiences over an extended period of time.

What Maintains Values?

One of the principal aims of this chapter is to give you the tools to help your clients cultivate long-term values-directed behavior patterns, or committed actions. A core element that we need to review as part of this discussion is the ACT and RFT theory concerning the maintenance of valued activity. As we've said before, values are rules that we choose freely or, in behavioral terms, rules chosen without being under aversive control. When we make behavioral choices under the influence of values rules, we generally come in contact with reinforcing consequences that make it more likely that we will make similar choices in the future and maintain a reasonably high level of this type of behavior as long as the consequences keep coming. When we live consistently with our values, we can contact two types of consequence—specific reinforcing consequences and values-consistent reinforcement—both of which are important in maintaining values. Both are potentially intrinsically reinforcing consequences, meaning the reinforcement comes from doing the activity, as opposed to being artificially provided by an external source; however, values-consistent reinforcement applies no matter what the outcome of taking valued actions, and it plays an important role in making those patterns of behavior more sustainable in the long term. Let's take a look at these two types of consequence.

Specific Reinforcing Consequences

When we're engaged in valued actions, one kind of reinforcement comes from the specific activity itself. Here are some examples of behaviors and related consequences that are likely to be reinforcing.

Valued Behavior	Specific Reinforcing Consequence
Telling my mother that I love her and that I'm glad she's in my life	Mom tells me all of the things she appreciates about me. I feel good.
Taking a walk outside on a warm, breezy evening and watching the sunset	I feel aesthetic pleasure and a sense of being connected to the world. My mind is calmer and I feel energized by what I'm doing.
Caring for my cat	I enjoy cuddling with my cat, having her greet me at the door, and feeling needed and able to help another creature.

As you can see, each of the valued behaviors in this table offers specific intrinsic reinforcers that might follow—a parent sharing love, a calming of the mind, and feeling the affection of a pet. The production of consequences such as these will make the valued behavior more likely to happen again. Furthermore, engaging in valued activities can be expected to produce positive consequences such as these on a fairly consistent basis. Indeed, this is why these activities are valued and why the domains in which they occur (in this case, family, spirituality, and caregiving) are valued domains.

Having said that valued activities such as these are likely to produce positive, reinforcing consequences on a consistent basis, there is, however, no guarantee that positive consequences will occur every time we engage in valued activities. Sometimes engaging in valued activities can even result in aversive consequences. For example, your mom might reply with "Well, why didn't you call sooner?" after you've told her that you love her; you might pull a muscle or get caught in a rainstorm on that "relaxing" walk; or your cat might scratch you when you try to cuddle her. These kinds of consequences are not quite as reinforcing as those outlined previously! In fact, all other things being equal, they might put you off engaging in those valued activities again. However, we believe there's another kind of consequence that results from engaging in valued activity that is powerful enough to keep us coming back to our valued activities even when we don't always get the positive specific reinforcing consequences we might expect.

Values-Consistent Reinforcement

A second type of consequence that results from valued activity, which we refer to as values-consistent reinforcement, comes from recognizing that our behavior is linked to our values. This may be explained as follows: Values are self-directed rules that necessarily involve a purposeful, chosen statement concerning what we want to be about in our lives. As such, they are central nodes in an extensive hierarchical relational network in which many if not all of our life activities, from the mundane to the most obviously vital and important, are categorized. When we deliberately do things that are consistent with our values, we tend to experience a sense of coherence. In technical RFT terms, there is a transformation of functions of elements of the relational network in accordance with relations of coherence ("This makes sense to me because I'm acting in accordance with my chosen life principles") and possibly also expected future reward ("I'm acting in accordance with my chosen life principles, which have directed me in the right way before and can ultimately continue to do so"). In this way, valued actions give our lives meaning. Essentially, coherence between the rule about acting in accordance with one's values and the response of actually doing so produces reinforcement which may stimulate continued values-consistent action. In short, behaving consistently with our values makes it more likely that we will do so again.

This source of reinforcement is most important when we don't immediately feel "good" when we perform committed actions: when your mom snaps at you, when you feel tired and sore after the walk, or when your cat scratches you. In each case, even though the experience itself may have an aversive property, the reinforcement you experience because your action was linked to a value means you might be more likely to do that behavior (or something similar) again. If you weren't in touch with that kind of reinforcement and your mom snapped at you, you might make a snide retort, end the conversation, or not tell your mom you love her again for a while (all actions that don't cohere with your value of caring for your mom). However, if you were aware of your value of sharing with your mom that you care about her, you might be more likely to persist at living consistently with your value by staying with the conversation, ignoring the comment, or finding some other way to express your caring to your mom at a later time. Psychologically, you're being flexible because you're making room for whatever response your mom may have to your statement. In addition, you might be more likely to act in accordance with this value again in the future because of the reinforcement from being consistent with your value in this particular instance.

Here are some examples of possible aversive consequences for the sample valued activities, along with a corresponding values-consistent reinforcer.

Valued Behavior	Specific Aversive Consequence	Values-Consistent Reinforcement
Telling my mother that I love her and that I'm glad she's in my life	Mom is angry that I haven't called in a few weeks.	I'm sharing with my mother that I care about her.

Taking a walk outside on a warm, breezy evening and watching the sunset	I feel tired and can't get my mind to stop spinning, and now it's pouring rain.	I'm living my value of getting exercise and taking some time for myself each day.
Caring for my cat	The cat scratches my ankles whenever I walk around, won't come when I call her, and meows all night.	I love caring for pets, and I enjoy watching the ever-changing behavior of cats.

You can see how doing something because it's linked to one's values is important. Although these behaviors are exactly the same as those discussed above, the consequences outlined here reveal that there are, in fact, two sets of consequences occurring for the person at the same time. In each case, an aversive consequence may happen, but another consequence also happens by virtue of the fact that the person connects with the value underlying the behavior. In each case, the person has lived consistently with a value and, through acceptance, defusion, and other processes, might choose to do so again, even if negative or otherwise unpleasant consequences sometimes occur. In ACT, we hope that clients will experience specific reinforcing consequences for their behavior a good deal of the time, but it is often the case that they first must learn to find the reinforcement from living consistently with their values.

When we use psychological flexibility in choosing valued actions, our choices will be based upon both workability and being consistent with our values, and our choices may evolve depending on their consequences. Eventually, however, at least some of our valued actions must be reinforced via specific reinforcing consequences; otherwise it becomes difficult to maintain valued behavior in the long term. And often, clients find themselves in personal environments that aren't very reinforcing: an abusive spouse, a miserable boss, or a less-than-desirable home, for example. It may be necessary to help clients find ways to obtain positive reinforcement, even in small ways, when positive reinforcement is lacking in the long term. For example, a client might do at least one self-care activity per day (taking a walk, eating a meal on the porch, listening to a favorite music album, and so on) in order to experience some specific reinforcing consequences. Over time, hopefully you can help clients find more areas of life that are similarly reinforcing, or guide them in developing willingness to make a change in their surroundings in order to gain specific reinforcing consequences in an alternative environment (for example, getting a new job, moving, or separating from an abusive partner).

On a related issue, committed action can involve working toward outcomes we never actually see, and in such cases values-consistent reinforcement is arguably even more important. However, even in these valued activities, it's still important that we experience specific reinforcing consequences.

Consider someone who values caring for the global environment. He might never see the outcome of a "healthy planet," but he will continue to recycle, carpool, and make his home more energy efficient based on his value. By acting in this way, he will certainly derive values-consistent reinforcement. However, in order to maintain behavior intended to produce an outcome that probably can't be achieved or discerned in his lifetime, it will also be important for him to obtain specific reinforcing consequences in the course of individual valued activities. For example, he might gain verbal reinforcement via a social network composed of fellow environmentalists, or experience satisfaction from maintaining an eco-friendly garden. This is the beauty of values: We may work toward something we never see but can maintain values-consistent behavior patterns by gaining reinforcement from instances of engaging in activities consistent with that value.

In the next section we explore specific ways to help clients create valued action plans. Using the last section of the Bull's-Eye Worksheet described in chapter 6, we will continue to follow Frank and his therapist as they work on Frank's valued action plan.

Stimulating Committed Action Using the Bull's-Eye Worksheet

The long-term aim of values-based therapy is to help clients contact long-term, sustainable values-specific intrinsic reinforcement and help them increase their behavior in the service of their chosen values. To get in contact with that reinforcement, clients must start taking steps that they *think* might take them in valued directions. As you may recall from chapter 3, clients often speak of wanting to have confidence, feel sure, or know the outcome before they take committed action. However, actions cannot be evaluated before they are taken, since there is no basis on which to evaluate them. All we have to rely on before we actually start to move is our minds, and we know that our minds aren't always a good source of information when it comes to values.

The last section of the Bull's-Eye Worksheet, part D, aims to help the client create a valued action plan that will hopefully bring the client in contact with sustainable, intrinsic reinforcers. This part of the work often occurs at the end of a session and can easily be translated into a homework assignment. Basically, this part of the worksheet asks the client, "What step are you willing to take now, in this moment, in the direction of the life you have described as your valued life, and in the presence of what you have described as obstacles?" Here's a dialogue from Frank's first session that provides an example of this therapeutic process.

Therapist: Frank, my question to you is what step or steps are you willing to take in order to live a more bull's-eye life?

Frank: This is hard… I guess I could talk to my wife and be more honest with her and stop shutting her out of my life and my problems.

Therapist: I don't want you to commit to something that you don't feel you are ready for. This is your life and you have to find your path here.

Frank: Yeah, true, but this is something I'm ready to do and something I want to do. At the same time, it scares me a bit.

Therapist: Okay, Frank. Is it okay to embrace this scary moment in the service of your values?

Frank: Yes it is. I can do that.

Therapist: Interesting. I can't wait to see how that worked out for you when we meet next week.

In this way, the client chooses a step he's willing to take in a valued direction. He commits himself to the step, and the therapist makes sure that the client has taken responsibility for his action and expresses an interest and a curiosity in how it may turn out.

Using the Bull's-Eye as a Valued Living Diary

The Bull's-Eye Worksheet can easily be translated into a homework assignment in which the bull's-eye is used to create a diary of valued activities outside the therapy room. It's helpful if the therapist and client have worked through the process of the entire Bull's-Eye Worksheet before using it as the basis for a homework assignment. The therapist instructions for working with the bull's-eye as a valued living diary include asking your client to take it home and write a value each morning reflecting an area in which he would like to work that day. Next, the client expands upon his intention for this value and makes a commitment for the day with respect to this value, regardless of internal barriers that might arise. At the end of the day, the client places an X on the dartboard indicating how close he came to bull's-eye living in regard to that value that day.

This homework assignment can help clients generalize all of the work they do in the therapy room to everyday life. However, some clients may not be eager to engage in homework of this (or any) kind. Here are some things to watch for as clients engage in this assignment, or any other homework you may create.

Be aware of the risk for pliance. As a therapist, you want clients to choose to take steps for their own sake and not simply based on pliance. However, some pliance is unavoidable and may even be of use to you in helping a client get moving. Many of your clients may start to do their homework solely because you asked them to.

If, via pliance, a client experiences something meaningful for him, help him find the intrinsic (not pliance-based) reinforcers that might help him persist with his valued action plan. This way, you can quickly move away from pliance and toward tracking what is of importance to the client in following a valued action plan.

Don't put pressure on the client to choose a more significant valued action. If the client feels hesitant about a step, it gives you important information. It is either too great of a step or a vital step entangled with emotional discomfort and troublesome thoughts. Try not to buy into the thoughts and fears, but at the same time don't push the client to do something that might be too big of a step for him at that point. Have the client carry the responsibility for his own actions and talk about how he would know the difference between a step that's okay for him and one that's too big.

Provide a "willingness booster" by predicting pitfalls. In ACT, we don't endorse the idea that there is any way in which a client can fail at anything, including not doing homework. However, it can be useful to work with the client to predict all of the pitfalls that might prevent him from keeping a commitment. The point of doing so is to help himself to prepare himself for uncomfortable barriers that might show up while he engages in his committed action. For example, Frank spoke of wanting to allow his wife into his life more. Possible pitfalls for Frank might include all of the ways in which he could choose to not do his valued action, or ways in which doing so could be uncomfortable. Predicting pitfalls can provide a "willingness booster." Before the client leaves session, you can work with him to make space for potential barriers and commit to engaging in his committed action anyway. Be careful, though, not to strengthen psychological barriers by giving them too much attention. With practice you will learn the difference between building willingness and focusing too much on possible difficulties, just like clients learn by evaluating steps after taking them.

The Bull's-Eye Diary

You may make copies of this worksheet and put them in a notebook that clients can bring with them every time they come to therapy. The diary will give you important information even if clients don't take the steps they committed to. This may reveal that the assignments are too difficult, that you need to do more work with other ACT processes, or that you need to slow things down and rethink your analysis. In any event, the reason a client didn't take a step is important information that you need to take into consideration. For example, if fear and thoughts are bullying the client and seem to present barriers, that pain is something you need to make room for in therapy.

BULL'S-EYE DIARY WORKSHEET

Each day, please complete this worksheet as best you can. You may need to look back at worksheets you filled out previously in therapy, where you wrote about your values within various life domains. Looking over those domains and your values in each, consider which area you would like to focus on and develop today and write it here. Then consider how you might live consistently with your value in that domain. In the section "Things I want to talk to my therapist about," write any questions or concerns you notice that you want to remember to share, or any other issues you want to discuss in your next session.

In what valued domain will I develop today?

_____

How do I want to be in this area?

_____

_____

_____

What specific step will I take today to fulfill my bull's-eye intention?

_____

_____

Things I want to talk to my therapist about:

_____

_____

_____

_____

_____

At the end of the day, assess how it went. Place an X at the spot that best represents how well your actions today coincided with your bull's-eye intention.

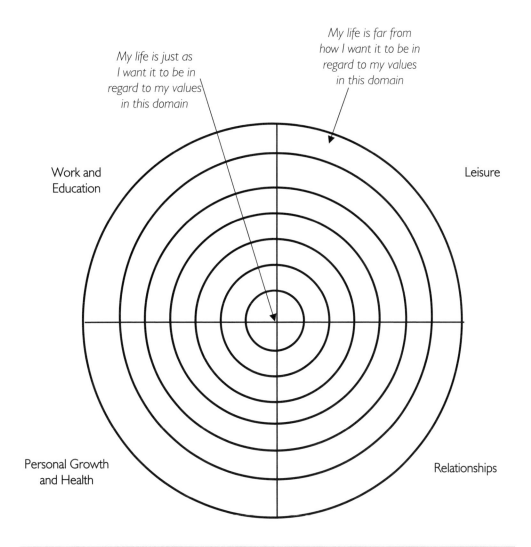

In this section, we've described how the Bull's-Eye Worksheet can be developed into a homework assignment. We have also examined possible therapeutic pitfalls when working with the Bull's-Eye Worksheet to create a valued action plan. As Frank chooses valued actions and then marks how close he's getting to his bull's-eye, his therapist's job is to help Frank notice what worked for him and what didn't. The overall aim of this homework is to help Frank learn to find what is reinforcing for him by selecting many different behaviors linked to his values. As he does so, he practices tracking his own experiences and looking for vitality. When he finds activities that work for him, he's more likely to continue down this valued path again—the intended goal for all of our clients.

Staying on a Valued Track in Therapy

In this section we examine how therapists can use a worksheet to stimulate values-directed actions in session even in the face of emotional difficulties. This worksheet can keep the therapist on a valued track in therapy and also help clients get going when they feel stuck. We've used this worksheet in the context of supervising therapists and in other clinical settings. When you use it, remember all of the things we talked about in chapter 5, on compassion and ways to improve the therapeutic relationship. This worksheet builds on those concepts. The content of the worksheet will come from your functional analysis of the client based on his values and barriers to living in a valued direction. The content of the worksheet is built on what the client needs you to do and hypotheses regarding how you might best do what is needed. The therapist must be willing to self-reflect when using this worksheet. In particular, it's important to consider the following questions, which can illuminate important elements in regard to the therapeutic process:

- What is most difficult for you with this client?

- Is there anything you avoid doing with this client because it might be uncomfortable or you feel uncertain about how to do it, or because of evaluations or judgments?

- What does this client evoke in you?

- Is there anything you might like to do with this client but you avoid it because you fear that pushing the client in that way might be too much or not warranted at this point in therapy?

Consider the following example. Linda, who is eighteen years old, and her therapist, Helena, have been working together for about four months and it is becoming clearer and clearer that they aren't moving forward in therapy. Linda has a history of being sexually abused by her grandfather, and over the last two years she has been cutting herself on her arms, legs, and stomach. Linda acts with anger and hostility when things get emotional in both the therapy room and also in everyday situations at the residential center where she lives.

Helena has a history similar to Linda's. She has been sexually abused, grew up in a foster home from the age of fourteen, and used to cut herself. Helena is very fond of Linda and the two of them have a relationship that both of them seem to value very much.

Helena's problems with Linda's therapy began after two months. According to Helena's case conceptualization, key elements in Linda's therapy are emotional exposure and daring to be vulnerable in relationships. Linda stated at the beginning of her therapy that she wanted to move to her own apartment and that she wanted to be able to build close relationships with both friends and boyfriends. However, when Helena suggests exercises that involve emotionally loaded material or talks about their relationship, Linda reacts with anger and hostility and even threatens Helena. When that happens, Helena gets quiet and passive and doesn't stand up for her analysis, herself, or her beliefs. These are old patterns for both Helena and Linda. As you can see, they are affecting each other's behavior, and as a result they aren't moving forward in the therapeutic process. When Linda and Helena talk about everyday things, they both feel relaxed and connected, and the fact that they both value their relationship is important and a therapeutic strength. However, that connection should be built on values, not on avoidance of emotions or fear of rejection. Helena senses that this isn't working, but she hasn't been able to find a way to break the vicious circle and move forward in therapy.

Here is a conversation between Helena and her supervisor in which they discuss Helena's therapeutic goals, which provide the content of the worksheet.

Supervisor: Helena, to me it seems like you have a special strength in your relationship with Linda, and at the same time you seem to struggle with your own emotions. I think you can be the perfect therapist for Linda. You have the possibility to model willingness to carry emotions and memories in a gentle way and at the same time stand up for what you need and what you believe in. What is it that Linda really needs from you?

Helena: You're right that I get stuck in my feelings. One thing I need and want to do is to continuously gently bring us back to what it is that's important in the therapy room. Right now I'm not doing anything but avoiding... When we're talking about everyday things, I want to ask her if we're doing the most important thing right here and now related to what she wants. Because I don't think we are mostly. It seems like we only talk about horses and everyday things. It isn't good for Linda, and it isn't good for me!

Supervisor: Okay, that sounds important. How can you gently bring Linda and yourself back to what's important in the therapy room?

Helena: I think that I can lean forward, maybe put my hand on hers, look into her eyes, and just ask. It feels scary when I think about doing it, but I need to break our pattern to be of service to her. When I do that, I think we need to stop and reflect on what's happening in the room... what happens inside ourselves and between us.

Supervisor: That sounds important, Helena—to use all of your compassion and acceptance to feel what you feel and make room for all thoughts, emotions, and fears that pop up. Break the emotional avoidance circle and see if it's possible to create a space for all emotions in the moment and just be there, right there with everything you might experience. Those are two important therapeutic moves you will develop that coincide with the analysis, right? Break emotional avoidance and make room for new experiences. I'll write those two moves as the first things you need to do. What else?

Helena: I'd also like to talk to Linda about working with acceptance of memories and emotions in the service of getting in contact with her values. I would like us to be about that and not be about avoidance.

Supervisor: Okay, so if I understand you correctly, you would like to go back and again give Linda a brief rationale of your work? Where is she going right now if you look at her behavior? What stands between her and her valued life? How do you think you can and need to work with this together? If I understand you correctly, that would mean going through your conceptualization with her continuously and working with psychological flexibility in the room. Sounds important. I'll write that down as well.

Helena: Yeah, and one more thing I want to do with her: I want to be able to self-disclose things with her when it can help her. Instead of avoiding and getting stuck in my own history, I'd like to be able to share my experiences with her. That way I'll model that it's possible to experience emotions and memories without defense, and I also think that we'd be acting more in the service of our common values of being open with each other.

Supervisor: Interesting idea. I'll write that down as well. Okay Helena, I would suggest this: Record your sessions with Linda and afterward look at the tape and record a tally mark for each time you do your chosen move. Bring the tape and the worksheet to the next supervision session and we'll see where you are and what we can do to help you. The worksheet will help us evaluate how well you did what you wanted to do. I also suggest that you start the next session by addressing what you hypothesize has happened between the two of you and how you want to continue from now on. How does that sound?

Helena: Sure thing. It creates a lot of feelings and some fears when we talk about it, but, yes, that's what I want to do and need to do.

Here's the worksheet that Helena and her supervisor developed together.

Therapeutic actions	Session 1	Session 2	Session 3	Session 4
Break emotional avoidance by leaning forward and breaking everyday talk, for example				
Stimulate new experiences				
Reiterate the rationale for therapy using simple ABC with values as reference, and work toward flexibility				
Self-disclose				

When you use a worksheet like this, we suggest that you make an audio or video recording of the therapy. When reviewing the tape, use tally marks to record each instance of doing your values-based moves in therapy. If video- or audio-recording isn't possible, then you can just estimate how often you did the target behaviors. (However, for maximum accuracy, we suggest that the sessions be recorded if at all possible.) We suggest making it a regular practice to use worksheets like this to help you gain perspective, and also to stimulate willingness to develop as a therapist. This type of worksheet can help you break vicious circles in therapy and get back on a valued track.

In this example, Helena had a good idea of what she needed to do with her client. Often, this isn't the case due to entanglement with thoughts and emotions that get in the way of perspective taking. The role of the supervisor is to help the therapist take perspective and formulate therapeutic actions. We suggest that therapists always be engaged in either group or individual supervision. This will greatly enhance the possibilities for powerful therapy that is in line with both client and therapist values.

Developing Valued Action Plans with Your Clients

Having looked at how to create a context in which valued actions were more likely in session, now let's examine how to help clients develop valued action plans. First we'll discuss the importance of setting short-term and long-term goals. Then we'll examine how to use motivative augmental rules to help clients find the value even within aversive properties of their environment. After that, we'll discuss creating a team around values and valued actions, using case examples and brief theoretical discussions to highlight the importance of including significant others in valued action plans.

Short-Term and Long-Term Goal Setting: Establishing a Pattern of Valued Action

As you recall from chapter 4, there are many ways in which clients can become overwhelmed during the process of setting goals. They may choose long-term goals related to their value but be unsure how to engage that value in the short term, or they may come up with only small, short-term behaviors that aren't oriented toward a larger goal related to their value. The following worksheet may help clients find the best way to plan out their valued activities. It can work very well in conjunction with the Bull's-Eye Diary, as it can help clients choose specific goals and activities in the service of their values, which can then be assessed using the Bull's-Eye Diary. Additionally, the worksheet encourages the client to clearly state both internal and external barriers that might arise when enacting valued action plans. This will help you work together on overcoming those barriers via the other ACT processes (acceptance, defusion, and so on).

WORKSHEET FOR ESTABLISHING SHORT-TERM AND LONG-TERM GOALS

This worksheet will help you figure out what goals may be appropriate for you as you move in your valued directions. You can copy this worksheet and use it to create a plan of committed action for any number of goals.

Value: _____

_____

Long-term goal: _____

_____

Short-term steps that will help you achieve that goal:

1. _____

2. _____

3. _____

4. _____

Internal barriers (uncomfortable or unwanted thoughts, feelings, sensations, or memories that show up):

_____

_____

_____

_____

External barriers (things outside of you, such as a lack of money or physical distance):

_____

_____

_____

_____

Are there ways to deal with the external barriers that could either be done right now, or that may take more time and patience? (For example, making a phone call, or saving money to visit a relative far away.) Write them here:

_____

_____

_____

_____

Are there external barriers that have parts of them that are internal barriers? (For example, feeling afraid of visiting someone important to you who you haven't talked to in a long time and who lives far away.) Write any internal barriers that may be linked to external barriers here:

_____

_____

_____

_____

What is something you can do today that would be in the service of this goal and this value? (Even the smallest activity can get you moving!)

_____

_____

_____

_____

I will do this activity *today*:

_____

_____

_____

_____

Motivative Augmental Rules: Finding the Value Within Aversive Behavior

As we mentioned earlier in this book, human behavior is under multiple sources of control most of the time. It is rare that we behave solely under appetitive control (doing something because we find it rewarding in some way) for very long. Even if we are doing something we care about, our minds can create ways in which we experience the situation at hand as aversive. For example, when a person is spending time with an intimate partner, her mind can generate such thoughts as "Ugh! Why is my partner still talking about his annoying boss? I'm tired and just want to go to bed," and then she isn't enjoying what could otherwise be a nice evening with her partner. Think of a time recently when you did something you didn't particularly want to do because someone you work for or care about asked you to. Think about what controlled your behavior as you did it. Most likely you did it because on some level you felt like you had to—because it was part of your role in that relationship with that person to comply. However, what else might have been controlling your behavior? Perhaps you also did it because you value being a good worker, a caring partner, or an accommodating friend. Here, again, is an opportunity for finding the values-consistent reinforcement in your daily activities. Sometimes it's difficult, particularly within each instance of behavior, to see that what you're doing comports with a larger value. For example, finding the value inside taking out the trash for your partner at midnight or making one hundred copies of a report for your boss during your lunch hour would be difficult for any of us without constant mindful awareness of the connection of such behavior to our values.

Finding the value inside a behavior is a good illustration of values as motivative augmental rules (see chapter 2), which is essentially how values are seen from an RFT perspective. In everyday terms, motivative augmental rules work by increasing the motivation to engage in a particular behavior. In the context of interventions aimed at finding the value inside a behavior, the target behavior is something that would normally be aversive; however, because a motivative augmental rule (the value) functions to counteract a large amount of the aversive "have to" property in that behavior, the person carries out the behavior despite its aversive quality.

There are many ways to create interventions based on finding the value inside a behavior. One way is to ask the client to list all of the reasons he did a particular behavior and then walk through each one to see if a value might be inside it. Consider Alexis, who was experiencing difficulty maintaining her values around being a parent. Her three-year-old son had just been diagnosed with autism, and she found dealing with his tantrums, cleaning up after his messes, and disciplining him (especially in public) very aversive and embarrassing. Exasperated, she came to therapy because she felt guilty for wanting to just cuddle and play with her son rather than follow the behavioral plan specialists had recommended. Working with her therapist, she was able to see that each and every activity (no matter how aversive, gross, or embarrassing) was linked to her love for her son, and that her full and active participation in his life was vital for supporting his growth—her most precious value. These realizations didn't take away the exhaustion or the embarrassment she felt in public when her son threw a tantrum, but linking all of her related behaviors to her value of being a caring parent helped create a context in which she was able to defuse from her negative evaluations and accept the discomfort it took to stick to her son's behavioral plan.

Here's an example of a worksheet that you might consider sending home with clients as they engage in activities they describe as "have to" situations.

FINDING VALUES IN UNENJOYABLE ACTIVITIES

There are many things we do that we don't particularly enjoy. Sometimes we do things that aren't enjoyable in the moment because they're linked to something we care about. For example, parents may not particularly enjoy changing their child's diaper, but they do it anyway because of their values in regard to caring for their child. This worksheet can help you to see if there's anything you care about inside some unenjoyable activities. There are no right answers here; this worksheet is simply designed to help you see if there is something of value to you in an unenjoyable activity. There may or may not be.

The unenjoyable activity:

_____

Consider the possible reasons why you do this behavior (for example, someone or something that is important to you in some way would be negatively affected if you didn't do it). Write these reasons down:

1. _____

2. _____

3. _____

4. _____

5. _____

In the space provided, record the thoughts, feelings, and bodily sensations you notice when you do this behavior.

Thoughts

1. _____

2. _____

3. _____

4. _____

5. _____

Feelings

1. _____

2. _____

3. _____

4. _____

5. _____

Bodily Sensations

1. _____

2. _____

3. _____

4. _____

5. _____

Is there a value inside even one of your reasons for doing this behavior? If so, describe it now:

_____

_____

_____

If yes, list three behaviors you can choose to do to live this value this week. You can include the original behavior above if you wish. In the spaces to the left, record your willingness to do each using a scale of 0 to 10, in which 0 indicates not at all willing and 10 indicates very willing:

_____ 1. _____

_____ 2. _____

_____ 3. _____

You can see how this worksheet helps clients keep track of what thoughts, feelings, and bodily sensations they notice when they make behavior changes. Using this worksheet or something similar to it, you can help clients find the underlying value in many instances of behavior and thereby make more contact with the values-consistent reinforcement in those actions. This is essential for establishing long-term patterns of values-based behavior.

Creating a Valued Action Team

Developing valued action plans in session is an important intervention in therapy; however, there are additional ways in which the therapist can stimulate and increase the likelihood of valued living. As you probably know by now, as ACT therapists we assume that human behavior occurs as interactions between a person and his inner and outer environment. Other people are an extremely important part of our environment. Therefore, one way to increase the likelihood that interventions such as action plans, homework assignments, and commitments will be successful is to ask the client to include significant others in his valued behaviors. In this context, significant others can include spouses, friends, relatives, other therapists, roommates, medical professionals, coworkers, or anyone affected by the client's valued actions or able to influence those actions. The inclusion of significant others aims at decreasing potential barriers and increasing the likelihood of reinforcement. For example, if a person wants to develop at work, this might require a change in his work assignments or work environment, so it's likely that her boss or her colleagues will be affected. Involving and preparing those who will be affected is one way to influence the environment and the environment's response to the valued act. Breaking patterns in life often affects others, and it's generally better to prepare the environment for the changes or, even better, to find a way to include important people in that environment to help support the changes the person wants to make.

We want to make something clear, however. In advocating the inclusion of significant others, we do not encourage either the therapist or the client to breach confidentiality concerning the fact that the client is in therapy. If the client chooses to involve others, that might be effective for certain individuals, such as a friend or a parent, but it's likely to be less effective with others, such as a boss. Help the client to find ways to involve others in his valued action plans outside of the therapy context simply as part of healthy communication with others about valued living without necessarily breaking confidentiality.

Following is a dialogue between Sasha and her therapist. They're talking about Sasha's work situation and how she can take valued actions at work. Sasha is trained as a nurse and has recently taken further education to become a psychotherapist. Due to a crisis in her family, she's been on sick leave for two months and during that time she's been in therapy. Sasha wants to go back to her job and work mainly as a therapist. Unfortunately, she has a hard time standing up for herself and what's important to her and has always taken care of others at the expense of her own self-care. Sasha's therapist asks her about her obstacles at work.

Sasha: Well, I think there are many things. I think they gave me this education without really knowing what to do with me when I was done. Someone has to do my other work duties. My boss told me he wanted me to do therapy as long as it didn't put the other nurses in difficult situations or give them an unrealistic workload. My boss is okay though; he is in most ways supportive. The most problematic obstacles are my nurse colleagues. I can work as a therapist; my boss has said okay to that. Also, my own experience tells me that it wouldn't be too much of a problem for my colleagues to help me out. The workload isn't that bad. I could easily work as a therapist two to three hours a day and they could cover for me. It wouldn't be a problem; it would actually help them and ease their workload because I would take care of the most troublesome clients… Actually, when I think about it and we talk about it, one of the other nurses has told me that she would support me, so I'm not really sure what the problem is… It is just that I feel so bad when there are things to do and I want to contribute, and I don't want the others to think badly of me.

Therapist: You want to work as a therapist and your boss has said okay. You have support from at least one of your colleagues. If I understand you correctly, what stands between you and developing at work are your feelings of not contributing enough and that others would think badly of you. When thoughts about not contributing pop up, you feel anxious and ignore your valued direction and do things to lessen your anxiety. Is that correct?

Sasha: Yes, I guess so. I think that I'm afraid of stepping out of my old patterns at work. I've always taken care of others and haven't really taken any space. If I started working as a therapist, I might feel like I had to leave the nursing job and my nurse colleagues.

Therapist: Sure, I understand that it would be emotional for you and something new, which is what you want and at the same time are afraid of, right?

Sasha: Yeah, and I really, really want to do it!

Therapist: What would be a good first step for you to do?

Sasha: I think I need to talk to my colleagues and tell them what I want and maybe also tell them what I'm afraid of. I want to tell them that being a therapist is important for me and that it might even develop our unit. We know each other well and we talk openly about all kinds of things, and I really think I can talk openly with them. I even think that they would help me more if I were open with them. However, I need to be prepared for a negative reaction from some of them.

Therapist: Okay, you're thinking of talking to your four colleagues in your nurse team and are prepared for both help and other reactions. Can you include them in more ways so that they can participate in this development and not only do it as a favor to you?

Sasha: Maybe I can ask them to refer clients that they think need therapy. Maybe we can work as a team around some of the clients that are really difficult and troublesome. My colleagues are open, and I think it might work.

Therapist: That sounds fun and interesting—including your colleagues and creating a treatment team. Do you think you could include your boss in some way?

Sasha: Hmm, I'm not sure. Maybe I can suggest that we try this out and ask for his thoughts about the idea. Maybe it would make him feel more involved and feel that he has the opportunity to influence and contribute. Actually, I can ask him if he has thoughts on how we can evaluate the work.

This conversation shows how entangled one can get in thoughts and feelings. It's as if thoughts were truth for Sasha. She started the conversation saying that her boss and colleagues were negative regarding the possibility of her working as a therapist. However, by the end of the conversation it became clear that what was keeping her from getting involved with her valued direction of working as a therapist was mainly her fear of feelings related to not contributing or not being part of a team, and a fear related to the risk of boldly stepping forward in valued directions. By asking Sasha what she wanted and what she was afraid of, the therapist helped her reflect upon her fears. Talking to her boss and colleagues might allow Sasha to create an expectation that could provide motivation for her to take steps toward her values. Furthermore, stating her values and asking for feedback from her colleagues and her boss invites them to affect the process, which might put some pressure on Sasha to actually take steps toward being a therapist. A role-play could be added to this therapeutic intervention to help Sasha start the valuing process in the therapy room.

Summary

In this chapter we discussed committed actions and how to increase the likelihood of taking actions congruent with one's stated values. Helping clients take steps in valued directions and then to maintain and increase such valued actions is one of the ultimate aims of ACT therapy. In this chapter, we explored how to use the last part of the Bull's-Eye Worksheet to develop a valued action plan and discussed two interventions that might be used to increase the likelihood of values-consistent behavior: finding the value inside a behavior and creating a valued action team. In the next chapter, we will continue to explore valued action by showing you how to use the values compass as a tool to orient both client and therapist to values throughout therapy. The values compass can be used in conjunction with the bull's-eye or in place of it, as you see fit. We present it as an additional model for attending to values and building long-term patterns of valued action. We will also discuss the positive and negative aspects of prioritizing versus balancing values.

CHAPTER 9

The Values Compass

Throughout this book we've discussed the functional meaning of values as well as the verbal barriers to valued living. We have discussed the core ACT interventions in relation to values and have provided strategies to foster and maintain valued actions. In this chapter, we pull everything together under one umbrella using the values compass, an organizing metaphor that we find useful in structuring the course of therapy from its earliest stages. Apart from some of the core benefits of metaphor as suggested by RFT (discussed in chapter 6), it has several functions as an organizing metaphor: First, it provides an introduction to each of the ACT processes by revealing the cost of unworkable strategies for dealing with difficult experiences and providing a glimpse of alternative responses to those experiences. Second, it establishes a framework for therapy that can be built upon and embellished in each session. Third, it provides a common language, consistent with the ACT work, that the therapist and client can use to discuss both old and new strategies for dealing with psychological discomfort.

Hence, in this chapter we present the values compass as one possible organizing metaphor for values-focused ACT work. This tool is extremely versatile, facilitating diagnosis, functional analysis, and intervention strategies throughout the course of therapy. Thus, it can complement the use of other values interventions presented throughout this book, including the Bull's-Eye Diary described in chapter 8. We hope that you will find the values compass helpful in your values work and that after reading this chapter you feel inspired to use it to assess not only your clients' values, but also your own.

The Values Compass: Creating a Course for Therapy

While most modern forms of therapy touch upon issues of quality of life in some way, ACT is different in that it *explicitly* addresses this via its values clarification component. As you have seen, one important goal of ACT is to provide a context in which clients are defused from their mental products and accepting of their experiences in the service of living consistently with their values. Achievement of this goal allows clients to discover their motivation for engaging in therapy, an awareness that helps them take responsibility for their therapeutic process and paves the way for them to continue to make values-consistent choices following therapy. In addition, it means that the therapist is able to concentrate more on the delicate art of therapy rather than having to act as motivator or coach.

At first glance, the values compass appears deceptively simple. However, if the therapist lacks prior knowledge and experience of the core processes of ACT, it will likely yield results that are at best superficial and at worst inaccurate with respect to the condition of the client. This is why we are discussing the values compass at the end of this book. At this point, you have gained some theoretical knowledge of ACT, particularly regarding the importance of values, and this knowledge will be useful in guiding your understanding with respect to the values compass.

We present the values compass in full detail, with examples, helpful hints, and discussion of potential problems at each stage of therapy. In so doing, we have two aims: to familiarize the reader with the instrument and to provide an in-depth understanding of the complexities of values work in ACT. The majority of the chapter focuses on a detailed presentation of the values compass and shows how it can be used at early, middle, and later stages of therapy. As a vehicle for this presentation, allowing discussion of both potential problems and possible solutions, we will use the hypothetical case of Karin, along with other minor examples.

The Values Compass

The values compass is presented in its entirety including instructions to the client. You are welcome to photocopy it and use it in clinical practice or research. Following presentation of the values compass, we will discuss how to use it section by section with respect to aims, practical guidelines, pitfalls, possible interpretations, and implications for therapy. We will also include some material from actual therapy sessions to further support you in your use of this instrument. The term "valued direction" (as opposed to "value") is used for clients in this worksheet because it makes the idea of a value a bit more concrete and links it to the compass metaphor and the concept of orienting to that direction constantly throughout one's life. It also underscores the distinction between values (a direction of travel) and goals (specific, achievable waypoints), as described in chapter 3.

When working through the values compass with a client, you may find it helpful to work together to fill out the worksheet. You may prefer to use a large whiteboard or presentation-sized notepad for more freedom. If you use the form, make photocopies so you'll have a blank form for future sessions. No matter which format you choose, you and the client should have pens or markers and work side by side.

THE VALUES COMPASS WORKSHEET

On the next page is a values compass, with a figure in the center representing you. From this figure, ten arrows emerge and aim at ten different life domains. Each of these domains may offer special and unique contributions to your life. This special meaning or quality is what you will look for using this worksheet. We will call these qualities valued directions. In the figure, labels such as "work" or "leisure" are used to represent these domains, but those words are only simple representations of these areas and you may think of them differently. For example, work can include homemaking or volunteer activities, and spirituality isn't confined to organized religion. The special meaning or quality within each domain that is meaningful to you (your valued direction in regard to that domain) has probably been present all your life and will continue to be present throughout your life, but how it is expressed or the form it takes is likely to change during your lifetime. For example, in the area of friends the importance of the valued direction of being an active part of a group of friends could be something that has been fairly constant in your life, but the particular friends or the form those interactions with friends take has probably changed quite a bit during your lifetime. In the area of caregiving, the constant quality might be the satisfaction of caring for someone or something, whether it was for a family pet when you were a child, caring for your own children after you became a parent, or volunteering at a school after you retired. There are seven steps to completing the values compass.

1. Identifying Valued Directions

In this first section, you are asked to reflect on and describe your valued direction in each of the ten domains. Even if some of the domains seem to overlap, see if you can find the unique contribution of each domain in your life. Don't limit yourself to how you are living right now in your life or what you think is possible; rather, describe the valued direction you'd choose if anything was possible. In other words, don't be realistic; instead, think about that special quality that you may have experienced at some time in your life when this particular domain was at its absolute best. Describe that quality as you would want it to be.

Describe this special quality in one to three words representing the essence of what you want from each of these ten domains. Write these descriptions in the boxes labeled "intention" in each of the ten domains. The following guidelines may help you as you write these descriptions:

- The description reflects a valued direction, not a goal you can achieve.

- It describes a quality rather than a quantity.

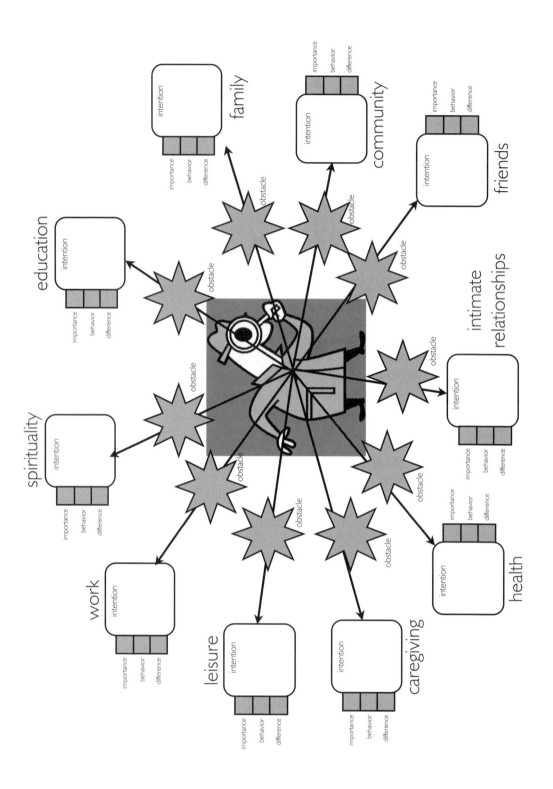

🐦 It's general and overarching rather than containing details regarding specific events, places, times, or conversations.

🐦 It represents a lifelong striving that transcends your age and life conditions.

🐦 It is only from your perspective and not based on what you think others expect or what is "right."

🐦 It pertains only to your behavior, not the behavior of others.

2. Ratings

Next to each of the ten intention boxes are three boxes labeled "importance," "behavior," and "difference." In this section you will place a rating in each of the three boxes. The first rating assesses the degree of importance this direction has for you. The second asks for an evaluation of how consistent your current behavior is with that direction. In the third box you'll fill in the difference or discrepancy between your importance rating and your behavior rating.

Importance. Consider each valued direction that you've expressed in your compass. For each, rate its importance in your life on a scale of 0 to 10 in which 0 means not at all important and 10 means of the greatest importance. Don't rank the domains; rate the importance of each independently of the others. All of them can be of equal importance if that's how you feel about it. As you consider the importance of your valued directions, try to see each one in terms of a higher overarching quality that may have had a certain meaning to you in the past that it still has today and will probably always have. In other words, try not to use your present situation as a reference concerning the importance of this valued direction. Ask yourself this question: "In the best possible scenario, how important is it to me to have this quality in my life?"

Behavior. Rate how consistent your behavior over the past two weeks has been with your valued direction. One way of thinking about this is to ask yourself how much you've invested your actions in creating opportunities for yourself to experience that quality described as your intention. Again, use a scale of 0 to 10 in which 0 means your actions have been entirely inconsistent with your valued direction and 10 means your actions have been as consistent with your valued direction as possible. So a high rating would probably mean that in the past two weeks you have invested substantially in creating this quality and have experienced this quality. A low rating means that you haven't invested much in creating opportunities for yourself, or you haven't experienced the quality you seek in this domain. If these past two weeks haven't been representative of your typical life in any way, choose two earlier weeks.

Discrepancy. Subtract the second rating (behavior) from the first (importance) and record the difference in the third box. This number represents the degree to which you are living consistently with your valued directions. The lower the number, the closer you are to living consistently with your value in a given domain.

3. Identifying Obstacles in Your Valued Path

In this section, you'll identify what stands in between you, here and now, and actually taking steps in the valued directions you have declared as important to you. Consider each domain that has any discrepancy between the importance of that valued direction and your actual behavior over the past two weeks. For many of us that might be several, if not all, domains. In the box labeled "obstacle," write a word or a short phrase that best represents the barrier between you and living consistently with your valued direction. In other words, describe the main reason why you aren't acting in a manner fully consistent with your declared valued direction in each domain with a discrepancy.

4. Rules About the Obstacles

In this section you'll identify your own rules about how you relate to the obstacles in the context of your valued directions. For example, consider a woman who believes that if she could only control her anxiety, she could then proceed to take steps toward an intimate relationship. Here are a couple more examples: "If I lose five pounds, then I might dare get into a relationship" and "If only I felt less tired, then I might further my education." As you can see, these rules are presented in the form of if-then statements, the form you'll use in this section of the worksheet. There is only room for three obstacles in this form. Choose three of the most central or common obstacles you experience and write them in the left-hand column. In the middle column, write the "if" portion of your rule, and in the right-hand column write the "then" portion of the rule.

Obstacle 1:	If I could get rid of	Then I would
Obstacle 2:	If I could get rid of	Then I would
Obstacle 3:	If I could get rid of	Then I would

5. How Has This Worked for You?

In this section, you'll look at your compass and choose three domains where you have discrepancies between your actions and your valued direction. These would be domains in which you clearly aren't acting in the ways consistent with your valued directions. Again, there's only space for evaluating three obstacles. In the left-hand column of the following table, record your valued direction, and beneath it record the main obstacle to living more consistently with that direction. In the next column, briefly describe the main strategies you've typically used to solve or manage your obstacles. In the next column, evaluate the short-term effects of your strategies. In other words, ask yourself whether you actually got immediate control over the obstacle as a result of using this strategy. In the right-hand column, evaluate the long-term effects of your strategies. In the long run, has using this strategy gotten you closer to or farther away from living consistently with a particular valued direction?

Here's an example:

Valued direction: education; **obstacle:** tiredness; **strategies used to manage the obstacle:** prioritize ongoing demands and postpone opportunities; **short-term effects:** relief from demands and feeling less tired; **long-term effects:** no education and little personal development.

Valued Direction and Obstacle	Strategies Used to Manage the Obstacle	Short-Term Effects	Long-Term Effects

6. What Does Your Experience Tell You?

In this section, you'll assess and describe what your experience tells you about how your strategies have been working with regard to these three valued directions specifically, and your quality of life in general. In the left-hand column, fill in the obstacle you were trying to manage or solve. In the middle column, circle either "closer to" or "farther away from." In the right-hand column, fill in which of your valued directions you were aiming for. An example would be "Trying to solve my pain problem has gotten me farther away from taking steps in my valued direction: being a loyal and conscientious worker."

Trying to solve	has gotten me closer to/ farther away from	taking steps in my valued direction:
Trying to solve	has gotten me closer to/ farther away from	taking steps in my valued direction:
Trying to solve	has gotten me closer to/ farther away from	taking steps in my valued direction:

7. How Willing Are You to Let Go and Move On?

In this last section, you're asked to rate your own willingness, right here and now, to let go of strategies in which you must solve the problem or get over an obstacle before living in your valued direction. Your degree of willingness to let go should be based on your own experience of how your strategies have worked for you. Trying something totally different means embarking on a new path, not more of these same strategies. So, here's the question: Based on the summary of your experience in the last step, how willing are you to abandon these strategies and try something totally different? Mark your willingness on the scale below:

Very willing ——————————————————————— Not willing
　　　　　　10　　　　　　　　　　　5　　　　　　　　　　0

The Purpose of the Values Compass

The purpose of the values compass is to enable the person using it to do the following:

- Identify the overarching value or valued direction (values identification).

- Assess how consistent her current behavior is with that valued direction.

- Take steps in valued directions (valued action).

- Identify verbally constructed obstacles to taking those steps (identify fusion).

- Identify patterns of experiential avoidance with respect to these obstacles.

- Make a functional analysis of these strategies of experiential avoidance in terms of short-term impact relevant to symptoms and long-term impact relative to declared valued directions.

- Practice willingness to accept and embrace these verbal obstacles and tendencies toward experientially avoidant behavior patterns *and* stay on the valued path.

The main figure used in the values compass features ten life domains. As discussed in chapter 4, these categories aren't meant to be prescriptive or the final say on what domains may hold a person's core values; rather, they are simply a useful guide for clients when choosing valued directions.

Right from the start, when clients are asked to identify valued directions, they are asked to distinguish between form and function. In the absence of guidance, clients might answer in terms of form by giving concrete and specific examples, probably from their current life. However, we're asking clients to look beyond the particular form valued action may presently be taking and describe a more constant quality of that value. For example, in the domain of intimate relationships, a client may tell us about her current partner; however, we want her to think about what intimacy means for her regardless of who her partner is. In the domain of work, a client might tell us about her current job; however, we want to know what she generally values about work, regardless of what her particular job may be.

As you can see, the aims of the values compass link closely with core ACT processes, allowing this instrument to be used as an organizing metaphor in all stages of therapy. The rest of this chapter will be primarily devoted to how to use the values compass at early, middle, and late stages of therapy using hypothetical sessions and exploring possible problems and pitfalls, interpretations, and implications for therapy.

Using the Values Compass at the Start of Therapy

The values compass can be introduced at any point in therapy. In our clinical research, we have often used it right from the first session. Many therapists question whether it is appropriate to introduce the instrument so early, wondering whether clients might be surprised that the first thing the therapist wants to talk about is their values rather than their presenting problem. In our experience, however, most clients seem pleasantly surprised when asked about what's important to them rather than being asked to describe a familiar problem once again. Ideally, this early communication about values should be built on the basis of an open, genuine, and compassionate therapeutic rapport with the client. Shortly, we will present two examples of what the early introduction of the topic of values can look like with a client who has other expectations.

Before presenting these examples, we will point out that in these and other hypothetical cases discussed in this chapter, we include observations concerning nonverbal aspects of behavior because we want to provide intervention skills that allow therapists to tap into nonverbal ways of doing ACT. As we have illustrated in earlier chapters, much information relevant to therapy, such as being connected to values or expressions of experiential avoidance, may be observed in nonverbal behavior. When the therapist is mindfully present in session, it's simpler to discriminate the difference between a client who shows genuine connection to valued directions and one who is being pliant or simply parroting what she has heard. Nonverbal expressions of experiential avoidance are very common during therapy sessions and provide opportunities for the therapist to do a functional analysis of behavior in the moment. As the client gets closer to valued directions by working with the values compass, the therapist is likely to observe avoidance behavior in all sorts of physical forms. Many people have learned how to speak as if they aren't being avoidant, but their body language may reveal that they are. This is why we include thoughts and other unspoken behavior in italics.

Setting the Stage for Introducing the Values Compass

The following dialogues show how the scene may be set for working with the values compass as early as the first session, and even at the very outset of the first session. The actual work with this instrument will be presented in a later section.

SETTING THE STAGE FOR VALUES WORK WITH JANE

Jane has sought therapy after having recently discovered that her husband has been having an affair with a friend of hers. She is coming to therapy for what she calls "a life crisis." She walks into the therapist's office, her face and eyes puffy and red from crying, and sits down stiffly in the client's chair. She takes out a tissue from a large pack in her purse, the presence of which may indicate that she's prepared for long periods of crying. She positions herself comfortably with several tissues at hand as if ready for the therapist to give her the signal to start telling her painful story.

Jane: I'm ready now.

Therapist: I can see that you are. I can also see that you've been suffering and are suffering right now. On the phone, you already told me briefly about what has happened in your life. I can see that you're prepared to tell me all about this, and I wonder if for the time being we could just put this problem over here on my shelf for safekeeping and instead, for right now, talk about you.

Jane: Wow, yeah, um, I thought you needed to know about what my husband has done, about the betrayal.

Therapist: To tell you the truth, Jane, you are my client, not your husband, and it is you I'm interested in. If it's okay with you, let's put your husband's actions on that shelf and allow me to get to know who you are and what's important to you. Would that be alright?

Jane: (*Puts down her tissues, sits back in her chair, and seems to relax as she looks curiously and almost with a smile into the eyes of the therapist.*) Yeah, sure.

At this point the scene is set for starting to work with the values compass.

SETTING THE STAGE FOR VALUES WORK WITH KATHY

Kathy is a teenage girl placed in a treatment home for her frequent suicide attempts. These attempts involve serious self-injury in the form of cutting her arms and legs. She has not sought therapy, but therapy is part of the treatment plan set up for her by the state. Just yesterday, Kathy made a deep cut in her arm and had spent most of the night at the emergency ward at the hospital. Today she has refused to leave her room. The therapist has come to her and is sitting on her bed ready to have the session there. Kathy stares at the ceiling and doesn't acknowledge the presence of the therapist. She's cradling her bandaged arm as if she were in pain.

Therapist: Kathy, is it okay if I sit here with you? I can see you had some trouble last night. I'm not here to talk about that.

Kathy: (*Nods a passive agreement.*) Good, 'cause I don't want to talk about it.

Therapist: You know, Kathy, I can see that you have cut yourself, and not only last night. I see from all of your scars that you've done this to yourself many, many times over a good part of your young life. I feel sad about this, but that isn't what I want to talk to you about. I want to talk about you, Kathy, the girl beyond those scars, beyond all these problems— it's that Kathy that I want to talk to. Is she here?

Kathy: (*Peeks at the therapist from the side of her eyes skeptically and speaks with a cautious voice.*) She is, but she's not talking to anyone right now.

Therapist: (*Relaxes with a smile on his face and speaks with a compassionate, gentle voice*) Do you think you could give her a message from me?

Kathy: (*Relaxes more and answers with more playful eyes.*) As long as I get to censor; she doesn't just let anyone say anything.

Therapist: Could you tell her that I already know that she's a girl who wants a life for herself. I can see that she wants to have friends and to feel a part of something, and to learn about things and create, to have boyfriends like everyone else and to be safe in her home. Tell her that this is some of what I see. Tell her that I can see that those parts of her life are far more important than the cutting, bandages, and scars. Could you tell her that?

Kathy: (*Looks at the therapist and nods with tears in her eyes.*)

At this point the scene is set for starting to work with the values compass.

Reflection

In these two examples, the therapist takes the client off guard by straying from the expected or traditional path. In both cases, the therapist asks permission to leave that path and embarks instead on a new path characterized by what's important and valuable to the client. The therapist gently and compassionately moves the focus from the urgent problem at hand to a higher level of values. This sets the stage for introducing the values compass, the purpose of which is to establish a context of values around the client, which will make it possible to see presenting problems and behavior patterns more generally from a values perspective.

Using the values compass with a client from the start provides the therapist with a sampling of behavior patterns relevant to the presenting problem, as well as keys to improving the client's quality of life. Doing this work at the beginning of therapy offers the advantage of giving the therapist the opportunity to establish, right away, what will be important for therapy. Rather than therapy being about storytelling or spending a great deal of time trying to fix a particular problem, remove symptoms, or reduce the client's pain, the therapist can establish a new path in which values are examined from the start. However, starting with values also has the potential to be painful, especially if the client has been deliberately avoiding valued areas of her life. It is important to support every client in the fact that she is suffering psychologically when she begins therapy, and clients may not be accustomed to support in the form of being asked what matters to them. Being aware that beginning with values can have this function will allow you to seek new ways to support clients in this often painful endeavor, or to find ways to begin therapy that work for you.

When using the values compass at the start of therapy, we generally watch for how the client moves between valued directions and experiential avoidance. We watch for verbal constructions representing obstacles to moving in valued directions that may emerge as the client approaches those directions, as well as gestures or statements indicating a willingness to approach those directions. In assessing how the client relates to obstacles, we look for flexibility or rigidity in relation to discussions of values or when practicing valued behaviors. Doing so may allow us to see what experiential avoidance and fusion might look like for that client (for example, particular rules regarding how to deal with values or valued behaviors).

Practice Watching Your Client's Nonverbal Behavior

As you start in on the first questions on the Values Compass Worksheet, observe the client's behavior. Watch to see whether she seems present in the task at hand or disturbed and focused on private events. This may be an opportunity to watch for degree of rigidity or flexibility in behavior patterns. Does she give over all power to you as the therapist or ask you what you think she should value? Either indicates high pliance. How fused is the client in telling her story? Fusion might be expressed as an unwillingness to do the values compass altogether, perhaps due to not seeing how the task is relevant.

As valued directions are investigated, important information may be gleaned by watching how the client approaches the various domains. Which does she address first and which last? Do some areas seem easier than others for her to contact? Does she show aversion or express avoidant behavior in regard to any domains? Either reaction might present the opportunity to address core ACT processes, such as defusion and acceptance. It might be useful to note, either during or after the session, examples of possible experiential avoidance and fusion, and the unique ways the client relates to values.

Often clients express rules while completing the values compass. For example, when a client with chronic pain looks at the domain of work, she might say, "If only I could get rid of my pain, I would love to get back to work." This response indicates a rule, which can be written next to the values compass under the heading "Rules." This can be a way of validating the client's expression without reinforcing her fusion to this rule. After writing down these rules, it's helpful to rewrite them in a way that clearly illustrates how the rule functions as a barrier to valued living. In this case, it isn't the pain itself that presents a barrier, but rather the rule about needing to get rid of the pain before working. From this perspective, valued action in the domain of work can occur even if pain is also present. For example, if the client says, "I would love to work if I could just get rid of this pain," this can be rewritten in a functional context as follows:

Valued direction: I value working.

Obstacle: The rule that I need to get my pain under control before I can work.

Impact: I don't work.

This analysis helps the client see that you aren't looking at the reasonableness of the value, the probability that something specific will happen, or her rules about the situation. Rather you are simply looking at what effect such rules have in the context of her value in regard to work. Toward the end of the session, as the last step in completing the values compass, the client is asked if she's willing to abandon her unworkable strategies in the service of starting to live in her valued directions. This is actually a question of commitment that asks the client if she's willing to stand up for what's of value to her. Is she willing to let go of a focus on symptom management and start focusing on taking steps in valued directions? Note the degree of persistence expressed in her answer. We can postulate that how an answer is formulated reveals degrees of commitment and persistence. Answers like "I'd like to" or "I could think about it" show a lesser degree of commitment than "I will go back to work" or "I'm committed to getting back in contact with my children." Notice and document the client's degree of willingness to have obstacles and still take steps in valued directions. Increasing acceptance, willingness, and commitment to valued living even in the face of difficulties is a general aim of ACT.

ACT Processes Present in the Values Compass: A Case Example

Coming into contact with valued directions via verbal processes, as is done in the values compass, is often experienced as painful, especially if the client has been avoiding these areas. In this case, experiential avoidance is likely to be evident, possibly fueled by fusion with rules about how the client should behave or what is possible for her life. Here's an example of how experiential avoidance and fusion looked in a session with Karin, a fifty-year-old woman with a presenting problem of chronic pain.

Karin is the oldest of her siblings, and after her mother died young, Karin spent her life taking care of her father and brothers, something she's still doing. She describes herself as dependable. She's never had an intimate relationship, and she hasn't had many friends. At one time she wanted to become a nurse, but there was never any time for her to get an education. She works as a home health aide for the elderly in their homes. Karin's therapist has already introduced her to the values compass, and now they're standing together at the whiteboard as Karin writes a few words in several of the intention boxes. The therapist carefully watches her and notices that Karin very quickly fills in her values in domains that have to do with helping others. She writes the following intentions in this order:

1. Family: Be helpful and supportive.

2. Caregiving: Be good, kind, and generous to those who depend on me.

3. Work: Be neat, helpful, and kind to my clients.

4. Community: Volunteer one day a week at the animal shelter.

After writing these values statements, Karin stops and hesitates as she looks at the other domains. Judging by her behavior, it seems as if the other areas are farther away for her than the first four. She stands looking perplexed for a minute or two, and then the therapist steps in to help her. The therapist comments on the observation that Karin appeared to have an easy time describing values when it came to serving others but skipped over any areas where she would value taking care of or devoting energy to herself. When the therapist asks her specifically about the domain of intimate relationships, Karin waves her hand and shakes her head in a manner suggesting that intimate relationships are irrelevant for her. The therapist looks closely at Karin, gently states that intimate relationships can make us feel very vulnerable, and asks if Karin has put aside personal relationships to take care of others. In response to this question, Karin covers her eyes and says with a quivering voice that she is most afraid of getting close to others or needing anything from anyone, and that taking care of others has always been easier for her.

LOOKING FOR EXPERIENTIAL AVOIDANCE

The mere contact with verbal content associated with the domain of intimate relationships was enough to trigger the reaction of experiential avoidance behavior in Karin. A plausible hypothesis is that the experiential avoidance seen here in session is an example of a more general pattern of behavior in her life. Using the values compass exercise showed an easy contact with all valued directions having to do with helping others (family, caregiving, work, and community) but difficulty in domains that might be categorized as involving self-care (spirituality, health, leisure, education, friends, and intimate relationships).

An early conceptualization might be that Karin's problems with chronic pain are related to this imbalance. She is valuing taking care of others but she isn't valuing taking care of herself. Of the ten domains, she is only actively pursuing her valued direction in four. She has shown in session that she avoids self-care domains in general and displays experiential avoidance in regard to intimate relationships in particular. The fact that she didn't fill out the values compass for these domains indicates that she may indeed be avoiding something in these areas. For Karin, experiential avoidance of anxiety around self-care activities has resulted in short-term relief, but over time Karin's life has narrowed to exclude self-care. As therapy progresses, her therapist will help her examine the cost of avoiding self-care activities.

Karin's example shows how using the values compass offers an opportunity to start early interventions using the ACT core skills. As we continue to follow Karin, we'll point out the relevance and use of core ACT processes. Let's go back to the therapy room, where Karin had just covered her eyes and told the therapist she was most afraid of intimate relationships.

Therapist: (Sits closer, puts her hand on Karin's hands, which are covering her eyes, and gently nudges them away from her eyes, allowing their eyes to meet.) Karin, I see that this is difficult for you. Can we stop right here and now so that you can help me understand what's happening?

Here we see an example of contact with the present moment. Karin seems to be in contact with painful emotions and thoughts related to intimate relationships.

Karin: (Now openly crying, but more relaxed.) It's just that this is so hard. It's so hard to talk about. It's so embarrassing. I try not to think about it.

Trying not to think about this painful area is an example of experiential avoidance right here and now.

Therapist: (Still sitting close, leans forward so as not to let go of this opening Karin has given her.) I think I just saw what you're talking about. You stood at the whiteboard and just skipped over this area of intimate relationships, along with other areas where you would be focusing on yourself rather than others. When I simply asked about this, you covered your eyes and said you were afraid and got upset. So, right here in this room, you tried not to think about this, and what happened?

Karin: (Alert, present, and teary-eyed but no longer crying, speaks with a little laugh.) I couldn't think about anything else.

Karin has seen an instance of the futility of trying to control her thoughts. This can be used as an example for further work down the line.

Therapist: (Stays close.) That's what happens to us when we struggle to control our thoughts. They come right back at us with even greater strength. We can talk more about that later. What I want to know right now, Karin, is about these areas: intimate relationships, friendships, your own education and health care activities, your leisure activities, and your own spirituality. One at a time, I want to know about these areas that you skipped over. I understand, because I've seen just now that getting closer to these areas may be painful for you. But I think, in fact, that what I have seen right here—the fact that you so easily expressed what you valued when it came to other people but showed such difficulty and even avoided when it came to areas that have to do with taking care of you—maybe has something to do with the chronic pain problems you're experiencing. What do you think?

Karin: (*Speaks with tears in her eyes and a quivering voice.*) Yeah, I guess somehow or other, I've had that feeling.

Karin has unconsciously discriminated the fact that not valuing self-care activities has come at a cost to her health.

Therapist: (*Stays close.*) Would you be willing to bring those feelings of embarrassment and fear that you just had, here with me, back into this room? Are you willing to open up to that pain you've been avoiding here with me? You would be doing it in the service of getting closer to the life you want to live.

Karin: (*Expresses her willingness and the two go on to explore further.*)

This interaction indicates Karin's willingness to accept painful experiences in the service of widening her quality of life. Even this short excerpt from an early session with Karin shows how working with values can elicit samples of experientially avoidant behavior patterns that are probably relevant to the presenting problem. Each instance of behavior that shows a widening of the client's repertoire in a valued direction, as opposed to continued experiential avoidance, should be reinforced and possibly used as an example in future work. This will help you start hypothesizing in terms of a functional analysis and subsequently begin an appropriate ACT intervention.

LOOKING FOR SELF-AS-CONTENT AND FUSION

When first using the values compass, clients tend to express values more in terms of concrete and specific goals rather than lifelong, overarching directions. For example, a client might write "becoming a nurse" in the work domain or "having children" in the caregiving domain. These are examples of conceptualizing values only in terms of specific goals, which is more of a self-as-content perspective. Clients often need help to see that these goals are specific expressions of content and are simply examples of a functional class, and that the function is what we're seeking. You may need to guide the client to the underlying function, or value. For example, when one client wrote "police officer" in the work domain, his therapist asked what being a police officer meant to him. If he were to become a police officer, what would this allow him to do that's of value to him? By helping clients see that specific goals aren't the same thing as the underlying value, you are using the core process of defusion and helping the client start moving from self-as-content to self-as-context.

Let's look at an example involving Karin, in which her therapist employs an early intervention involving defusion and moving toward self-as-context. The therapist and Karin are standing facing the whiteboard following Karin's statement of willingness to allow her pain and suffering into the room. The therapist asks Karin if it's okay to return to those areas of the compass in which she had difficulty identifying her values. The therapist points to the words "intimate relationships" and asks Karin to revisit that area: "Let's go back to these areas that are difficult for you. What happens when I point to the words 'intimate relationships'?" Karin winces and looks away, tensing and bracing her body, and then takes a deep breath. The therapist asks Karin to just notice what is happening to her at the sight of the words "intimate relationships." Karin admits to the therapist that just seeing the word "intimate" elicits a response of fear and avoidance. At that point, in response to the therapist's prompting, they both start to write the letters of the word upside down and backward and with different colors. Playing with the letters, Karin laughs that these letters aren't so meaningful and marvels at how much they've made her afraid of living her life.

There can be many opportunities even early on in therapy to use these types of defusion techniques. In Karin's case, the early interventions are based on a preliminary hypothesis that Karin is avoiding the thought of intimate relationships, and even the words "intimate relationships." This avoidance is likely being maintained by an immediate relief from the anxiety provoked by thoughts or sensations associated with the idea of a possible intimate relationship. As Karin's therapist was, be ready to use mindfulness, acceptance, and defusion techniques as soon as experiential avoidance and fusion with content show up in the therapy room. Use every opportunity to help the client move from self-as-content to self-as-context.

Potential Problems When Working with the Values Compass

We have found that there are many ways in which clients may get off track when completing the values compass. Many of the difficulties we have seen as clients complete the values compass are presented in detail in this section, often using the case example of Karin to illustrate them. We have also provided some possible conceptualizations for problematic ways in which clients apply ratings when completing the compass. When you encounter these types of pitfalls in your own practice, we hope that they don't discourage you or the client, but rather provide an opportunity for you and the client to find ways to continue to choose to live consistently with vital, valued directions.

PITTING VALUED DIRECTIONS AGAINST EACH OTHER

Most clients rank or prioritize their values when using the values compass, despite instructions explicitly asking them to refrain from doing so. For example, if a client rates her values in the domain of family as a 10, she may give values related to work a lower rating if she prioritizes family over work, even if she feels equally strongly about her values in each domain. It may be due to the common habit of prioritizing in Western culture. Most of us have been taught that we need to have priorities and make sacrifices for future rewards in life. When a client allows herself to assign a relatively high importance rating to many or all of the domains, this shows an awareness of the potential reinforcing quality in diverse areas of life even if she isn't active in all of them. The advantage of doing the values compass together rather than assigning it as homework is that you can watch how the client approaches rating the importance of her valued directions. Which of the areas does she rate first or last? How long does it take her to rate particular areas? Watch for signs of connection with a valued area, as well as painful memories and experiential avoidance. Write down any rules the client expresses while making these ratings. (For example, "I would spend more time with my family if I wasn't so busy with work.")

FUSION WITH RULES

As you commence work with the values compass with a client, listen for rules the client expresses regarding how she relates to her valued directions as well as obstacles to those directions. Notice her degree of fusion with these rules. Here are some examples of expressions that may indicate fairly high levels of fusion:

- That isn't just a thought; it's true!

- I don't just think I have pain; I have a diagnosis written by a specialist.

- I can't help it. I've always been this way.

Karin expressed a number of rules in the first session. Here are two that she expressed as she filled in her ratings, each followed by a functional analysis.

Domain: Health

Rule: "When I finally get home, I'm just too tired to walk or make a healthy meal like I should."

Functional Analysis

Valued direction: Taking care of myself by exercising and eating more healthy foods

Obstacle: The thought "I'm too tired."

Impact: No exercise, and no healthy homemade meals

Domain: Intimate relationships

Rule: "I'm too old now and it isn't important anymore."

Functional Analysis

Valued direction: Wanting to be open, vulnerable, and close both physically and mentally

Obstacle: The thought "I'm too old and it isn't important anymore."

Impact: No intimate relationships

Karin's fusion with these and other rules allows experiential avoidance. The rules serve as reasons to avoid moving in a valued direction. In this early intervention, Karin's therapist uses the values compass to find examples of persistence in valued living and to reinforce that persistence. For example, Karin is always dependable, willing to help others around her, and seeks out consistent opportunities to volunteer in her community. Karin has been very persistent in helping domains, but less persistent in personal care domains. In cases where she has been less persistent, Karin identifies the overarching value; takes a step in her valued direction; intercepts conditioned aversive thoughts, feelings, and memories; and persists in her valued direction while experiencing these reactions. Any new pattern of persistent values-directed behavior appearing in session can be used as a guiding metaphor outside the therapy room and later in therapy.

RATING QUANTITY, NOT IMPORTANCE

Rating the importance of a valued direction doesn't depend on any behavior or activity actually occurring in that area. But declaring something as important and at the same time knowing there is little or no activity in that area may cause some psychological discomfort (see chapter 8 for an RFT-based discussion of the importance of values-consistent reinforcement). Clients may avoid such discomfort by simply assigning low importance ratings to those areas in which they aren't active. Consider Karin's case: She rates the importance of her values in each domain according to her current level of activity in that domain. It's difficult for her to see that her values in an area could be important without her actually being active in it. This is an example of the influence of verbal rules in the form "If I declare some area to be important, then I should be active in it" or "If I'm not active in an area, then it isn't important to me."

RATING WHAT SEEMS REALISTIC, NOT IMPORTANCE

Some clients see rating importance as being equivalent to rating how realistic it might be to have valued qualities in their everyday life. For example, in the domain of education (which includes personal growth), Karin feels that developing her own creativity is important, but in light of how her life looks right now and how she imagines it will look in the future, she judges developing her creativity as unrealistic, so she assigns it a low importance rating.

LOW IMPORTANCE RATINGS

We don't mean to imply that all intentions recorded on the values compass must be rated highly. However, as mentioned, a higher rating in each domain, regardless of level of activity, does show an awareness of potential reinforcing qualities, and in our experience, a greater diversity of reinforcement is better. Again, we are simply referring to an awareness of the intrinsic reinforcing quality of valued actions, rather than any particular form, content, or quantity of those actions. Using the values compass is one way to foster this awareness in clients.

In general, we recommend discussing having an open stance toward domains with low ratings; this will allow the client to find new areas reinforcing if opportunities to enjoy these domains arise in the future. Over time, different domains may become more important as avoidance and fusion become less a part of the client's repertoire.

In our experience, low ratings often indicate a therapeutically relevant issue in relation to valuing. A low rating might also be a sign of avoidance, a lack of awareness of this domain as a potential source of reinforcement, or a lack of experience in this area. Therefore, it is important for you to further investigate the nature of the low rating, even if you decide to wait to address this area until later in therapy. Let's take a look at how Karin's therapist intervenes when Karin assigns low importance ratings in several domains on her values compass.

The therapist and Karin are sitting side by side looking at the ratings on Karin's compass. The therapist has just explained that the reason these ten domains are on the values compass is because these areas are generally found to have some importance for people, and Karin says that she can see that. The therapist points out Karin's lower ratings, and especially the 0 rating for intimate relationships, and asks her to explain these ratings. Karin replies that because she lacks experience and confidence in these areas, she has learned to just shut them out of her life. The therapist says that most of us assign some importance to areas such as intimate relationships, and also experience some accompanying anxiety about them. She asks Karin if she thinks it's possible to deem values in the area of intimate relationships important and at the same time have little experience in that area and have the thought that one has no confidence in that area. Karin concedes that this is indeed possible. The therapist then uses the example of their therapeutic relationship as a means of experiencing valuing qualities that could be relevant to intimate relationships while at the same time having thoughts of limited experience and confidence in that domain.

Karin and her therapist have examined what might be controlling Karin's behavior of assigning a low importance rating to her values in some domains. Karin's low ratings are impacted by fusion with the thought that she lacks experience and needs to feel confident, especially in regard to seeking out intimate relationships. By examining what controls these low ratings, they have uncovered additional therapy targets and established that Karin's values in the domain of intimate relationships actually have some level of importance.

LOW DISCREPANCY SCORES

Discrepancy scores indicate the degree of difference between the rated importance of a value and the steps taken to live consistently with that value, and can go in either direction; a high importance score coupled with a low behavior score will result in a positive discrepancy score, and a low importance score coupled with a high behavior score will result in a negative discrepancy score. Positive discrepancy scores due to high importance ratings and low behavior ratings are most common. In either direction, ideally, the discrepancy should be as small as possible. For example, if Susie rates her values in regard to community as important and rates her values-consistent behavior in this area as high, she has a low discrepancy score. Not all cases are as clear-cut as Susie's, though. Another way to get a low discrepancy score is to assign low ratings to both importance and values-consistent behavior. How might this be a problem? Consider Marianne, who is depressed and rates her values for intimate relationships and friends as unimportant and also assigns a low rating to her values-consistent behavior in these areas. The resulting low discrepancy score doesn't highlight the fact that she actually lacks reinforcement in these areas of her life, which might well be a factor in her current state of depression. If her therapist ignores this domain altogether because of her low discrepancy score, they would both be missing opportunities to discuss possible areas in her life from which she might gain reinforcement.

HIGH DISCREPANCY SCORES

A high discrepancy score generally shows a greater degree of inconsistency between the importance of declared valued directions and the person's behavior. A high positive discrepancy score is clearly problematic, but a high negative discrepancy score, in which values-consistent behavior receives a high rating but the value is deemed relatively unimportant, is also of concern. This indicates that there is a high level of committed action without a good connection to an underlying value, which is likely to lead to burnout, resentment, greater distress, and possibly a growing sense of meaninglessness over time. Consider John, who rated his values in the domain of work as relatively unimportant and actually sees work as a necessary evil in his life. He works two jobs in order to make ends meet for his family and hasn't found a valued direction or long-term reinforcement in the domain of work. Nevertheless, his behavior in working long hours every day is highly consistent with his limited value of making ends meet, even though doing so means forcing himself, on a daily basis, to engage in an activity he doesn't intrinsically value. In this way, John conditions aversion to the domain of work each and every day. Spending so much of his time working at jobs that he doesn't find reinforcing (which therefore isn't actually in line with his values) is probably a significant factor in his anxiety and depression.

Generally speaking, high discrepancy scores reveal suitable places to start therapy work. Reports of high discrepancy in a particular domain indicate client awareness of an inconsistency between what she values and how she is actually behaving. In other words, the client is acting in a way that doesn't give her access to the long-term reinforcement she wants in her life. Studies of cognitive dissonance (e.g., Egan, Santos, & Bloom, 2007) show that this type of awareness of inconsistency motivates behavior change in the direction of consistency. In RFT terms, recognition of such a discrepancy may add the aversive stimulus of relational incoherence to the motivative augmental effect of value rules. In other words, when a client recognizes both that she values something deeply (a motivative augmental rule) and that she is acting inconsistently with her valued direction (relational incoherence), she may be more likely to change her behavior to move in the direction of her declared value. Avoidance of inconsistencies or discrepancies such as these, on the other hand, might ultimately lead to greater psychological distress.

Developing a Functional Analysis from the Values Compass

Once a client specifies her valued directions, the therapist has a sense of what long-term positive reinforcement might look like for that client. Being aware of that valued direction, the client may intend to or actually take steps in that direction. While doing so, she is likely to encounter uncomfortable feelings and notice thoughts that provide her with various reasons why she can't continue her journey on her valued path. If she listens to these thoughts or sees them as reality, they become psychological barriers and she may leave her valued path. Let's look at an example of a functional analysis in regard to Karin's struggles in the domain of intimate relationships. We've seen that Karin values several qualities found in intimate relationships. However, when she even just thinks about taking steps in that direction, she becomes frightened and buys into thoughts about the surety of rejection. These fears and fused thoughts lead her to avoid that risk by not engaging her values. This avoidance gives her a short-term feeling of relief from fear, but it also means that she misses out on opportunities to establish an intimate relationship.

Using the values compass with clients should help with both diagnosis of presenting problems and creating guidelines for treatment. In general, the compass should reveal important valued directions, degree of consistency between declared valued directions and current behavior, and the particular verbally constructed obstacles to acting consistently with important values. In the process of working with the values compass, the client is likely to provide critical examples of how she relates to these obstacles, which may reveal the strategies she typically uses in regard to her obstacles. Having the client summarize the workability of these strategies allows her to draw conclusions about the outcome of her actions and change her behavior where those actions are seen as ineffective. The process of acceptance of obstacles and emergence of willingness to abandon old strategies cannot be forced. Choosing and clarifying valued directions and choosing to abandon old strategies must take place again and again, in every session of therapy.

Applying the Values Compass Midtherapy

The values compass is a process, not an end result. It's like a GPS that tracks your travels, continuously updating your position and assessing whether you're on course or how far you're diverging from your intended path. Just like a GPS, the values compass can't provide useful guidance if you don't use it to check in on your position and direction from time to time. Ideally, the client identifies valued directions using the values compass at the beginning of therapy, but this is an ongoing process, and for every new situation the client faces, the questions are the same: "What is my overarching value here? Are the steps I am now taking or wish to take consistent with my valued direction? Alternatively, are these steps functioning in the service of experiential avoidance of some unacceptable feeling or thought? Were any steps I took consistent with my valued direction? Did they bring me closer to my valued direction or move me farther away? How willing am I to allow and even embrace obstacles that show up in my path as I take steps in my valued direction?" These questions reflect the ongoing process of working with the values compass.

Just as the client practices taking valued steps many times with you in session and then evaluating them in this way, she should practice the same process outside the therapy room. In early sessions, Karin identified that she wanted to take steps toward a goal of getting an education and becoming a nurse and stated that her obstacles were mainly focused on solving her pain problem first. By the seventh session of therapy, Karin had started taking steps toward her goal outside the therapy session. Let's take a look at what happened during the seventh session.

Karin is usually early for therapy, waiting for the therapist to arrive. But on this occasion Karin comes running in a couple of minutes late. She seems both excited and stressed. Once seated, she buries her face in her hands and breathes out a sigh of relief. At the end of the previous session, Karin had committed to making an appointment with an adult education counselor. She now appears so agitated that the therapist starts the session by asking Karin to do a mindfulness exercise where she connects to her value involved in getting an education. Well in contact with that value of wanting to develop and challenge her abilities, she tells the therapist that she did, in fact, go for a meeting with the adult education counselor and experienced many difficulties.

The therapist places the now-familiar life line scarf on the floor and asks Karin to role-play what happened as she took steps in her valued direction. The therapist asks Karin to stand at one end and, standing at the other end of the scarf, asks Karin to identify the valued direction in her homework exercise. Here, Karin reaffirms her commitment to developing her potential, with the current goal of becoming a nurse. The therapist writes Karin's value on a piece of paper and places that on the wall opposite Karin to indicate her valued direction. The therapist then stands beside Karin, who is now on her valued path, and asks her what happened. As she takes a step forward, Karin explains that she went to meet the counselor even though her head was full of reasons not to. She could feel arguments such as "You will be sneered at" tugging at her, trying to bully her away from the counselor's office, but went there anyway. She nearly had a panic attack in the waiting room, but in response she closed her eyes, looked for her valued path, and found it—and stayed in the waiting room, with her discomfort.

Exercises such as the life line and the values compass can be used in each and every session as a means of helping clients return to their valued path, recommit to their valued directions, identify obstacles, and explore how they're relating to these obstacles. In this way, clients can see themselves practicing psychological flexibility toward a great diversity of obstacles while walking in their valued direction.

Applying the Values Compass Near the End of Therapy

Toward the end of therapy, the values compass can be used to help the client generalize her values-consistent behavior to the greatest extent possible so she will continue to thrive in her life after therapy. If the values compass has been used in every session to guide and calibrate the client's behavior, at this point it should be integrated into the client's pattern of living. If the client has also used the Bull's-Eye Diary, this would also contribute to an increase in daily valued actions. In general, by the end of therapy the client should have learned to approach unpleasant life events with acceptance and flexibility and be aware of her overarching valued directions in every new life situation. The client should also be aware of her typical verbally constructed obstacles and be able to see them for what they are (mind products), rather than what they say they are (which would indicate fusion).

At the end of therapy, the values compass can be used to predict future events and subsequent obstacles. Here's an example of how the values compass might be used in sessions taking place toward the end of therapy, again using Karin, who has now started her adult education with a view to obtaining her high school diploma. She's very motivated and her grades are excellent despite her constant fears of failing. She has made a number of good friends at school, which pleases her. The therapist and Karin have decided that they're nearing the end of therapy. Karin has a well-worn values compass with her and lays it on the table. Together, the two look at each domain to see what has happened over the course of the past four months. They examine it, one domain at a time, for any changes in rating of importance and values-consistent behavior. Together, they make predictions about what's likely to happen in the future based on these observations. The therapist likens this to looking at a road map before going on a trip. The therapist tapes the values compass on the wall and suggests that it might be more effective to act out the road map rather than just talk about it.

The therapist suggests using the life line exercise to examine each domain on the compass, one at a time, and over the course of the last three sessions, Karin works through the entire values compass. She redefines her values in each domain and rates the importance of those values and how consistent her behavior is with her values. She also takes a fresh look at familiar obstacles and how she now relates to them. Karin makes new commitments in many of the domains, and together they make predictions about what types of obstacles are likely to show up and attempt to bully her off course.

Living in Accordance with Values: Some Important Issues

Having discussed how to use the values compass in early, middle, and late phases of therapy, we will now discuss some of the problems clients commonly encounter when working with this instrument to live in accordance with their values. There are two issues we have discussed previously in the book that we wish to bring up once more—function versus form, and balancing versus prioritizing.

Form and Function

A typical client reaction when looking at the ten domains on the values compass is a feeling of overwhelming stress. This reaction may be the first sign of fusion with form rather than function regarding valued living. Here are some examples of these reactions:

- If I had to cover all those bases, I would really be stressed out.

- Just looking at all ten of those areas gives me the jitters.

- You've got to be kidding! A new list of "musts"? That's all I need...

These types of reactions are usually a response to the form of certain content related to the name of various domains. It's easy to understand why a stressed client would balk at the sight of what she thinks are more demands on her. Imagine that upon seeing the word "family," a client is reminded of all the duties she believes she should be performing but isn't currently doing. Not only is she confronted with a list of "shoulds," she is also showered with feelings of guilt for not doing these things. Likewise, imagine what happens for a client with chronic pain who's been on sick leave for some time when she sees the word "work." She's likely to be overwhelmed by a mixture of longing and aversion for her workplace and perhaps guilt for having left it, along with reminders of the back pain that she experienced there. She might also be reminded of her current financial straits and the emptiness of her days. It is generally impossible to not elicit form and content associations with the words labeling each of the valued domains, and often what the client is reacting to is these associations.

This is one reason why many ACT therapists choose to wait to work with values until after the core processes of defusion and self-as-context are introduced. That way clients may be more likely to identify constant valued directions from a perspective of self-as-context rather than self-as-content. In our experience, you can work with values from the start, but doing so requires that the therapist use all of the ACT core processes in each and every step. As we've shown in the examples, the therapist does this by moving with the client as she contacts the verbal processes involved in valued directions, observing patterns of fusion and experiential avoidance and stopping to help the client become aware of these. Thus, the values compass is used as a means of conceptualizing unworkable behavior patterns in the light of valued directions, which requires the use of all of the core ACT processes.

One of the first tasks when using the values compass is to help the client discriminate form from function and quantity from quality in valued directions. Many of the interventions and experiential exercises presented in chapters 7 and 8 can aid in work with the values compass and help move the client from fusion with content to a higher position from which she can see a valued quality that transcends any particular content. This quality is function. As soon as a client is able to see that a valued quality or function transcends the specifics of time, place, and people, she has made the transition from form to function. Prior to making this transition, clients may say things like "I really value family ties, but I don't see my family very often because they live far away from here" or "I used to love being with my friends, but we've all gotten busy and I haven't been able to make much time for them."

These sorts of statements show that the client has experienced the value in certain domains, but because she is fused with a particular form of valued behavior that isn't possible, she has stopped taking action in those valued directions. Such clients have lost access to sources of reinforcement and their lives have narrowed as a result. Once they understand their value in terms of function rather than form, they can begin to behave in accordance with their value again. For example, one of the authors of this book (JD) has lived as a single mother of three children in a foreign country without her extended family. Understanding that family served an important function for herself as an uncertain young mother and for her young children, she advertised for a grandmother figure and got one. This shows how the function of a value in regard to family may be created more easily if one isn't fused with a particular form or concept of how it should look. Many who have adopted children can attest to the success of this bonding of a created family. This is a good example of behavior serving the function of a value in a way afforded by the current context.

Similarly to the case of chronic pain, some clients come to therapy firmly believing that their lives are constricted by immutable outside circumstances. Consider Marietta, a young single mother living in her mother's basement and working two jobs to support her two young children. She scoffed at the idea that she might find reinforcement from her job, as she felt tired, worn down, and disheartened by her job prospects. Marietta's therapy focused on helping her become more flexible in how she expressed and enacted her values. She started by finding the value in working hard to give her children a better life than she'd had and found some reinforcement in showing them a strong work ethic. In addition, she focused on strengthening the consistency of her behavior in regard to a value she subscribed to immediately when doing the values compass: loving and caring for her family. She practiced both in her behavior with her children and by becoming more open with her mother and thankful for her mother's support. As therapy progressed, Marietta and her therapist weighed the pros and cons of seeking further education or finding a less exhausting job with better pay. Marietta found that she had the tools to look for a new job but accepted the discomfort of working at her current job until she was able to find a new one.

Valued living is essentially about opening up to the potential for positive reinforcement in one's environment, which becomes much more immediately accessible through mindful awareness of the present moment. Little or no effort is required to experience the richness life offers us, provided we are paying attention to the world around us and are free from the bonds of fusion, avoidance, and attachment to the conceptualized self. The values compass aims at helping the client orient away from a quantitative and form-based perspective and toward a qualitative and function-based perspective in which the process of living consistently with one's values (regardless of the outcome) itself is valued. Working with the values compass should help the client become newly aware of reinforcement in a variety of life domains. Bringing the client to a point at which she is aware of her overarching values and is consciously choosing to live in accord with those values is the ultimate aim of using the values compass.

Prioritizing and Balancing

Most of us have learned that the ability to prioritize is helpful in managing stress and reaching our goals. In fact, this is a skill taught in many stress reduction courses. What we mean by "prioritizing" in this context (as opposed to balancing) is designating one valued direction as more important than another and choosing to engage in activity in the apparently more important direction at the expense of activity in other directions. Different forms of prioritizing are seen in different stages of life. Students often prioritize studying and partying over more health-related activities such as getting adequate sleep, fresh air, and exercise. Young parents often prioritize activities with their children over socializing with friends or engaging in leisure activities. A person establishing her career might prioritize work above everything else.

We all prioritize to a degree when we choose one activity over another at any particular time. However, if over a long period of time a person consistently prioritizes activities in the service of certain values while curtailing or even completely omitting others, this may cause problems. When people prioritize, they often believe it's a temporary measure. A student may believe that her unhealthy behavior will be confined to her college years, and as soon as she graduates she'll get back into healthy habits. A young parent may believe that when her children are grown up, she'll reclaim her own interests and connect with her friends again. A woman establishing her career may believe that once she's achieved a certain position, she'll get her normal life back. However, what starts as a temporary imbalance may become more permanent, and the result may be less diversity in sources of reinforcement, a narrowing of the behavioral repertoire, and a reduction in quality of life.

Furthermore, there is empirical evidence of the risks of prioritizing with respect to valued directions. For instance, a number of studies have shown that role diversity is positively correlated with mental and physical health and perceived quality of life (Aube, Fleury, & Smetana, 2000; Park & Liao, 2000). One study of women's health (Lee & Powers, 2002) found that women who were active in three or more roles (for example, parent, employee, caregiver, physically active person, socially active person, and community volunteer) had significantly better health than those with fewer roles. Another study (Moen, Ericsson, & McClain, 2000) showed that elderly retirees who continued to have multiple active roles such as volunteering in the community, socializing, learning (through ongoing education), or exercising had significantly better health and quality of life than did those with fewer roles. Such studies seem to indicate that a diversity of roles and behaviors has an enhancing effect on health and well-being. Conversely, a narrowing of roles or sources of reinforcement may ultimately produce poorer psychological health, and possibly poorer physical health.

Evidence of the deleterious effects of prioritizing was also seen in a study of middle-aged women with chronic pain conducted by one of the authors of this book (Dahl, Wilson, & Nilsson, 2004). Over the course of this study, the authors noted that the physical and psychological vulnerability consistently evidenced by these clients was accompanied by a relatively consistent pattern of imbalance among valued activities. In the case of each of these women, valued action was restricted to work and caring for children, extended family members, and others. Meanwhile, all of the women had a gaping lack of valued activities in the domains of friendship, spirituality, health, leisure, education, and intimate relationships (grouped together as "self-care" activities).

The values compass allows the therapist to quickly see whether a client has prioritized valued directions, and quite often, any such prioritization is directly connected with the presenting problem. What we sometimes refer to as values narrowing or values maladjustment is simply the imbalance that can arise due to prioritizing. In all likelihood, this prioritizing is based on rules specifying the importance of values in one domain over others. Clients may find themselves prioritizing and cutting themselves off from sources of reinforcement as a result of fusion with rules dictating that they give all of their energy to one particular area.

An example of such a rule might be "I need to get out and see my friends more, but work is my highest priority right now. I can start going out again after I get that promotion." In such a case, the person cuts herself off from her friends and from important sources of reinforcement, which diminishes her social repertoire and constricts her life. Furthermore, even when she reaches her supposed goal of promotion, she may continue to be deeply fused with rules dictating the importance of her career, so the pattern continues and perhaps worsens, rather than improves. The long-term effect is a less vital life and a greater risk of psychological maladjustment and physical ill health.

We prioritize every time we choose one activity over another, and this is inevitable. However, in terms of a mix of activities over time, psychological research suggests that we should maintain a balance. Here, we define balance as an equilibrium or homeostasis of the mind and body. This relates most closely to the concept of workability, which we have mentioned a few times, and which can be seen as a measure of quality of life. Most of us usually know when we're living in a way that's unworkable; irritation, frustration, or physical symptoms often result when we're out of balance. However, possibilities for valued living are all around us. Balancing values simply requires an awareness of what a particular context has to offer. The values compass can orient any of us to attend to all of the possibilities for balancing our values. Using the values compass, we learn to balance rather than prioritize as we consciously choose to act on a moment-by-moment basis. Mindfulness can help us maintain our balance, and although rules and routines may help us value healthy activities, they aren't a replacement for a mindful awareness of what is needed in the present moment.

Summary

In this chapter we have presented the values compass as a useful tool and a metaphor around which to organize therapy. In our experience, clients easily relate to the idea of life as a whole that encompasses various domains that offer the potential for meaning and value. Presented with branches of the values compass, for example by using the life line exercise in the therapy room, the client can gain experiential insight into what is involved in moving in a valued direction. Using the values compass from the start of therapy and throughout the process helps the client identify and clarify the special qualities of each of her valued directions, along with the particular language traps and obstacles that threaten to pull her off course. We have also discussed how to help clients move from fusion with concepts of valued actions taking certain forms to a broader awareness of values as lifelong functions. In addition, we looked at how prioritizing one or more valued directions over others can lead to an imbalance and narrowing of life, while mindful awareness can help a person maintain balance and quality of life.

Acknowledging the depth and breadth of our values tends to broaden and enrich our lives. In ACT, the therapist weaves together the client's values, visions, and willingness to create a sense of purpose and meaning that will help the client get out of a stuck place and get on with life. In this way, choosing to move in valued directions is a commitment made with full knowledge of life's inevitable difficulties. It is rare that any of us are perfectly able to live consistently with our values, but with practice we can become much better at recognizing when we aren't doing so and take steps to rectify the discrepancy. We set this type of mindfulness as the goal for each of our clients. Some of them reach it and others don't. True to our values as therapists, however, it is not the outcome that matters but the process. When we commit to engaging the ACT model in the service of helping our clients live the lives they want, then we have lived in alignment with our values.

References

American Psychiatric Association. (2000). *Diagnostic and statistical manual of mental disorders* (4th ed, text revision). Washington, DC: Author.

Aube, J., Fleury, J., & Smetana, J. (2000). Changes in women's roles: Impact on and social policy implications for the mental health of women and children. *Development and Psychopathology, 12*(4), 633-656.

Barnes, D. (1994). Stimulus equivalence and relational frame theory. *Psychological Record, 44,* 91-124.

Barnes, D. (1996). Naming as a technical term: Sacrificing behavior analysis at the altar of popularity. *Journal of the Experimental Analysis of Behavior, 65*(1), 264-267.

Barnes-Holmes, D., O'Hora, D., Roche, B., Hayes, S. C., Bisset, R. T., & Lyddy, F. (2001). Understanding and verbal regulation. In S. C. Hayes, D. Barnes-Holmes & B. Roche (Eds.), *Relational frame theory: A post-Skinnerian account of human language and cognition* (pp. 103-117). New York: Klewer Academic/Plenum.

Barnes-Holmes, Y., Barnes-Holmes, D., McHugh, L., & Hayes, S. C. (2004). Relational frame theory: Some implications for understanding and treating human psychopathology. *International Journal of Psychology and Psychological Therapy, 4*(2), 355-375.

Barnes-Holmes, Y., Barnes-Holmes, D., & Smeets, P. M. (2004). Establishing relational responding in accordance with opposite as generalized operant behavior in young children. *International Journal of Psychology and Psychological Therapy, 4*(3), 559-586.

Beck, A. T., & Emery, G. (2005). *Anxiety disorders and phobias: A cognitive perspective.* Cambridge: Basic Books.

Berens, N. M., & Hayes, S. C. (2007). Arbitrarily applicable comparative relations: Experimental evidence for a relational operant. *Journal of Applied Behavior Analysis, 40*(1), 45-71.

Dahl, J., & Lundgren, T. (2007, May). Bull's-eye: Validity and reliability. In J. C. Plumb (Chair), *Engaging in life: Values and valued action as catalysts for change.* Symposium presented at the annual convention of the Association for Behavior Analysis, San Diego, CA.

Dahl, J., Wilson, K. G., & Nilsson, A. (2004). Acceptance and commitment therapy and the treatment of persons at risk for long-term disability resulting from stress and pain symptoms: A preliminary randomized trial. *Behaviour Therapy, 35*(4), 785-801.

Dymond, S., & Barnes, D. (1994). A transfer of self-discrimination response functions through equivalence relations. *Journal of the Experimental Analysis of Behavior, 62*(2), 251-267.

Dymond, S., & Barnes, D. (1995). A transformation of self-discrimination response functions in accordance with the arbitrarily applicable relations of sameness, more than and less than. *Journal of the Experimental Analysis of Behavior, 64*(2), 163-184.

Dymond, S., & Barnes, D. (1996). A transformation of self-discrimination response functions in accordance with the arbitrarily applicable relations of sameness and opposition. *Psychological Record, 46,* 271-300.

Egan, L. C., Santos, L. R., & Bloom, P. (2007). The origins of cognitive dissonance. Evidence from children and monkeys. *Psychological Science, 18*(11), 978-983.

Feldner, M. T., Hekmat, H., Zvolensky, M. J., Vowles, K. E., Secrist, Z., & Leen-Feldner, E. W. (2006). The role of experiential avoidance in acute pain tolerance: A laboratory test. *Journal of Behavior Therapy and Experimental Psychiatry, 37*(2), 146-158.

Feldner, M. T., Zvolensky, M. J., Eifert, G. H., & Spira, A. P. (2003). Emotional avoidance: An experimental test of individual differences in response suppression using biological challenge. *Behaviour Research and Therapy, 41*(4), 403-411.

Hayes, S. C. (1989). *Rule-governed behavior: Cognition, contingencies, and instructional control.* New York: Plenum.

Hayes, S. C. (1991). A relational control theory of stimulus equivalence. In L. J. Hayes & P. N. Chase (Eds.), *Dialogues on verbal behavior* (pp. 19-40). Reno, NV: Context Press.

Hayes, S. C. (1994). Relational frame theory: A functional approach to verbal events. In S. C. Hayes, L. J. Hayes, M. Sato, & K. Ono (Eds.), *Behavior analysis of language and cognition* (pp. 9-30). Reno, NV: Context Press.

Hayes, S. C. (with Dahl, J., Wicksell, R. K., & Sonntag, R. F.). (2007). *Values and action* (120-minute DVD). Oakland, CA: New Harbinger.

Hayes, S. C. (2008, May). *The roots of compassion.* Keynote address presented at the fourth Acceptance and Commitment Therapy Summer Institute, Chicago, IL.

Hayes, S. C., Barnes-Holmes, D., & Roche, B. (2001). *Relational frame theory: A post-Skinnerian account of human language and cognition.* New York: Klewer Academic/Plenum.

Hayes, S. C., Bissett, R., Roget, N., Padilla, M., Kohlenberg, B. S., Fisher, G., Masuda, A., Pistorello, J., Rye, A. K., Berry, K., & Niccolls, R. (2004). The impact of acceptance and commitment training and multicultural training on the stigmatizing attitudes and professional burnout of substance abuse counselors. *Behavior Therapy, 35*(4), 821-835.

Hayes, S. C., Brownstein, A. J., Haas, J. R., & Greenway, D. E. (1986). Instructions, multiple schedules, and extinction: Distinguishing rule-governed from schedule-controlled behavior. *Journal of the Experimental Analysis of Behavior, 46*(2), 137-147.

Hayes, S. C., & Hayes, L. J. (1989). The verbal action of the listener as a basis for rule-governance. In S. C. Hayes (Ed.), *Rule-governed behavior: Cognition, contingencies, and instructional control* (pp. 153-190). New York: Plenum.

Hayes, S. C., & Hayes, L. J. (1992). Verbal relations and the evolution of behavior analysis. *American Psychologist, 47*(11), 1383-1395.

Hayes, S. C., Luoma, J. B., Bond, F. W., Masuda, A., & Lillis, J. (2006). Acceptance and commitment therapy: Model, processes and outcomes. *Behaviour Research and Therapy, 44*(1), 1-25.

Hayes, S. C., Strosahl, K. D., & Wilson, K. G. (1999). *Acceptance and commitment therapy: An experiential approach to behavior change.* New York: Guilford.

Hayes, S. C., Wilson, K. W., Gifford, E. V., Follette, V. M., & Strosahl, K. (1996). Experiential avoidance and behavioral disorders: A functional dimensional approach to diagnosis and treatment. *Journal of Consulting and Clinical Psychology, 64*(6), 1152-1168.

Kaufman, A., Baron, A., & Kopp, R. E. (1966). Some effects of instructions on human operant behavior. *Psychonomic Monograph Supplements, 1,* 243-250.

Kohlenberg, R. J., & Tsai, M. (1991). *Functional analytic psychotherapy: Creating intense and curative therapeutic relationships.* New York: Plenum.

Lee, C., & Powers, J. R. (2002). Number of social roles, health, and well-being in three generations of Australian women. *International Journal of Behavioral Medicine, Special issue: Women's health, 9*(3), 195-215.

Leigland, S. (2005). Variables of which values are a function. *Behavior Analyst, 28*(2), 133-142.

Lowe, C. F. (1979). Determinants of human operant behavior. In M. D. Zeiler & P. Harzem (Eds.) *Advances in analysis of behavior. Vol. 1. Reinforcement and the organisation of behavior (pp. 159-192).* Chichester, England: Wiley.

Luciano, C., Gomez-Becerra, I., & Rodriguez-Valverde, M. (2007). The role of multiple exemplar training and naming in establishing derived equivalence in an infant. *Journal of the Experimental Analysis of Behavior, 87*(3), 349-365.

Lundgren, T., Dahl, J., & Melin, L. (2007, May). Using the bull's-eye to measure values attainment and believability. In J. C. Plumb (Chair), *Assessment of ACT processes: Values and psychological flexibility.* Symposium conducted at the annual conference of the Association for Behavior Analysis, Chicago, IL.

Luoma, J. B., Walser, R. D., & Hayes, S. C. (2007). *Learning ACT: An acceptance and commitment therapy skills-training manual for therapists.* Oakland, CA: New Harbinger.

Matthews, B. A., Shimoff, E., Catania, A. C., & Sagvolden, T. (1977). Uninstructed human responding: Sensitivity to ratio and interval contingencies. *Journal of the Experimental Analysis of Behavior, 27*(3), 453-467.

McAuliffe, D., Barnes-Holmes, D., & Barnes-Holmes, Y. (2004, May). Excessive rule-following and depressive symptomology. In S. Smyth (Chair), *Acceptance and commitment therapy: Core principles and measures.* Symposium conducted at the annual conference of the Association for Behavior Analysis, Boston, MA.

Michael, J. (1982). Distinguishing between discriminative and motivational functions of stimuli. *Journal of the Experimental Analysis of Behavior, 37*(1), 149-155.

Moen, P., Ericsson, M., & McClain, D. (2000). Social role identities among older adults in a continuing care retirement community. *Research on Aging, 22*(5), 559-579.

Park, J., & Liao, T. F. (2000). The effect of multiple roles of South Korean married women professors: Role changes and the factors which influence potential role gratification and strain. *Sex Roles, 43*(7-8), 571-591.

Pepper, S. (1942). *World hypotheses.* Berkeley, CA: University of California Press.

Roche, B., & Barnes, D. (1996). Arbitrarily applicable relational responding and sexual categorization: A critical test of the derived difference relation. *Psychological Record, 46,* 451-475.

Roche, B., & Barnes, D. (1997). A transformation of respondently conditioned stimulus functions in accordance with arbitrarily applicable relations. *Journal of the Experimental Analysis of Behavior, 67*(3), 275-301.

Shimoff, E., Catania, A. C., & Matthews, B. A. (1981). Uninstructed human responding: Sensitivity of low-rate performance to schedule contingencies. *Journal of the Experimental Analysis of Behavior, 36*(2), 61-68.

Skinner, B. F. (1938). *The behavior of organisms: An experimental analysis.* Englewood Cliffs, NJ: Prentice Hall.

Skinner, B. F. (1974). *About behaviorism.* New York: Vintage Books.

Skinner, B. F. (1989). The origins of cognitive thought. *American Psychologist, 44*(1), 13-18.

Steele, D. L., & Hayes, S. C. (1991). Stimulus equivalence and arbitrarily applicable relational responding. *Journal of the Experimental Analysis of Behavior, 56*(3), 519-555.

Stewart, I., & Barnes-Holmes, D. (2001). Understanding metaphor: A relational frame perspective. *Behavior Analyst, 24*(2), 191-199.

Vilardaga, R., Hayes, S. C., Levin, M. E., & Muto, T. (2008). *Creating a strategy for progress: A contextual behavioral science approach.* Manuscript submitted for publication.

Vowles, K. E., McNeil, D. W., Gross, R. T., McDaniel, M. L., Mouse, A., Bates, M., Gallimore, P., & McCall, C. (2007). Effects of pain acceptance and pain control strategies on physical impairment in individuals with chronic low back pain. *Behavior Therapy, 38*(4), 412-425.

Wegner, D. (1994). Ironic processes of mental control. *Psychological Review, 101*(1), 34-52.

Weiner, H. (1970). Human behavioral persistence. *The Psychological Record, 20,* 445-456.

Wilson, K. G. (with DuFrene, T.) (2009). *Mindfulness for two: An acceptance and commitment therapy approach to mindfulness in psychotherapy.* Oakland, CA: New Harbinger.

Wilson, K. G., & Murrell, A. R. (2004). Values work in acceptance and commitment therapy: Setting a course for behavioral treatment. In S. C. Hayes, V. M. Follette, & M. M. Linehan (Eds.), *Mindfulness and acceptance: Expanding the cognitive behavior tradition* (pp. 120-151). New York: Guilford.

Zettle, R. D., & Hayes, S. C. (1982). Rule-governed behavior: A potential theoretical framework for cognitive behavior therapy. In P. C. Kendall (Ed.), *Advances in cognitive behavioral research and therapy* (pp. 73-118). New York: Academic.

JoAnne C. Dahl, Ph.D., is associate professor and senior lecturer in the psychology department at the University of Uppsala in Sweden. She is a leading acceptance and commitment therapy (ACT) researcher who has applied ACT to various conditions, including chronic pain. Dahl is author of *Living Beyond Your Pain* and *Acceptance and Commitment Therapy for Chronic Pain*.

Jennifer C. Plumb, MA, is an advanced clinical psychology doctoral student at the University of Nevada, Reno, working with Steven Hayes, Ph.D. She has practiced ACT since 2004, working primarily with patients who have anxiety, depression, and interpersonal relationship difficulties. Her primary interest is psychotherapy process and outcome research with a specific focus on applying values to clinical work from a clinical behavior analysis, relational frame theory, and ACT perspective.

Ian Stewart, Ph.D., received his doctorate from the National University of Ireland, Maynooth, and is a faculty member in the psychology department at the National University of Ireland, Galway. His academic research focuses on the analysis of language and cognition from a relational frame theory perspective, and he has authored multiple peer-reviewed publications on this topic.

Tobias Lundgren, MS, is a licensed clinical psychologist specializing in cognitive behavior therapy and ACT. He is an active clinician and a researcher in the areas of behavior medicine, psychometrics, and self-destructive behavior. Lundgren is affiliated with the psychology department at the University of Uppsala in Sweden, and has conducted research in many developing countries.

Index

A

abuse: physical, 59, 109; sexual, 59, 109, 176-177; substance, 110-111

acceptance, 25-27, 93-98, 154-159; examples of avoidance vs., 93-95, 96-97; importance of practicing, 97-98; indicators of, 159; recognizing in sessions, 158-159; therapeutic benefits of, 95-96; values as context for, 157-158

acceptance and commitment therapy (ACT), 22-41; acceptance in, 25-26, 27, 154-159; assessing values in, 112-114; behavior analysis and, 4-5; cognitive defusion in, 28-29, 134-146; committed action in, 38, 161-190; compassion and self-compassion in, 84-85; declaration of therapist values in, 101-103; diagram of processes in, 40; intervention strategies in, 133-159; present moment awareness in, 30, 146-149; process of valuing in, 63-82; psychological flexibility and, 39; self-as-context in, 31-32,

149-154; therapeutic relationship in, 83-104; values and, 1-2, 8-9, 32-35, 39-41

Acceptance and Commitment Therapy: An Experiential Approach to Behavior Change (Hayes, Strosahl, and Wilson), 9

ACT. *See* acceptance and commitment therapy

action: creating patterns of, 80-82; depressive withdrawal from, 106-107; plan for valued, 124, 179-189. *See also* committed action

adaptive rules, 135

agape love, 95

alcohol abuse, 110-111

and-statements, 55, 137

anxiety, 108-109

appetitive stimulus, 6

arbitrarily applicable relational responding, 14

assessing values: Bull's-Eye Worksheet for, 120-130; questions used for, 112-114; therapeutic pitfalls in, 130-131

audio recordings, 179

W

"Which Master Do You Serve?"
    exercise, 73-75
willingness, 155-156, 173, 198. *See also*
    acceptance
withdrawal, depressive, 106
workability, 38
worksheets: Bull's-Eye Worksheet,
    120-130, 171-176; Establishing
    Short-Term and Long-Term

Goals, 181-182; Finding Values in
Unenjoyable Activities, 185-186;
Values Compass, 193, 194. *See also*
exercises
worldviews, 3-5; contextualism, 4-5;
    mechanism, 3-4

Z

Zettle, Robert, 19